TH FUTURES
OF
EVANGELICALISM

For Fred Hughes

THE
FUTURES
OF
EVANGELICALISM

ISSUES AND PROSPECTS

CONTRIBUTORS INCLUDE:
ALISTER McGRATH
EUGENE PETERSON
GRAEME GOLDSWORTHY
KEVIN VANHOOZER

EDITED BY
CRAIG BARTHOLOMEW,
ROBIN PARRY AND ANDREW WEST

Inter-Varsity Press

INTER-VARSITY PRESS
38 De Montfort Street, Leicester LE1 7GP, England
Email: ivp@uccf.org.uk
Website: www.ivpbooks.com

First published 2003

British Library Cataloguing in Publication Data
A catalogue record for this book is available
from the British Library.

ISBN 0-85111-399-0

Set in Monotype Garamond 11/13pt
Typeset in Great Britain by Servis Filmsetting Ltd, Manchester
Printed and bound in Great Britain

*Inter-Varsity Press is the publishing division of the Universities and Colleges Christian
Fellowship (formerly the Inter-Varsity Fellowship), a student movement linking Christian
Unions in universities and colleges throughout Great Britain, and a member movement of the
International Fellowship of Evangelical Students. For more information about local and
national activities write to UCCF, 38 De Montfort Street, Leicester LE1 7GP, email us at
email@uccf.org.uk, or visit the UCCF website at www.uccf.org.uk.*

CONTENTS

CONTRIBUTORS

Craig G. Bartholomew is Senior Research Fellow in the School of Humanities at the University of Gloucestershire. He specializes in Old Testament wisdom literature and biblical interpretation. He is the author of *Reading Ecclesiastes: Old Testament Exegesis and Hermeneutical Theory*, editor of *In the Fields of the Lord: A Calvin Seerveld Reader*, and co-editor of *Christ and Consumerism*. He is series editor of the Scripture and Hermeneutics Series.

Graeme Goldsworthy lectured in biblical theology and Old Testament at Moore Theological College, Sydney. He now lives in semi-retirement on the far north coast of New South Wales, and continues as a visiting lecturer in hermeneutics at Moore College. He is the author of *According to Plan*, *Preaching the whole Bible as Christian Scripture*, *Prayer and the Knowledge of God*, and three books on biblical studies collected as *The Goldsworthy Trilogy*.

Gregory J. Laughery is associated with the Swiss branch of the L'Abri Fellowship. He is the author of *Living Hermeneutics in Motion: An Analysis and Evaluation of Paul Ricoeur's Contribution to Biblical Hermeneutics*, 'Language at the Frontiers of Language', in *After Pentecost*, and a commentary on the book of Revelation.

Stephen Lazarus is Senior Policy Associate at the Center for Public Justice in the Washington, DC area. The Center is a non-partisan Christian public policy organization that seeks to develop policies that ensure the just treatment of people of all faiths in the public arena. Staff at the Center have served as advisors to the White House and to state governments as part of the Faith-Based and Community Initiative.

I. Howard Marshall is Honorary Research Professor of New Testament at the University of Aberdeen where he taught from 1964 to 1999. He is the author of many academic articles and books including commentaries on the Greek text of Luke and the Pastoral Epistles, and recently he edited the sixth edition of Moulton and Geden's *Concordance to the Greek New Testament*.

Alister E. McGrath is Professor of Historical Theology at Oxford University and Principal of Wycliffe Hall. He is a distinguished theologian and speaker and has written numerous books, including several on evangelicalism. His most recent publications are the first two volumes ('Nature' and 'Reality') in the three-volume *Scientific Theology*.

Robin Parry taught 'A' Level Religious Studies for ten years at a Sixth Form College in Worcester until, after finishing a PhD on Old Testament narrative ethics, he became commissioning editor for Paternoster Press.

Eugene H. Peterson is Professor Emeritus of Spiritual Theology at Regent College, Vancouver, Canada. He is the author of the paraphrasing translation of the Bible in contemporary language, *The Message*, and numerous other books including *A Long Obedience in the Same Direction*, *The Contemplative Pastor* and *Leap Over a Wall*. He founded Christ our King Presbyterian Church in Bel Air, Maryland, where he was pastor for twenty-nine years.

Jonathan Ruthven is Professor of Systematic Theology at Regent University School of Divinity, Virginia Beach, Virginia, USA. He previously pastored for twelve years and served as a missionary in Kenya. His most recent book is *The Prophecy That Is Shaping History: New Research on Ezekiel's Vision of the End*. He enjoys feedback from readers: ruthven@regent.edu

Nigel Scotland is Field Chair of Theology and Religious Studies at the University of Gloucestershire where he has lectured since 1984. An ordained Anglican, he was chaplain and lecturer at the College of St Paul and St Mary from 1975 to 1984. Before that he served as rector of the parish of Lakefield in the diocese of Montreal. He is the author of a number of books. Among the most recent are *John Bird Sumner: Evangelical Archbishop*, *Charismatics and the New Millennium*, *Sectarian Religion in Contemporary Britain*, *Good and Proper Men: Lord Palmerston and the Bench of Bishops* and *Evangelical Anglicans in a Revolutionary Age*.

Kevin Vanhoozer is Research Professor of Systematic Theology at Trinity Evangelical Divinity School, Chicago. Previously he taught theology for eight years at New College, University of Edinburgh, where he was Senior Lecturer in Theology and Religious Studies. He is the author of *Is There a Meaning in this Text?*, *First Theology: God, Scripture and Hermeneutics*, and the forthcoming *The Drama of Doctrine: A Canonical-Linguistic Approach to Theology*.

Andrew West, a former school teacher, is at present Chaplain at the University of Gloucestershire. He is, with Craig Bartholomew, co-editor of *Praying by the Book: Reading the Psalms*.

Christopher Wright is the International Ministries Director for the Langham Partnership International – a group of ministries founded by John Stott for the support of churches and seminaries in the Majority World. Previously Principal of All Nations Christian College, he also lived and taught in India. He has written several books on the Old Testament, including *Living as the People of God*.

INTRODUCTION: A TIME TO REFLECT

Craig G. Bartholomew

When I studied for a year in Toronto, my friends and I used to gather at a marvellous coffee shop called 'Futures'. Full of students in term time, it served up great coffees and a wonderful variety of cakes and nutritious meals in a pleasant ambience. Perhaps it was from there that the title of this collection of essays came to me.

It is certainly appropriate – for all of the authors of these essays evangelicalism is a good thing which has nourished us deeply and which we wish to recommend. It is not uncommon to hear of prominent Christians who have been brought to faith in Christ through evangelicalism, but later come to distance themselves from it as they embrace alternative traditions of Christianity. Here in the UK recent days have also seen discussions of 'post-evangelicalism' and some attempts by (former) evangelicals to reshape evangelicalism so fundamentally – often in a radically postmodern direction – that it is denatured. These are not the approaches of this collection of essays.

For all of us evangelicalism is the Christian tradition we regard as most biblical and true to the Christian faith. Of course, we know the difficulties of defining evangelicalism – indeed there are

a variety of groupings of evangelicals and that diversity is represented among us.[1] Some of us are Anglican evangelicals with a
strong commitment to the Reformation tradition. Others are charismatic evangelicals – some Anglican some not – and Pentecostals.
And so on and so forth. Yet all of us would recognize a family
resemblance between our various 'evangelicalisms', however hard
it is to define that with precision.

This does not mean that we are uncritical of evangelicalism. On
the contrary the assumption of this book is that evangelicalism
has much to reflect upon, much to repent of, and a great deal to
learn. But our critique is prophetic critique in the sense that like
the Old Testament prophets it comes, not from those who in
despair have left evangelicalism, but from those who remain
within and passionately so. Where we weep over aspects of contemporary evangelicalism we do so in the spirit of Jeremiah and
Hosea. We have a sense of the abundant riches of evangelicalism
and we long to see it fulfil its great potential.

Indeed, as is well documented, evangelicalism has made huge
strides in the second half of the twentieth century so that it is now
'the largest and most actively committed form of Christianity in
the West'.[2] But that very growth has brought its own problems

---

1. There are many discussions of the nature of evangelicalism and various
typologies of the different types of evangelicals. Two books that I have
found helpful in this respect are Knight 1997 and McGrath 1988. Both
discuss ways of defining evangelicalism and both refer to the typologies
of evangelicals that have been proposed. Both note helpfully that the
word 'evangelical' has acquired different meanings since the Reformation.
Knight 1997: 20 points out that in the Reformation evangelical was more
or less synonymous with Protestant. However, around the time of the
evangelical awakenings in the eighteenth and nineteenth centuries
evangelical became associated with personal conversion, holiness of life,
mass evangelism and often, social reform. Since the 1940s evangelical has
come to refer to a post-fundamentalist movement also known as neo-
evangelicalism, i.e. evangelicalism is here at pains to distance itself from
fundamentalism.

2. McGrath 1996: 9.

and there is a widespread feeling that evangelicalism in the West is at a crossroads at present. Stanley Grenz begins his recent assessment of the current state and future of evangelicalism by noting that, 'The future of evangelicalism is in doubt. At least this is the assessment of many of today's evangelical pulse-takers, prognosticators, and prophets.'[3] This crossroads is closely related to the shifts that Western culture is undergoing at present – the challenge of so-called 'postmodernity'. Certain types of evangelicalism are closer to modernity than to postmodernity when it comes to issues like how we know whether something is true or not – that is, in relation to epistemology.[4] During the twentieth century evangelicals recovered an interest in culture, but, with the fragmentation and pluralism of postmodernism, that fragmentation has come to characterize evangelicalism too.

Whatever the precise reasons for the present challenges to evangelicalism, this is certainly a time to reflect, a time for evangelicals to assess the route we have come and the gains made, as a means of assessing what we need to attend to if our future is to be bright. The title 'The *Futures* of Evangelicalism' deliberately evokes the possibility of diverse futures for evangelicalism. In this respect we have asked our authors to address a key topic in relation to the progress evangelicals have or have not made in that area, with a view to outlining a programmatic agenda for a way forward.

We are not under any illusions that these essays pronounce the final word on the topics addressed or that all the important topics are addressed. Rather, the aim is to stimulate evangelicals and other interested parties to reflect upon evangelicalism and its possible futures. We do think that the areas addressed are fundamentally important – theology, the church, biblical interpretation, biblical

---

3. Grenz 2000: 11.

4. Knight 1997 contrasts Carl Henry's approach with that of Donald Bloesch in this respect. Grenz 2000: 85–116 compares Henry with Bernard Ramm. On the contemporary relevance of Ramm see Vanhoozer's introductory essay to Ramm's *The Evangelical Heritage*. The point is that with the emergence of postmodernism these differences have become far more significant than one might have imagined previously.

theology, mission, ethics, world-view, spirituality, philosophy, the charismatic movement, and politics. Our hope is that the volume will provoke healthy reflection and debate about good ways forward for evangelicals in the years of possibility that lie ahead.

A milestone in the production of this volume was a very stimulating day conference at the University of Gloucestershire on the Futures of Evangelicalism, funded with the generous help of the University Fellows. I remain grateful to our Principal, Dame Janet Trotter, and to the University for providing a stimulating and supportive environment in which to pursue this sort of work. Without the help of my co-editors Robin Parry and Andrew West, both associated in different ways with the University, the volume would never have seen the light of day. Philip Duce of IVP has been a great help and encouragement throughout the process and has kept us on track to completion.

We dedicate this book to Dr Fred Hughes. Fred was Head of Theology and Religious Studies at the University of Gloucestershire from 1997 until 2003, a post he has now relinquished as Theology and Religious Studies has been integrated into the new School of Humanities. Fred remains on the staff at the University. He led Theology and Religious Studies with integrity and wisdom and it is a great pleasure for us to dedicate this collection to him.

Bibliography

Grenz, S. J. (2000), *Renewing the Center: Evangelical Theology in a Post-Theological Era*, Grand Rapids: Baker Academic.

Knight III, H. H. (1997), *A Future for Truth: Evangelical Theology in a Postmodern World*, Nashville: Abingdon.

McGrath, A. (1988), *Evangelicalism and the Future of Christianity*, London: Hodder & Stoughton.

—— (1996), *A Passion for Truth: The Intellectual Coherence of Evangelicalism*, Leicester: Apollos.

Vanhoozer, K. J. (2000), 'Foreword: The Pattern of Evangelical Theology: Hommage à Ramm', in B. Ramm, *The Evangelical Heritage: A Study in Historical Theology*, ix–xxvii, Grand Rapids: Baker.

1. THEOLOGY AND THE FUTURES OF EVANGELICALISM

Alister E. McGrath

It is particularly appropriate to offer some reflections on the role of theology for evangelicalism by congratulating the University of Gloucestershire on its new status, and the opportunities for ministry and service which this offers. And who could give a lecture on the relevance of theology for evangelicalism without honouring James I. Packer, who was born in this county of Gloucestershire in 1926?[1] Packer has devoted his long and distinguished career to reminding evangelicals of the importance of theology in relation to evangelism, worship and spirituality, and it is appropriate to begin this essay by celebrating a man who has much to say to us on this theme.[2]

---

1. McGrath 1997.

2. See especially his classic work *Knowing God* (Packer 1973) and also his remarkable lecture 'An Introduction to Systematic Spirituality' (Packer 1990). This lecture is reprinted, with comment, in McGrath 1999: 194–209.

Christian hostility to theology: a general overview

The best point at which to begin exploring our theme is the growing indifference to academic theology within the mainline Western churches. Why has academic theology suffered the indignity of marginalization within its home communities? A number of reasons may be offered. The most obvious is the strongly pragmatic nature of American academic culture, which still has immense influence throughout the world. Academic theology might be the victim of what some have called the 'evasion of philosophy', which can be thought of as a tendency to address cultural problems, rather than to undertake philosophical analysis. 'It is no exaggeration to say that in American intellectual life, irrelevant thinking has always been considered to be the cardinal sin.'[3] The general evasion of theology reflects a broader cultural trend which casts doubt on the merits and necessity of theoretical analysis, and prefers to engage directly with the issues of the day.

The importance of this point is easily appreciated. If a Californian megachurch is in the process of expansion, it is likely to be considering developing better pastoral techniques, better car parking facilities, better conferencing facilities, increased income flow, and more efficient use of its pastors' time. The past history of academic theology offers little indication that it might have any bearing on the practical issues of church life. Except, of course, preaching and teaching.

Surely theology has a significant role to play in connection with the sermon and Christian education courses – immensely important elements of church life, especially in growing congregations. Here, surely, theology might expect to find a place of honour. As I know from many visits, not a few clergy studies still have weighty tomes of theology on their shelves. The standard joke among theologians about the clergy goes like this. You have a look at their bookshelves, and you notice that there is a cut-off point. After a

---

3. Smith, 1963: vii. The importance of the instrumentalism of John Dewey (1859–1952) should be noted here. See also the excellent account in West 1989: 5.

certain date, they seem to stop buying theological works. 'And that's when their brains died!' goes the joke.

I used to find this amusing, until I visited a former student of mine, who was academically brilliant and seemed to have a glittering academic career ahead of him. But he had spent the last five years in parish ministry. As we drank coffee together in his study, I scanned his bookshelves, and noticed the inevitable cut-off point. I commented on this, and prepared to deliver the standard punchline. But he beat me to it. 'Yes,' he said, more in sadness than in anger. 'That's when I realized that those books had nothing to say to the people I serve, or myself as I serve them.' He then proceeded to pull out some books that he did find helpful, and explained why. His brain was clearly alive and active. It was just that theology seemed to fail to make the connections that mattered to him and his people.

The problem is that too many mainline academic theologians for comfort seem to speak a different language to the rest of us, and have completely different agendas. This point was made back in 1960 by Bishop Hans Lilje, in an address to students at Union Theological Seminary, New York – then one of the most highly regarded seminaries in the world.

> The Christian Church seems to have lost . . . the capacity to speak about
> its beliefs in a manner which should convey the impression of
> something real and alive. The language of the theologians seems to have
> become so artificial, so self-centered and so remote from real life that
> one can only dream of the times when theology took the lead in the
> universities and was the most formative influence in the intellectual life
> of Western nations.[4]

It has not got any better. I recall an occasion back in the 1970s when a leading British theologian gave an address to a group of us who were preparing for ministry in the Church of England. He offered us a few personal reminiscences of his own time in ministry, before moving on to deal with some erudite matters of

---

4. Details in Hendry 1960: 216.

theology. He related how he regularly had to visit little old ladies in his parish, and was obliged to converse with them over cups of lukewarm overbrewed tea. We all politely tittered (as we were clearly meant to) at the thought of such an immensely distinguished theologian having to suffer the indignity of talking with little old ladies whose subject of conversation was grandchildren, the price of groceries and the pains of old age.

After his lecture, we wished he had spent rather more time with these people. The bulk of his lecture was unintelligible, and made no connections with real life – the issues of relationships, the cost of living, and the pain of the world. It was academic in the worst possible sense of the word – stated in hopelessly pompous language, and failing to connect up with the issues that affected and concerned the vast bulk of the nation. It was a luminous example of what Charles Newman would later call 'the inflation of discourse', in which verbal pretentiousness is deliberately cultivated and any relationship to public utility or relevance is abandoned.[5] It was after that lecture I decided that I did not want to be a theologian, and would go into parish ministry as a corrective to my academic tendencies – but that is another story.

In England, the perception that academic theology is something of an irrelevance to the church can be dated from 1977, when a group of academic theologians published a book entitled *The Myth of God Incarnate*. To the contributors, it was doubtless an interesting essay in theological experimentation, and a landmark contribution to academic study. Sadly, the book is not viewed in that way; rather, it is now seen as illustrating rather nicely how theology had painted itself into a corner. A conservative riposte, written in great haste, was generally regarded as academically superior.[6] *The Myth* delighted non-Christians, perplexed an increasingly irritated Christian public, and convinced many that the dominant religious liberalism had nothing to offer the church or the world. As Adrian Hastings observes in his highly praised history of English Christianity:

---

5. Newman 1985.

6. Hick 1977, and also Green 1977.

If *The Myth* produced excitement, it was principally the smirking excitement of an agnostic world amused to witness the white flag hoisted so enthusiastically above the long-beleaguered citadel of Christian belief, the stunned excitement of the rank and file of weary defenders on learning that their staff officers had so light-heartedly ratted on them. It was hardly surprising that more than one of the contributors soon after ceased, even in a nominal sense, to be Christian believers, or that Don Cupitt, one of the most forceful and publicity minded of the group, published only two years later his commitment to objective atheism.[7]

If this work was intended to increase the status of academic theology in the eyes of Christianity, it most signally failed to do so. It represented an own goal, a piece of self-publicization that merely convinced its audience of the intellectual shallowness and spiritual irrelevance of English academic theology.

The growing gap between academic theology and the church is best seen in the fact that much recent theology seems to focus on issues which appear to be an utter irrelevance to the life, worship and mission of the church. Adrian Hastings notes the importance of this point in evaluating the weakness of much Anglican theology of the last generation:

No church can continue for long without a theology possessing a fair measure of internal coherence, one related organically both to the actual religious practice of believers and to certain basic requirements of credibility or utility posited by contemporary society . . . By the 1970s the central tradition of English academic theology as taught at Oxford and Cambridge, was hardly fulfilling these needs. There had long been a notable gap between academic theology and what one may call a theology of the pew, but in previous ages there had remained a link between them. The theology of [Charles] Gore, [William] Temple, [Arthur Michael] Ramsey or [Austin] Farrer was, most certainly, one the church could live and thrive with. The same cannot be said for that of [Dennis] Nineham, [John] Hick or [Don] Cupitt . . . It is no refutation

---

7. Hastings 1986: 650–651.

of their work to say that there is simply no future for a church which can produce no reasoned expression of its faith stronger than what the dominant theologians of the seventies were able to muster.[8]

The point Hastings makes is, sadly, irrefutable. The situation has simply deteriorated since those words were written, leading many to wonder whether academic theology has now lost its credibility with believers completely.

Evangelicalism and theology: some significant factors

What, then, about evangelicalism? Has it managed to avoid this elitism, and secure the pastoral and spiritual relevance for Christian theology?[9] Despite its long history of theological reflection, evangelicalism is widely regarded as the new kid on the academic block. For many, it has not been a welcome arrival. In part, this is because of evangelicalism's insistence upon the importance of Scripture in theologizing: one of the most fundamental and essential distinctives of the evangelical approach to theology is its insistence that theology must be nourished and governed at all points by holy Scripture, and that it seeks to offer a faithful and coherent account of what it finds there. To understand the theological enterprise in such terms is to insist that theology is fundamentally, no more and no less, than attentiveness to Scripture, and a desire to express and communicate what is to be found there to the church and the world. Christian theology is under an obligation to pay respectful and obedient attention to the biblical testimony, and allow itself to be shaped and *re*shaped by what it finds expressed here.

The word 'evangelicalism' continues to evoke images of the anti-intellectualism especially associated with North American fundamentalism during the 1920s and 1930s. Yet evangelicalism has long since moved on from the defensive posturing and

---

8. Hastings 1986: 662–663.

9. McGrath 2000.

overreactions of this critical period. Since the Second World War, evangelicalism has increasingly shown itself to be concerned about intellectual issues, without in any way weakening or compromising its concern for pastoral and spiritual matters.

On account of its recent history in North America, a significant constituency within evangelicalism has had a markedly ambivalent attitude towards theology in the last generation. Since its emergence as a major presence in global Christianity after the Second World War, at least a large section of the evangelical movement has not seen sustained theological engagement as a pressing priority on its substantial agenda. Why is this? Four major reasons may be given, each of which merits further exploration. Three of these are particularly associated with North American, rather than with British, evangelicalism, which accounts to some extent for the very different intellectual ethos associated with the American and British wings of the movement.

The lingering influence of fundamentalism

The fundamentalist heritage of North American evangelicalism distanced it from academic theology for a generation. This factor is of little significance in Britain, where there has been a long history of evangelical involvement in academic theology. The rise of fundamentalism in North America during the 1920s is of decisive importance in relation to understanding the ambivalent attitude within evangelicalism in this region to theology. The rise of fundamentalism had an impact on the evangelical commitment to scholarship in general which shows distressing parallels with events during the so-called 'Cultural Revolution' in the People's Republic of China. Both divorced a generation from mainline academic engagement, making the subsequent process of reintegration both painful and hazardous. And in the meantime, American universities and colleges have generally drifted still further away from their foundational Christian moorings, making that reintegration additionally problematical.[10] Evangelicalism, which seems to have yet to recover fully from the lingering influence of the fundamentalist

---

10. See the kind of considerations set out in Marsden 1994; Sloan 1994.

insistence that it was exempt on religious grounds from any kind of thinking or cultural engagement,[11] still retains a reputation for intellectual shallowness in some quarters.

A pragmatic approach to theology and church life

The fundamentalist legacy is not, however, totally to blame for evangelicalism's lack of commitment to intellectual engagement. It is arguable that it is the present fixation of the movement on the American therapeutic culture of 'feel-good-ism' which is as much to blame for the intellectual weakness of the movement. Particularly in North America, evangelicalism has come to place emphasis on pragmatic criteria of success, which has led to a retreat from theological engagement on account of its questionable utility for pastoral and evangelistic practice. In a penetrating and important recent study, David F. Wells has argued that evangelicalism has lost whatever grasp it once had of the importance of theology.[12] The strongly pragmatic nature of the movement has, he suggests, led to an emphasis on church growth, feel-good preaching and styles of ministry informed largely by secular psychology. The role of classical theology has become seriously eroded, with evangelical seminaries failing to allot it the place of honour it was once universally acknowledged as possessing. No longer, according to Wells, is theology regarded as integral to maintaining and nourishing Christian identity in the world, or as a seminal resource in forging new approaches to ministry. Wells is now widely regarded as having overstated his case. Evangelicalism has in fact produced a substantial and sustained theological output since the Second World War, and shows no particular inclination to abandon its theological heritage.[13]

-----

11. Note the perceptive comment on evangelicalism within the Church of England during the 1940s: 'Evangelicals inclined to the view that they were excused culture, scholarship and intellectual exercise on religious grounds': Manwaring 1985: 55.

12. Wells 1993.

13. See the important review essay of Braaten 1996. For a definitive guide to evangelical theology during the twentieth century, see Elwell 1993.

Yet there are other issues involved here, not least the manner in which academic theology is viewed as having become adrift from the life of the Christian community. If evangelicalism has marginalized academic theology, the problem lies at least in part with that theology itself, which has failed to ensure that it understands for itself, let alone communicates to others, its distinctive role within the evangelical community. Theology cannot expect evangelicals to assume that it possesses relevance, given the widespread contempt for academic theology within the church at large. It must *demonstrate* that relevance to a constituency whose very success has rested on its insistence that relevance is an issue.

Evangelicalism has always been aware that no revival in history has ever been born out of a renewed interest in purely academic theology. The renewal of evangelical *theology* depends upon the renewal of *evangelicalism*. It is not theology which brings a revival into being. Theology is what erupts from a self-confident and reflective community of faith, in possession of a vision of why it exists and what it proposes to do. It is the expression, not the cause, of that vision. As Ninian Smart has perceptively pointed out, 'doing theology, in the proper sense, is articulating a faith'.[14] If there is no faith to articulate, theology has nothing to convey or express. Theology may help the evangelical community to judge, reformulate, contextualize and better articulate its vision – but it cannot create that vision in the first place. A vibrant tradition of theological reflection is the outcome, rather than the cause, of a dynamic community of faith.[15]

This point can be seen clearly from the 'Death of God' controversy, which erupted during the 1960s. Much attention was then paid to its theological ideas. However, it is now clear that too little notice was taken of what is now being recognized as a lack of religious vitality within the mainline churches which seems to have occasioned the emergence of this theology.

---

14. Smart 1973: 6–7.
15. For reflections on this theme with specific reference to Anglicanism, see McGrath 1993.

While most of the philosophy and theology contained in the 'Death of God' literature seems to be very second-rate or worse, it is very necessary to reflect on how absolutely deadly must have been the experience which the writers of this literature must have had, both in the worshipping and in the theological lives of their churches. For example, the God whose death is proclaimed in Thomas Altizer's *The Gospel of Christian Atheism* is a very sick God indeed. But someone must have given him this idea of God. The evidence suggests that it comes from a very sick church.[16]

A church without any sense of vision and purpose, lacking any expectations of what God could do with it, inevitably leads directly to a weary, unfocused and irrelevant theology.

This observation would therefore seem to suggest that the future wellbeing of evangelicalism lies in evangelistic activism, perhaps – but by no means necessarily – coupled with the vigorous pursuit of sustainable spiritualities and an increased engagement with social and political issues. An emphasis on the issue of personal salvation, such as that which lay behind the complex network of regional revivals usually linked together as the 'Second Great Awakening',[17] is therefore widely regarded as integral to evangelical consolidation and expansion. The preaching styles associated with such revivals – populist sermons aimed at an emotional response – reflect the wish to bring audiences to the point where they were prepared to make commitments of personal conversion, on the basis of an immediate existential decision rather than a careful process of reflection. On the basis of the highly pragmatic criteria which evangelicalism has tended to use to measure its successes, theology had little discernible role to play in the serious business of conversion.

Evangelicalism has become a mass movement precisely because evangelicals have been concerned to identify and promote its popular appeal. Its activist, immediate and somewhat individualist approach to the Christian faith has ensured that it has maintained a high presence and profile in a culture increasingly tending towards democratic individualism. So who needs theology? There is no

16. Cited in Ramsey 1972: 21.
17. See Boles 1972; Bilhartz 1986.

place for a version of the Christian faith which has become so cerebralized that it has become the preserve of a small academic élite, and has lost any clear links with the concerns and issues confronting Christians in their everyday lives. And that, in the view of most evangelicals, is where theology takes us.

When all is said and done, however, this remains a critique of a particular style of theology – what one might loosely call 'academic theology', not in the sense of an informed and thoughtful theology, but a theology whose agenda is dictated by the values and goals of the academy; an academy which is not merely preoccupied with a series of purely 'academic questions' (in the negative sense of this phrase), but which conducts its debates on the basis of a series of non-Christian or anti-Christian assumptions. We shall explore this point in what follows.

The élitism of 'academic theology'

Academic theology is under an obligation to respond to the secularizing agenda of the professional academy, which distances it from the life and concerns of the Christian churches. The days are long since past in which 'the academy' was equated with learning, wisdom and personal integrity. Evangelicals have noted with concern some increasing indications that the modern American academy seems to have more to do with élitism, ideological warfare and rampant anti-religious propaganda than with the advancement of learning or excellence.[18] Especially in the United States, some academic theologians have often seemed to be little more than acolytes to these trends, articulating what often turn out to be profoundly illiberal theologies and firing both their opponents and less than totally enthusiastic colleagues, rather than engaging in the dialogue for which the academy was once noted, honoured and valued.[19] The strongly institutionalized liberal ethos of the modern American university, which is widely perceived to

---

18. The most widely read criticism remains Bloom 1987. This should be supplemented by more recent studies, such as D'Souza 1991.

19. For both a personal narrative and a critique of this trend, see McGlasson 1994.

be anti-Christian (although it is arguably hostile to public commit-ment of any kind, religious or otherwise), has reinforced both the determination of evangelicals to remain faithful to the gospel, rather than the latest cultural trend, and their perception that 'academic theology' is at best an irrelevance to be avoided, condi-tioned and sustained by a series of secularizing and relativizing assumptions. These evangelical perceptions may not always be entirely justified, and may occasionally reflect misreadings of complex situations. Nevertheless, it is clear that the academy has a substantial way to go before it allays evangelical fears that its agenda is, whether in intent or merely in effect, anti-evangelical.

Academic theologians occasionally refer to evangelicalism as 'naïve'. Yet this epithet requires translation. On closer examina-tion, this generally turns out to mean something like 'refusing to acknowledge the authority of the secular academy', or 'failing to accept the norms of a self-serving and closed academy'. In short, the term has little to do with intellectual ability or scholarly activ-ity; instead, it focuses on the refusal of evangelicalism to become subservient to the ideology of what is coming to be seen as an increasingly marginalized and anti-religious academy.

In this environment of growing scepticism concerning the merits and viability of academic theology, evangelicalism has insights to offer which are of relevance beyond its own bounda-ries. Theology is the servant of the church. Evangelicalism has always seen theology as part of a greater whole, rather than as a professionalized department which is isolated from the life of the church as a whole. The theologian is not someone who stands above the community of faith, but someone who is deeply involved in its life of worship, prayer, adoration and evangelism.

For evangelicalism, the theologian is one who is called to serve the community of faith from within. Part of that service is criti-cism of its ideas and outlooks – but it is a loving and caring criticism on the basis of shared Christian beliefs and commitments, rather than the modern criticism of the Christian community by academic 'theologians' on the basis of secular beliefs and values, often radically agnostic or atheistic, which that community feels no pressing reason to share. For evangelicalism, academic theology is as élitist as it is irrelevant; indeed, its irrelevance may have a direct proportional relation to its élitism. In view of the importance of the perceived élitism of the academy, we may turn to deal with this point in more detail.

Theology is potentially élitist, often contemptuous of the concerns of ordinary Christian believers, and thus finds itself strongly in tension with the populist character of North American evangelicalism. The élitism of theology raises serious concerns for evangelicalism, especially in North America. As we noted earlier, North American evangelicalism is a strongly populist movement, with a genuine heartfelt concern for the issues which are of importance to ordinary Christian believers. It takes seriously the ideas of ordinary people. Nobody has thought that about academics of any kind for a very long time; indeed, the popular stereotype of academia as being an 'ivory tower' detached from – and even contemptuous of – popular culture is too close to the truth for comfort. The detachment of the academy from the realities of everyday life is widely linked, at least in popular perceptions, with the élitism of the academy.

Evangelical theology is rooted in popular piety

Evangelicalism, then, has little time for the élitism of academic theology, and is primarily concerned with addressing the issues faced by ordinary people.[20] Yet it must be appreciated that 'populism' has its limits. Evangelicalism has ensured that the relevance of the gospel to popular culture is never sidelined through an improper concern for purely academic issues. Popular culture, however, often shows an alarming trend towards shallowness. This intellectual superficiality often means that the ideas of one generation – or even decade – are discarded in the next. Evangelicalism needs to ensure that its concern for popular appeal is never gained or maintained by throwing overboard the deep theological roots of the Christian faith, which provide it with stability and depth across generational divides. A purely 'academic' theology is élitist and irrelevant; a populist theology may well have mass appeal without having any depth. Theology, rightly understood, is about intellectual

---

20. See here the excellent study of Mouw 1994.

and spiritual depth and staying power. Given both the widespread contempt for the concern of ordinary Christians by academic theologians and the shallowness of populist theology, evangelicalism would do well to encourage the emergence of sustained serious theological reflection from a committed standpoint within the Christian community, and see the theologians as believers who think for themselves and for others within the community of faith.

A similar approach was advocated by the Marxist writer Antonio Gramsci (1891–1937), who used the sixteenth-century Reformation as a paradigm for his notion of the 'organic intellectual'.[21] This idea is of considerable importance to evangelicalism, as it reflects on the proper place of theology within its ranks. Gramsci argues that two distinct types of intellectuals can be discerned. In the first place, there are those who are imposed upon a community by an external authority. These 'traditional intellectuals' were not chosen by that community, and have influence only in so far as that authority is forced upon the community. In contrast to this, Gramsci notes – and commends – the idea of 'organic intellectuals', understood as thinkers who operate and are respected within a community, and who gain authority on account of their being seen to represent the outlook of that community. Their authority is thus not imposed, but emerges naturally, reflecting the esteem in which the community holds them and its willingness to regard them as its representatives and thinkers. This model of the theologian resonates with the experience of many evangelicals, who have come to regard 'professional theologians' with intense scepticism as a result of the irresponsibility of the 1960s and 1970s, during which much academic theology showed itself to be the willing prisoner of the latest cultural whim and treated the pastoral and spiritual needs and concerns of the churches with a scarcely disguised contempt.

The British evangelical writer John R. W. Stott is an excellent example of an 'organic intellectual' in this respect. He possesses no academic or institutional authority worth speaking of, but rightly enjoys enormous status within the evangelical community

---

21. For a detailed study of this point, see McGrath 2001: 144–155.

(and beyond) on account of his having earned that respect. People regarded him as having authority because he had been accepted as being worthy of possessing authority. There was an organic and natural relationship between this person and the community for whom he spoke, and to whom he so clearly holds himself responsible. Echoing the outlook of the Reformation, a careful reading of Gramsci's work will encourage evangelicals to look towards the community of faith, to seek and find authority in individuals with a proven record of fidelity to the Christian tradition, a concern for the *consensus fidelium*, a love for the gospel, and a responsible and informed concern to relate it to the world – whether this is recognized by the academy or not. The best intellectuals may exist and operate outside the academy! Evangelical theologians are conscious of a dual responsibility, in that they are writing both for other theologians, yet also on behalf of the evangelical community, with all the responsibilities which this brings.

The benefits of theology for evangelicalism

What benefits does theology bring to the evangelical community? Many! In what follows, I will explore only three ways in which this can happen:

- by bringing about an enhanced appreciation of the profundity of Christian doctrines
- by engaging with our emotions, allowing theological formulations to move us, for example, to tears of sorrow or joy
- by enabling us to behave in ways which reflect a deepened personal appropriation of the truth of the gospel

There are, of course, many other ways in which theology may serve the evangelical community; my concern here is simply to illustrate, rather than exhaust, the possibilities.

Enhancing our appreciation of our faith
First, let us consider how we may go about gaining an enhanced appreciation of Christian doctrines. I shall explore this point with

reference to one of the more difficult aspects of Christian theology – the doctrine of the Trinity.

The doctrine of the Trinity gathers together the richness of the complex Christian understanding of God, to yield a vision of God to which the only appropriate response is adoration and devotion. The doctrine knits together into a coherent whole the Christian doctrines of creation, redemption and sanctification. By doing so, it sets before us a vision of a God who created the world, and whose glory can be seen reflected in the wonders of the natural order; a God who redeemed the world, whose love can be seen in the tender face of Christ; and a God who is present now in the lives of believers. In this sense, the doctrine can be said to 'preserve the mystery' of God, in the sense of ensuring that the Christian understanding of God is not impoverished through reductionism or rationalism. The Brazilian liberation theologian Leonardo Boff makes this point as follows:

> Seeing mystery in this perspective enables us to understand how it provokes reverence, the only possible attitude to what is supreme and final in our lives. Instead of strangling reason, it invites expansion of the mind and heart. It is not a mystery that leaves us dumb and terrified, but one that leaves us happy, singing and giving thanks. It is not a wall placed in front of us, but a doorway through which we go to the infinity of God. Mystery is like a cliff: we may not be able to scale it, but we can stand at the foot of it, touch it, praise its beauty. So it is with the mystery of the Trinity.[22]

'Your God is too small!' There is a serious danger that theology may have precisely the reverse effect from that which is intended. At its best, theology is intended to deepen our appreciation and understanding of the richness of the Christian revelation, offering us fresh perspectives on its contents and inner dynamics. In this sense, a trinitarian theology challenges us to expand our vision of God, by reflecting on the person and works of the God who has called us and redeemed us. Yet that same theology can also limit our vision, if

---

22. Boff 1988: 159.

we define theology as the mere repetition of formulae without engagement with the realities which lie behind them.

Let me cite from a classic Reformed catechism, which sets modern evangelicalism an exciting and challenging agenda. 'What', asked the *Shorter Westminster Catechism*, 'is the chief end of man?' The answer given is rightly celebrated as a jewel in evangelicalism's theological crown: 'to glorify God and enjoy him for ever'. This brief statement sets us on a journey of theological exploration – to gain a fresh apprehension of the glory of God, so that we might return that glory to God and have our spiritual lives enrichened by the knowledge of such a God. To catch such a glimpse of the full splendor of God is also a powerful stimulus to evangelism. Was it not by catching a glimpse of the glory of God in the temple that Isaiah reponded to the divine call to go forth in service? There is a need for us to allow our minds, imaginations and emotions to be stimulated and informed by theology. Rightly grasped, it will force us to our knees in adoration and praise, as we catch a glimpse of the immensity of this God who loves us and has called us to be his own.

Engaging our emotions responsibly

It is often suggested that the British male is characterized by a 'stiff upper lip' – meaning that he refuses to show any emotions, regarding this as unmanly, demeaning, humiliating, or a worrying sign of immaturity. I am no psychologist, and cannot comment on whether this is wise or healthy. But, as the reaction to the death of Princess Diana in 1997 makes clear, the British seem perfectly capable of emotional release when the occasion is seen to demand it. So why, I find myself wondering, do so many evangelicals seem to believe that any form of emotional engagement is a worrying sign of spiritual immaturity?

I do not for one moment wish to suggest that public displays of emotion are to be encouraged, as a matter of principle. Yet surely it is not just impossible, but unthinkable, to read the accounts of the suffering and death of Jesus Christ without being moved – perhaps moved to tears? Isaac Watts (1674–1748) was convinced that much of the Christianity of his day was superficial. He longed to go deeper, and learn more. His advice to his readers reflects this concern: 'Do not hover always on the surface of things, nor take up suddenly, with mere appearances; but penetrate into the depth of matters, as far as your time and circumstances allow.' We see this concern to 'penetrate into the depth of matters' in his devotional hymns, which stimulate personal devotion through active engagement with their themes.

His best-loved hymn takes the form of a meditation on the cross, intended to evoke a sense of sorrow, wonder and commitment on the part of its audience. In 'When I survey the wondrous Cross', Watts offers a reflection on the cross, designed to allow its audience to see the attractions of the world in their proper perspective. In addition to painting a vivid word-picture of the cross, Watts stresses that all else pales into insignificance in its light. By building up a verbal picture of the sufferings of Christ for his audience, Watts hopes to move them deeply – to repentance, sorrow, and an increased commitment to their Saviour:

> When I survey the wondrous Cross
> On which the Prince of Glory died,
> My richest gain I count but loss,
> And pour contempt on all my pride.
>
> Forbid it, Lord, that I should boast
> Save in the Cross of Christ my Lord
> All the vain things that charm me most,
> I sacrifice them to his blood.
>
> See from his head, his hands, his feet
> Sorrow and love flow mingled down;
> Did e'er such love and sorrow meet?
> Or thorns compose so rich a crown?
>
> Were the whole realm of nature mine,
> That were an offering far too small;
> Love so amazing, so divine,
> Demands my soul, my life, my all.

Notice how Watts leads his readers to meditate on the cross. The hymn builds up a verbal picture of the cross, focusing attention on the pain experienced by the dying Christ, and the fact that this is the means by which the redemption of the world has been accomplished. An example may make this point clearer. 'Forgiveness' is a simple idea to understand. Yet *we need to experience the reality to which that word points.*

It is fatally easy to think that we have 'understood' the word, without entering into the real world of experience and life to which it refers. 'Forgiveness' is what restores a relationship that really matters, when you have messed it up. It is about the restoration of something which means everything to you, and which you thought you have lost forever on account of your foolishness. If you have ever been through that situation, the word 'forgiveness' will mean the transformation of your life, evoking powerful emotions and calling to mind the situation which made it necessary. Someone who has never needed to be forgiven will never know the full richness, wonder and joy of that simple word 'forgiveness'.

This point is made powerfully by J. Randall Nichols, who wrote of an experience he had while visiting the Greek island of Corfu:

> Some of the most beautiful music I ever heard was the chanting of Greek peasant women, tears streaming down their lined and hardened faces, in a church on Corfu one Good Friday. I asked someone why they were weeping. 'Because', he said, 'their Christ is dead.' I have often thought that I will never understand what resurrection means until I can weep like that.[23]

Nichols' point is that we can never appreciate the joy and hope of the resurrection, unless we have been plunged into the sense of hopelessness and helplessness which pervaded that first Good Friday. What is true of the resurrection is also true of forgiveness. Christian spirituality is grounded in an awareness of being a condemned sinner – an experience which is utterly transformed by divine forgiveness. We can never understand what forgiveness really means until we have wept the tears of condemnation.

Now suggesting that we allow our theology to impact on our

---

23. Nichols 1987.

emotions in no way detracts from its intellectual integrity. It simply helps us to identify a legitimate emotional component to our theology. Music (for example, J. S. Bach's passion chorales) and art (for example, Matthias Grünewald's depiction of the crucifixion) can help us in this quest for a proper emotional engagement with our theology. Some evangelicals are critical of any tendency to allow music and art to have any role in the life of faith, echoing similar concerns expressed in the patristic and Reformation periods.[24] Yet I believe that these can be seen as means of grace which, rightly used, have potential for helping us to focus on the person and work of Christ, and thus deepening the quality of our faith.

Enabling us to behave appropriately

Theology affects the way in which we live and behave. An excellent example is provided by the Christian vision of the New Jerusalem, which is meant to encourage us to lift our eyes upwards, and focus them on where Christ has gone before us. Paul makes this point as follows in his letter to the Colossians:

> Since, then, you have been raised with Christ, set your hearts on things above, where Christ is seated at the right hand of God. Set your minds on things above, not on earthly things. For you died, and your life is now hidden with Christ in God. (Col. 3:1–3)

Our belief concerning the New Jerusalem ought to encourage us to behave as people who are looking forward to finally being with Christ, and to view the world accordingly. This point is made, in different ways, by two great evangelical writers: Jonathan Edwards and John Stott.

One of Edwards's most compelling works is a sermon entitled 'The Christian Pilgrim'. In this sermon, Edwards is concerned to help us orientate ourselves correctly as we travel along the road of faith. As we pass through the world, what should be our attitude towards it? Because it is God's creation, we cannot reject it as evil. Yet because it is not God, it falls short of the true glory of the

---

24. See, for example, Routley 1978; Blume 1975.

ultimate goal of our journey. Edwards reminds us that our final goal is God, and that nothing else has the power to satisfy or right to be adored other than that same God.

Edwards thus declares that 'God is the highest good of the reasonable creature; and the enjoyment of him is the only happiness with which our souls can be satisfied.' We may therefore pass through the world and enjoy all that it has to offer, while realizing that the final delight of being with God will totally overwhelm whatever joy and delights this world may offer. Edwards sets out this approach in his sermon:

> We ought not to rest in the world and its enjoyments, but should desire heaven . . . We ought above all things to desire a heavenly happiness; to be with God; and well with Jesus Christ. Though surrounded with outward enjoyments, and settled in families with desirable friends and relations; though we have companions whose society is delightful, and children in whom we see many promising qualifications; though we live by good neighbors and are generally beloved where known; yet we ought not to take our rest in these things as our portion. . . . We ought to possess, enjoy and use them, with no other view but readily to quit them, whenever we are called to it, and to change them willingly and cheerfully for heaven.[25]

Edwards thus offers us a new perspective on our journey. As we travel, we are not being asked to ignore the beauties of the world through which we are passing. We may appreciate it, and see it as a foretaste of the beauty of God, whom one day we shall see in all his radiance. Nor are we being asked to withdraw from the company and love of other people. Rather, we are asked to value and appreciate this, seeing it as an anticipation of being in the presence and love of God. One day we shall have to relinquish that which is good for that which is the best. But in the meantime, we may begin to anticipate how wonderful that entry into the presence of God will be, and allow that thought to encourage and excite us as we travel on our journey.

---

25. Edwards 1966: 136–137.

A related point is made by John Stott, brings out clearly how the hope of future glory illuminates and transforms the present. In a series of addresses given to the Inter-Varsity Mission Convention at Urbana, Illinois in 1976, Stott developed the importance of the hope of glory for theology, spirituality and especially evangelism. His addresses issued a clarion call for the recovery of this leading theme of the Christian faith, and its application to every aspect of our present Christian lives.

> Lift up your eyes! You are certainly a creature of time, but you are also a child of eternity. You are a citizen of heaven, and an alien and exile on earth, a pilgrim travelling to the celestial city.
> I read some years ago of a young man who found a five-dollar bill on the street and who 'from that time on never lifted his eyes when walking. In the course of years he accumulated 29,516 buttons, 54,172 pins, 12 cents, a bent back and a miserly disposition.' But think what he lost. He couldn't see the radiance of the sunlight, and sheen of the stars, the smile on the face of his friends, or the blossoms of springtime, for his eyes were in the gutter. There are too many Christians like that. We have important duties on earth, but we must never allow them to preoccupy us in such a way that we forget who we are or where we are going.[26]

Stott encourages us to renew our acquaintance with the glory that awaits us, and begin to anticipate its wonder – and allow that to impact upon us now.

Conclusion

Throughout his lecture courses on Christian doctrine at Tyndale Hall (later Trinity College), Bristol in the 1960s and 1970s, J. I. Packer argued that theology served three functions:

> First, it deepens our understanding of Scripture, God, human nature, the church, the world, and so forth;

---

26. Stott 1977: 90.

Second, it controls our thinking and living as Christians;
Third, it assists communication of the Christian faith in mission and evangelism.[27]

On Packer's view, theology is thus essential to the life, thought and ministry of the church – a view which I have warmly endorsed throughout this essay. Theology offers evangelicalism a firm foundation upon which we may build, ensuring that the great riches and truths of the gospel stimulate and nourish our minds, emotions and imaginations. In this essay I have tried to outline some of the ways in which theology can serve the evangelical community as it advances and develops in this new millennium.

Bibliography

Bilhartz, Terry D. (1986), *Urban Religion and the Second Great Awakening*, Rutherford, NJ: Fairleigh Dickinson University Press.

Bloom, Allan (1987), *The Closing of the American Mind*, New York: Simon & Schuster.

Blume, Friedrich (1975), *Protestant Church Music: A History*, London: Victor Gollancz.

Boff, Leonardo (1988), *Trinity and Society*, London: Burns & Oates.

Boles, John B. (1972), *The Great Revival, 1787–1805: The Origins of the Southern Evangelical Mind*, Lexington, KY: University Press of Kentucky.

Braaten, Carl E. (1996), 'A Harvest of Evangelical Theology', *First Things* 61: 45–48.

D'Souza, Dinesh (1991), *Illiberal Education: The Politics of Race and Sex on Campus*, New York: Free Press.

Edwards, Jonathan (1966), 'The Christian Pilgrim', in *Basic Writings*, New York: New American Library.

Elwell, Walter A. (ed.) (1993), *Handbook of Evangelical Theologians*, Grand Rapids: Baker.

Green, Michael (1977), *The Truth of God Incarnate*, London: Hodder & Stoughton.

---

27. McGrath 1997: 182–183.

Hastings, Adrian (1986), *A History of English Christianity 1920–1985*, London: Collins.

Hendry, George S. (1960), 'Theological Table-Talk', *Theology Today* (July).

Hick, John (ed.) (1977), *The Myth of God Incarnate*, London: SCM Press.

McGlasson, Paul C. (1994), *Another Gospel: A Confrontation with Liberation Theology*, Grand Rapids: Baker.

McGrath, Alister E. (1993), *The Renewal of Anglicanism*, London: SPCK.

—— (1997), *To Know and Serve God: A Biography of James I. Packer*, London: Hodder & Stoughton.

—— (1999), *The J. I. Packer Collection*, Leicester: IVP.

—— (2000), 'Evangelical Theological Method: The State of the Art', in John G. Stackhouse (ed.), *Evangelical Futures: A Conversation on Theological Method*, 15–37, Grand Rapids: Baker.

—— (2001), *The Future of Christianity*, Oxford: Blackwell.

Manwaring, Randle (1985), *From Controversy to Co-existence: Evangelicals in the Church of England, 1914–1980*, Cambridge: Cambridge University Press.

Marsden, George (1994), *The Soul of the American University: From Protestant Establishment to Established Non-Belief*, New York: Oxford University Press.

Mouw, Richard J. (1994), *Consulting the Faithful: What Christian Intellectuals can Learn from Popular Religion*, Grand Rapids: Eerdmans.

Newman, Charles (1985), *The Post-Modern Aura: The Art of Fiction in an Age of Inflation*, Evanston: Northwestern University Press.

Nichols, J. Randall (1987), *The Restoring Word: Preaching as Pastoral Communication*, San Francisco: Harper & Row.

Packer, James I. (1973), *Knowing God*, London: Hodder & Stoughton.

—— (1990), 'An Introduction to Systematic Spirituality', *Crux 26/1*: 2–8.

Ramsey, A. M. (1972), *The Christian Priest Today*, London: SPCK.

Routley, Erik (1978), *The Church and Music: An Enquiry into the History, Nature, and Scope of Christian Judgement on Music*, London: Duckworth.

Sloan, Douglas (1994), *Faith and Knowledge: Mainline Protestantism and American Higher Education*, Louisville, KY: Westminster/ John Knox Press.

Smart, Ninian (1973), *The Science of Religion and the Sociology of Knowledge*, Princeton: Princeton University Press.

Smith, John E. (1963), *The Spirit of American Philosophy*, New York: Oxford University Press.

Stott, John (1977), 'The Biblical Basis for Declaring God's Glory', in D. M. Howard (ed.), *Declare His Glory Among the Nations*, Downers Grove: IVP.

Wells, David F. (1993), *No Place for Truth: or, Whatever Happened to Evangelical Theology?*, Grand Rapids: Eerdmans.

West, Cornel (1989), *The American Evasion of Philosophy: A Genealogy of Pragmatism*, Madison, WI: University of Wisconsin Press.

2. EVANGELICALISM AND THE CHURCH: THE COMPANY OF THE GOSPEL

Kevin J. Vanhoozer

Introduction: the best and worst of evangelical times

'The century of the church'. This was how many hopeful onlookers, impressed with Vatican II, the ecumenical movement and the charismatic movement, characterized the twentieth century. How did evangelicals fare? Charles Dickens is as good a place to start as any in describing the current situation of evangelicalism with regard to the theory and the practice of church: 'It was the best of times; it was the worst of times.'

It is the best of times
Evangelicals at the dawn of the third millennium can look around and justifiably conclude 'We have arrived.' In society, evangelicals have arrived in terms of influence. In North America evangelicals see themselves as a 'moral majority'. The political clout of evangelicals was publicly recognized by *Time* magazine when it proclaimed 1976 the Year of the Evangelical. Evangelicals have also arrived academically. They have started their own institutions of higher education and they have responded to the external

threats of biblical criticism, secular humanism and scientific naturalism. Finally, with regard to the church, evangelicals have arrived in the sense that the evangelical church has become a success story. Evangelical churches are growing numerically, employing new technologies, and developing myriad programmes for personal, familial and social development. We have arrived; we are megafamily.

There are now evangelicals not only in confessional churches but whole new evangelical denominations for those impatient with reform. Yet another sign of evangelical arrival is that evangelicals now have a seat at the ecumenical table. That Roman Catholics and evangelicals can negotiate doctrinal settlements is a sure sign that the latter have been acknowledged as having the right to exist! Finally, evangelicals have arrived culturally; instead of fleeing the world, evangelicals are trawling the cultural landscape, mining its resources for ways in which to relate the gospel to the needs of the present.

It is the worst of times

'We have arrived.' Yes, but where? The surface success of the evangelical church masks a conspicuous lack of biblical and theological substance when it comes to reflecting critically upon the nature and function of the church. The evangelical church may be wealthy, but the quantity and quality of evangelical ecclesiology is at near poverty level. To make matters worse, there is all too often a pronounced disconnect between what we say we believe (logos, world-view) and the way we live (ethos, lifestyle).

Poor reflection

Ecclesiology is the poor cousin or, in Stanley Grenz's words, 'the neglected stepchild of evangelical theology'.[1] George Vandervelde concurs: 'If there is one theological area in which evangelicalism is weak, it is ecclesiology.'[2] The reasons for this vulnerability will be discussed below, but they include the parachurch nature of the

---

1. Grenz 1993: 165.
2. Vandervelde 1999: 30.

evangelical movement and its emphasis on the salvation of the individual.

Among the many examples of neglect that could be given, two must suffice. In *Across the Spectrum*, Gregory Boyd and Paul Eddy present divergent views held by evangelicals on a number of divisive issues.[3] Included in the book's eighteen chapters are treatments of baptism, the Lord's Supper, charismatic gifts, and women in ministry, yet there is nothing on the nature and mission of the church as such. Similarly, in *This We Believe*, a book written as a kind of commentary on the much-heralded 1999 statement 'The Gospel of Jesus Christ: An Evangelical Celebration', there is no chapter on the church.[4] There is a chapter on 'unity' in the evangelical family, but the focus is on being united in the truth of the gospel. The chapter has nothing to say about the role of the church in maintaining or displaying this unity – a striking departure from the creedal affirmation, 'I believe in the holy catholic church, the communion of saints'. This, however, is precisely the problem: evangelicals by and large do not know what they believe about the church – neither about what it is, nor what it should be doing.

Poor practice

One function of the church, as we shall see, is to nurture Christians in the faith. We can assess how well an ecclesial incubator is working by examining the lives of its members. What kind of character is being formed in evangelical churches? What is the evangelical church doing with its new-found success – its influence, its numbers, its wealth? By their fruit shall ye know them. This dominical saying presents a rather stark rule for assessing spiritual health, whether of an individual or of a tradition, such as evangelicalism.

Robert Gundry has recently argued that the 'success' or arrival of North American evangelicals was won largely through an accommodation to worldly culture. This is as true of evangelicals

---

3. Boyd & Eddy 2002.
4. Akers, Armstrong & Woodbridge 2000.

in the academy, where biblical scholars often employ the same exegetical tools and methods as their liberal counterparts, as it is of evangelicals in society generally, where the shape of evangelical life often appears to be little or no different from that of non-evangelicals:

> With nonevangelicals' increasing recognition of our contributions to biblical and theological scholarship and with the consequent whetting of our appetite for academic, political, and broadly cultural power and influence are coming the dangers of accommodation, of dulling the sharp edges of the gospel, of blurring the distinction between believers and the world . . . of only whispering the Word instead of shouting him.[5]

Gundry fears that evangelicals have lost their fundamentalist edge, that they are no longer opposed to worldliness but in bed with it. What began as a faithful 'sect' – a marginal community in tension with the world – has deteriorated into an 'institution' that is quite comfortable with its new niche in the world and with its concomitant respectability. What is needed, according to Gundry, is a good dose of Johannine sectarianism: a radical commitment to the Word of God, together with a willingness to confront the 'world' for the Word's sake.

David Wells concurs. Writing in a volume entitled *The Compromised Church*, Wells laments: 'Evangelical abundance on the surface, and boundless evangelical energy, conceals a spiritual emptiness beneath it.'[6] The emptiness is partly the result of an evisceration of the doctrinal substance and moral fibre of the faith. Wells's diagnosis is similar to Gundry's: evangelical churches are increasingly inclined to adapt to culture rather than sustain an intellectual and spiritual antagonism towards it. The irony, says Wells, is that in order to be relevant, the church has to be *different*, otherwise it has nothing significant to offer.

---

5. Gundry 2002: 74.
6. Wells 1998: 22.

Poor worship

The poverty of evangelical theory and practice of the church shows up most spectacularly, perhaps, in the poverty of its worship. Our worship is an index of our knowledge of God and of the extent of the cultural accommodation of our faith.[7] Worship also 'reveals and forms our identity as persons and communities'.[8] Marva Dawn is concerned that evangelicals may be 'dumbing down' the church, choosing user-friendly styles and techniques that lack the necessary intellectual substance and spiritual fibre to nurture excellence in our attempts to know and praise God.

The idea that the church should change its worship in order to attract people to Christ is a fallacious notion, as is the idea that worship should attract people to church because it meets their felt needs. 'Success is the most dangerous idolatry the Church must resist in its worship.'[9] Worship is primarily about God, not us. According to Dawn, the failure of the church's worship stems not from offering people too much or something too deep, but from offering too little or something too shallow: 'The only means for keeping worship free of idolatries is to keep God the subject.'[10] The point is to ask the right questions: not 'How can we get more people to come to our 9 o'clock service?' but rather, 'How can we best praise God and form faithful disciples?'

Marketing strategies typically do not focus on what is essential (viz. the gospel 'product') but on what is peripheral (viz. the congregational 'packaging'). Dawn cites a study by William Hendricks which discovered that many people stop participating in worship because of boredom.[11] Much of what our churches offer – music, entertainment, therapy, food – is available elsewhere. What is not available elsewhere, however, is the preaching and celebration of the gospel in word, sacrament and worship. What is not available

---

7. See Vanhoozer 2002: 3–16.

8. Dawn 1995: 4.

9. Ibid.: 285.

10. Ibid.: 285.

11. Ibid.: 287.

elsewhere is *theology*: 'Our worship should cause us to ask . . . Who is God? How does God want to use me and the community to which I belong for his purposes in the world?'[12] Genuine worship that focuses on the reality of God will be subversive to the extent that it confronts denizens of contemporary culture with the way of Jesus Christ rather than with Christian variations upon a secular theme.

It is the most urgent of times

So which is it: best or worst? boom or bust? A case can be made on both sides, according to what aspect of evangelicalism one has in mind. What does appear to be incontrovertible, however, is that we are living in urgent times. Christendom no longer exists in the West. Religion has been privatized. Decisions now being taken about how best to respond to these changes will lead to habits and trends that will in turn shape the future character of evangelicalism. The church is confronted with an either-or of Kierkegaardian proportions: shall we compromise or shall we remain faithful? Faithfulness, I hasten to add, is not incompatible with creativity. The decision is not between preserving the forms and contents of the past and experimenting with the new, so much as it is between being a people of the culture rather than of the gospel, between (to put it in the starkest terms) being a people of the world rather than of the Word.

Virtually every other issue addressed in the present volume has a direct bearing on our understanding of the church, *and vice versa*. The church – the way evangelicals live out their faith together – is a veritable *summa* of evangelical experience and evangelical theology. Confusion about the nature and function of the church is thus a symptom of a more serious confusion, a confusion about evangelical identity and evangelical vocation. This is no time to rest on our laurels. It is rather the time to rediscover the privilege and responsibility of being a member of Christ's church, of being a person in the people of the gospel. Hence my thesis: the best of times for evangelicalism must be *church* times, and the best church

---

12. Dawn 1995: 295.

times must be *evangelical* times. But what is the church, and what does it mean to be evangelical?

'Mere ecclesiology': the problem and the project

To begin with, there is no such thing as 'the' evangelical church. Evangelicals are found in many denominations, only some of which explicitly wear the label. Yet every genuine church must be evangelical in some sense inasmuch as the people of God must also be people of the gospel: a people gathered together from all the nations by the preaching of the Word, a people summoned and empowered by the Holy Spirit to be the body of Christ. Precisely because evangelicals do not have any single ecclesiology of their own, it is preferable to think in terms of 'mere ecclesiology'.

The problem: the vanishing evangelical identity
I freely admit to being part of the problem. For years I actively avoided teaching the required course on ecclesiology, and not only because it was paired with eschatology! No, I wanted no part of a course whose syllabus seemed to consist of a hit parade of controversies, a series of the doctrines that divide.[13] Nothing is more depressing than constant family squabbles. As a result, my grasp of ecclesiology was both ambivalent and ambiguous.

Ecclesiological invisibility
I was not alone. Evangelical ecclesiology was largely invisible on the radar screen of twentieth-century theology. But the real problem lay in another kind of invisibility, namely, the notion that the true church is an invisible fellowship of believers, seen only by God. Stanley Grenz traces this emphasis back to evangelicalism's Pietist heritage: 'In setting the new birth as the principal article of faith while challenging the efficacy of churchly rites

---

13. I am thinking of issues such as the mode of baptism, the role of women in ministry, the place of charismatic gifts, the nature of ordination and church polity.

such as baptism and mere adherence to church doctrine, the Pietists inaugurated a new vision of what it means to be a Christian.'[14] Henceforth, the church was a spiritual fellowship of the truly converted, a group that transcended particular ecclesiastical affiliations.[15]

Evangelical ecclesiology typically tends to be an account of the invisible church. 'The operative principle of evangelical ecclesiology from its inception has been the distinction between the invisible church of the truly converted and the church as a visible institution, whose members include both true believers and nominal Christians.'[16] The priority given to the individual's decision of faith, and to the individual's invisible relation to Christ, goes a long way towards accounting for what George Marsden has observed: 'One of the striking features of much of evangelicalism is its general disregard for the institutional church.'[17] Bloesch, too, attributes the 'appalling neglect' of ecclesiology in evangelicalism to the emphasis on the individual's decision of faith rather than the community's subsequent nurture of faithful individuals.[18]

'The invisible church must increase, but the visible church must decrease.' Is it really the case that evangelicals have elevated the invisible church at the expense of the visible church? I shall suggest below that we recast the invisible–visible distinction in terms of the eschatological already–not yet. The immediate task, however, is to explore the consequence of privileging the invisible church. The most glaring consequence is easily identified: the

---

14. Grenz 2000: 291.

15. Cf. Mohler's comment (1990: 530) that 'The evangelical movement itself ... was largely a parachurch movement. The momentum and defining characteristics of the movement came from the parachurch institutions which shaped the evangelical consciousness.' Among these organizations, one might cite the Inter Varsity Fellowship movement, the Tyndale Fellowship, and such publications as *Christianity Today* and *The Evangelical Quarterly*.

16. Grenz 2000: 297.

17. Marsden 1991: 81.

18. Bloesch 1983: 127.

visible church is, for all soteriological intents and purposes, irrelevant. The result: participation in the visible church appears optional. Furthermore, perception that the church is soteriologically irrelevant is symptomatic of a more troubling problem, namely, a diminished understanding of salvation. Can salvation really be boiled down to an individual's personal relation to Christ? As we shall see, there is good reason to think that such an individualist emphasis owes as much to modern culture as it does to the biblical gospel.

Why do we need the institutional church if we have direct access to heaven? Why not rely on one's own individual relation to Christ and on parachurch organizations? Why indeed? Evangelicals would do well to ponder Calvin's remarks on the necessity of the visible church. Though he acknowledged that the church was the invisible company of the elect, Calvin also stressed the importance of the visible body of believers who participate in, and benefit from, the ministry of word and sacrament. The title of Book IV of Calvin's *Institutes*, which is also the longest part, says it all: 'The external means or aids by which God invites us into the society of Christ and holds us therein.' The point is not that we need a human institution to mediate salvation, but rather that the church is a God-ordained means for inculcating and cultivating the salvation that we have in Christ. Thinking primarily of its nurturing role, Calvin goes so far as to speak of the church as our 'mother', from whom we must learn and be comforted all our lives. The church is part of God's providential plan; nay, the church is part of divine providence, part of God's provision for human sin and weakness. For the Christian life is not simply a matter of faith's one-time decision, but of faith's ongoing nurture – hence the necessity and significance of the visible church.

Evangelical identity

To propose an evangelical ecclesiology is to presuppose that we know what 'evangelical' means. In fact, the two problems – clarifying the meaning of evangelical identity and the role of the church in fostering and expressing evangelical identity – are interrelated. Consider, for example, Stanley Grenz's recent suggestion that evangelical self-understanding is torn between pietism and propositionalism.[19] He argues that the unity of evangelicalism is more properly established on the basis of a common experience of faith rather than in a common affirmation of doctrine. Convertive piety is prior to orthodox doctrine.[20]

Grenz's proposed understanding of what it means to be an evangelical carries obvious implications for theology and ecclesiology alike. In the first place, theology is to be 'communitarian'. Because the beliefs (or faith) one holds 'are dependent on the community in which we are situated',[21] theology becomes the 'articulation of the belief-mosaic' of the Christian community.[22] The church is thus central for Grenz in two ways: first, the community shapes individual experience and identity (faith); second, the community is a necessary condition for undertaking theology (faith seeking understanding). We can restate Grenz's communitarian ecclesiology in terms of a material and a formal principle. Materially, the church is central because God's whole purpose in salvation is to form a new people. The conclusion to the story of salvation is, in a word, community. Formally, the church is central because theology is the articulation of the community's 'mosaic of beliefs'. On Grenz's account, the church stands at the core of evangelical identity and theology alike.

Grenz makes his case for the primacy of ecclesiology from two different directions at once: in the first place, he accepts the postmodern point that meaning, knowledge and truth are community constructions: 'As church dogmatics – as the faith of

---

19. Grenz 2002.

20. Interestingly, Grenz (2002: 63) notes that the Pietists' concern regarding the experience of new birth and the assurance of salvation ('experimental religion') may have been influenced by eighteenth-century empiricism, but he does not appear to be worried by it.

21. Grenz 2000a: 132.

22. 'Articulating the Christian Belief-Mosaic' is the title of Grenz's chapter in Grenz 2000a. This belief-mosaic is informed by biblical narrative. But it appears that it is the community's, not Scripture's, web of belief that theology is to articulate.

the community seeking understanding – theology is inherently communitarian.'[23] In the second place, he argues that community is theology's integrative motif, 'the theme around which a systematic theology is structured'.[24] For God's ultimate goal in human history, according to Scripture, is precisely the formation of community.

Clearly, Grenz gives a compelling account both of evangelical identity and of the centrality of the church to evangelical theology. Yet there is reason to wonder whether his solution to the endemic dilemma of pietism and scholasticism is adequate. If part of the church's remit is the nurture of Christian identity, then it makes a considerable difference whether that identity is viewed in primarily cognitive, moral or affective terms. Must evangelicals choose 'heart' over 'head'? Should the evangelical church have to choose between doctrine and life? Grenz's solution gives pride of place to convertive piety, with the result that theology becomes something like the 'articulation of religious feelings set forth in speech' – Schleiermacher's definition of doctrine. Grenz differs from Schleiermacher in one important respect, namely, by emphasizing the role of the community both in shaping and in articulating the experience of faith.

What kind of Christian identity should evangelical churches seek to nurture? I am unhappy with the dichotomy between piety and propositions. I want my truth, and I want to feel it too. Grenz's account of a bifurcated evangelical identity recalls Kant's similarly bifurcated analysis of modernity. Kant's problem was how to synthesize his theory of knowledge (facts) with his theory of morality (values). He, too, was not sure how to bridge the divide between head and heart, the cognitive and volitional, metaphysics and morals. Grenz, like Schleiermacher, simply chooses to rank Kant's ethics and *Critique of Practical Reason* over his metaphysics and *Critique of Pure Reason*. Yet Kant himself introduced a third term: the imagination. I believe that evangelicals should do something similar.

---

23. Grenz 2000a: 133.
24. Ibid.: 132.

Intellectualism and moralism alike are fatal to genuine faith; evangelical churches must avoid them both. It is fatal, on the one hand, to equate faith with intellectual assent. Too many people in our churches identity themselves as evangelicals because they can give mental assent to a list of doctrines. We have far too many believers and far too few disciples. Bonhoeffer was right: 'cheap grace' – the preaching of forgiveness but not of discipleship – is the enemy of the evangelical church. Moralism – the notion that to be an evangelical is to behave a certain way – is equally damaging. Going through external motions, even when they are moral, is not the equivalent of having one's inner being renewed and transformed. To this extent, Grenz is right to highlight convertive piety, an experience of the Spirit's work.

Evangelical identity, I submit, is best viewed as formed by what we might call the evangelical imagination, namely, by the biblical narratives that display the world as it really is: created, fallen and redeemed. By imagination I am referring not to the capacity to produce images of things that are not there, but rather to the capacity to apprehend a dimension of reality that eludes sensory perception. The imagination is a distinct cognitive faculty that grasps diverse persons and events together in a kind of synoptic vision; it is the ability to grasp diverse parts in terms of a unified whole (or story). Evangelicals locate their identity in the gospel story concerning what God was doing in Jesus Christ. The gospel story should enjoy epistemic and existential primacy, serving as the norm for knowledge and ethics alike. In short: the imagination is the way to integrate the head and the heart: the unities it grasps are both thought and felt.[25]

The imagination is linked to another whole-grasping activity: the gaining of wisdom. It is not enough to know the facts of the Bible; one has to know how to apply and relate to them. The imagination is in this respect an ally of wisdom: the ability to see how things fit together and to know how one may oneself rightly fit in. Evangelicals must define themselves in terms of the gospel; the

---

25. Cf. C. S. Lewis on the superiority of story as a synthesis of 'seeing' (knowing) and 'tasting' (experiencing).

story of Jesus is the evangelical norm and criterion for understanding the true, the good and the beautiful.[26] 'Evangelical' thus simultaneously names a renaissance of faith (born-again), a reformation of doctrine (Bible-believing), and a revitalization of the imagination (Bible-indwelling).

The project: 'mere ecclesiology'

I have now repented of my sin of omission, my earlier disregard of ecclesiology. Ecclesiology has become one of the most exciting doctrines I teach. Why? What changed? Two things. First, I decided to focus not on the areas of disagreement that bedevil evangelicalism but rather on the essential core of the doctrine of the church, namely, on understanding the basic nature and the basic mission of the church: 'mere ecclesiology'. Second, I came to see that the church both cultivates and illustrates what it is that evangelicals believe, not least about the gospel. The church is not merely a doctrine but the life Christians live before God to God's glory. It is in this sense that the evangelical church is a living *summa* of evangelical theology. One of the major contentions of the present essay is that the church is a *theological* community.

Mere ecclesiology and mere evangelicalism go hand in hand. Each focuses on primary truths rather than on the secondary matters that so often divide evangelicals. I am using the term 'mere' not in the sense of 'trivial' but rather, with C. S. Lewis, in the sense of *essential*. The way forward for the evangelical church is to recover the truth and power of the gospel: the promise and summons of God's saving purpose to create a people with whom to fellowship. For the church is a fellowship: *ekklēsia* in the New Testament always mean 'assembly' or 'gathering', never 'building'.[27] The church is thus the people of the gospel, a people assembled by the gospel in order to proclaim the gospel.

---

26. On the role of beauty in the church, see Vanhoozer (2003b).
27. Tinker (2002: 149) exhorts us to use the term 'church' more precisely in order to avoid such misunderstandings.

'Mere' evangelicalism

To be a 'mere' evangelical is to correspond to the gospel. It is to confess its message (the written word) and to conform to its matter (the living Word): 'An evangelical theology is one which is evoked, governed, and judged by the gospel.'[28] Mere evangelicalism affirms the twin convictions that God has acted salvifically (there is good news) and that God has spoken truthfully (this news comes to us through the inspired Scriptures). According to Bernard Ramm, 'evangelical Christianity refers to that version of Christianity which places the priority of the Word and Act of God over the faith, response, or experiences of men'.[29] 'Evangelical' in this sense is more a statement of an objective than an already attained goal, more of a theological prescription than a sociological description. The aim is to be biblical: to correspond in word, thought, and deed to the canonically attested gospel.

I have a dream . . . that the evangelical church will recover its vision for mere evangelicalism. I work and pray for a new day for evangelicalism, for a mere evangelicalism that would be characterized by three distinguishing features.

(1) Mere evangelicalism is *radical* in its insistence that we continually return to faith's root, the Scriptures. A radical evangelicalism holds the canonical Scriptures, as the cradle and indispensable context of the gospel, as the primary criterion of truth and life. The biblical testimony to what God the Father has done and is doing in and through God the Son and God the Spirit is the touchstone for determining what is true, good and beautiful. Mere evangelicalism is radical, secondly, in the sense of being willing to confront contemporary culture with the claims of the gospel. Radical evangelicalism is thus rooted in objectivity (Word) and passionate in its subjectivity (Spirit).

(2) Mere evangelicalism is *irenic* in granting that the gospel is not the sole possession of evangelicals. While we must strive to preserve the integrity of the gospel from false interpretations, we must also acknowledge our own cultural conditioning and strive to be at

---

28. Webster 2001a: 191.

29. Ramm 2000: 13.

peace with as many other confessing Christians as possible. Mere evangelicalism is irenic because it focuses on the essentials (i.e., what is necessary to maintain the integrity of the gospel) and evinces both humility and charity with regard to the non-essentials.

(3) Mere evangelicalism is *joyful* because it knows that of all the words that can be heard, the gospel is the best. Evangelicals celebrate the fullness of life made possible by Jesus Christ. A 'dour' evangelicalism is thus a contradiction in terms. Evangelical joy is not simply an emotion but a whole person response to what God has done in Jesus Christ. The *euangelion* issues in *eucharist*, thanksgiving. Mere evangelicals see their highest calling in life in terms of praising, glorifying and enjoying the God of the gospel. The church is integral to this task.

Mere ecclesiology

There is no such organization as 'the' evangelical church. There are evangelical denominations, to be sure, but the church of Jesus Christ is one. It is precisely because evangelicals exist in many confessional churches and denominations that we can speak of a 'mere ecclesiology'. The role of evangelicals with regard to the church is to promote and preserve the integrity of the gospel. The evangelical understanding of church should thus be oriented towards mere ecclesiology, towards becoming a people of the gospel. Our loyalty must be to the one church of which Jesus Christ is the head, not to this or that denomination.[30]

'Always reforming' and 'always renewing' should be the watchword of the evangelical with regard to the church. Evangelicalism was originally a renewal movement within mainstream confessional Christianity. Indeed, one way of construing evangelicalism would be to view it as a renaissance (the experience of rebirth in the Spirit) and reformation (the practice of biblical authority). What is distinctively evangelical about this movement of reform and renewal is its source and norm: the gospel. To speak of mere ecclesiology is to envision a people dedicated to continuing the initiative of the

---

30. I shall discuss the implications of this position for the question of church order and leadership later in this essay.

gospel (evangelism), to protecting the integrity of the gospel (theology), and to practising the gospel by living in its light (church). A mere evangelical ecclesiology sees the church as the people of the gospel, charged with witnessing to the gospel, with displaying the wisdom of the gospel and with worshipping the God of the gospel.

The church between gospel and culture: the perennial crisis

A people of the gospel – a bold claim, to be sure, and to a large extent, premature. For the witness, wisdom and worship of too many evangelical churches have been compromised by an accommodation to culture. Here we may recall Niebuhr's famous typology charting the possible relations of church and culture: Christ above culture; Christ against culture; Christ of culture; Christ the transformer of culture. Into which type do evangelicals fit? Probably there are individual evangelical churches that fit into every type. I want to focus, however, on what I take to be the constant temptation and besetting sin of evangelicalism, namely, that of confusing gospel and culture.[31]

Evangelicals have long been in the trenches of the Western front, fighting off the giants of modernity's intellectual landscape: Hume, Hegel, Freud, Marx, Darwin, Bultmann, Tillich and the like in order to preserve the integrity of the gospel. However, while evangelicals were successfully resisting modern notions, they were at the same time conspiring with modern values, methods and practices. The great irony of twentieth-century evangelicalism has been its capacity simultaneously to resist modern thinking and to accommodate modern culture.

'Like all the nations'
My children discovered the secret for becoming popular or cool in secondary school: act like everybody else; do what the cool kids do. All too often, this means compromising one's principles, but

---

31. See the very helpful collection of essays on this subject in Hunsberger & Van Gelder 1996.

this is a price many are prepared to pay. Israel, too, was constantly tempted to be like the other nations, 'keeping up with the Joneses' of Canaan and Egypt by worshipping false gods. And, in what is perhaps the most revealing instance, the elders of Israel decided they wanted a human ruler rather than to be ruled by God after the divine fashion: 'now appoint for us a king to govern us like all the nations' (1 Sam. 8:5).[32]

'Like all the nations'. Evangelicals, like Israel before them, apparently want to be like all the cool institutions. 'Give us new management techniques and marketing tools!'; 'Give us magazines and television and movies!'; 'Give us programmes and specialists!'. There is a rush to adopt and adapt the latest business, psychological, media and even entertainment strategies for the church. There is a rush to imbibe the wisdom of the world and use it to promote Christ. James Turner's book on the origins of unbelief in the modern world contains a surprising conclusion. Instead of assigning blame to science or secularization, Turner pins the primary responsibility on religion itself. Specifically, faith was lost not because churches failed to adapt to changes in the culture around them, but precisely because they did adapt, often to the point of capitulation.[33] The basic problem was not the fact that the church was threatened by outside forces (such has always been the case), but rather the way in which the church responded to these threats. Cultural accommodation is a fateful step towards self-imposed irrelevance.

The question is whether culture is not a Trojan Horse, a gift from the world to the church that the church invites in (= accommodates) only at risk of self-destruction. At the same time, we must be careful not to make summary judgements. Can we simply identify 'culture' with the Johannine *cosmos*, with the light-hating dark-loving world that opposes the Word throughout the Fourth Gospel?[34]

---

32. Biblical quotations in this chapter are from the NRSV.

33. Turner 1985.

34. As Gundry (2002: 56–62) points out, only God loves the world in the Fourth Gospel. Neither Jesus nor his disciples are depicted as loving (or even praying for!) the world. Sectarians are precisely those who identify themselves by their opposition to the world, to the secular powers that be.

Everything hinges on how we understand 'culture' and 'world', and on the extent to which we admit the possibility of common grace.[35] There is clearly an antithesis between the love of God and the love of self, between the City of God and the city of Man; but can we simply identify this opposition with the tension between church and culture? Or might the tension rather be located between the two powers: the power of sin and the power of grace? In the latter case, it follows that the antithesis may not be between the church and world *simpliciter* so much as between sin and faithful obedience – a dichotomy that, sad to say, pervades the visible church too.

Even if we cannot simply identify culture with worldliness, the church must still exercise great caution and wise discernment before buying into cultural presuppositions, preferences and practices. The spirit of the age, just like any other spirit, must be tested (1 John 4:1). For example, the church should work for justice and freedom, but it must also ensure that these are not simply the cover stories for sub-Christian ideologies. Practically speaking, however, the church will rarely adopt a stance that is either totally against culture without losing its sense of mission, or a stance that is totally of culture without losing its sense of identity. The church instead lives in the precarious interstice *between gospel and culture* precisely in order to engage culture with the gospel.

Even when we take all the nuances and subtleties into consideration, however, it is becoming increasingly apparent to those with ears to hear and eyes to see that the evangelical church has frequently let culture transform the church rather than vice versa. Let me count the ways . . .

Modern individualism
One of the most prominent and potent challenges to the evangelical church comes straight off a page of modernity: individualism. The Enlightenment viewed society as the voluntary contract between autonomous individuals. Indeed, Kant defined the Enlightenment in terms of the ability to think and choose for oneself rather than submitting to some authority. Individualism is

---

35. See Mouw 2001.

a distinctly modern ideology that promotes the sacred value of the self: individual freedom, private property and personal wealth, personal fulfilment, self-improvement and the self-made man, the right to pursue one's own happiness.[36]

Modern social contract thinking about the state has had its impact on the church as well. It was easy for nineteenth-century evangelicals to see the church as a voluntary association of individuals who were believers before they were members of the church. On this model, the individual believer is prior to the church: 'Rather than constituting its members, the church is constituted *by* believers, who are deemed to be in a sense complete "spiritual selves" prior to, and apart from, membership in the church.'[37] One's personal relationship with Jesus is, similarly, prior to one's relation to the church. The problem with this picture is that it reduces the church to something dispensable, to what Robert Bellah calls a 'lifestyle enclave': a group of persons united by their shared interest in a project that they believe will contribute to their individual good.[38]

Where individualism goes, consumerism follows. To elevate the individual is to focus on *my* needs, *my* wants, *my* fulfilment. Individualism encourages people to shop around for the church best tailored to meet their needs. But the very notion of 'designer churches' that cater to the demand of the market belies the true nature of the church. Let me be clear. I am not asking evangelicals to surrender their individual personhood in order to merge into some grand ecclesial collective. I am rather questioning whether the modern understanding of personhood is compatible with the Bible's emphasis on life in community. One aspect of what God was doing in Christ is forming a new community; community is part of God's plan. In the words of George Vandervelde: 'The challenge for evangelical ecclesiology is to develop a more integral

---

36. See Roxburgh 1996: 322–323 for an examination of the ways in which pastoral ministry has been affected by therapeutic approaches and by 'technical rationality'.

37. Grenz 2000: 314.

38. See Bellah 1986.

understanding and practice of the communal reality of the new reality inaugurated by Christ.'[39] Individuals may have a personal relationship with Jesus in the privacy of their own homes, but they cannot find community in their closets.

Modernization and McDonaldization

George Rizter suggests that society is being transformed by 'McDonaldization': 'the process by which the principles of the fast food restaurant are coming to dominate more and more sectors of American society as well as of the rest of the world'.[40] McDonaldization is an apt metaphor for the modernization of society in general, for these social forces and forms – secularization, industrialization, bureacratization – embody the Enlightenment ideals of rationality and progress.

Modern society is a triumphalistic exercise of instrumental rationality in the domain of social life. Instrumental rationality is the operative concept; seeing its success in the realm of nature, modern thinkers have sought to apply a similar kind of means–end reasoning process to society. The scientific method has enabled us to gain mastery over our physical environment; perhaps reason might enable us to gain mastery over our social environment as well? What does this have to do with McDonald's? Just this. The aim of McDonald's is to 'master' the manufacture and marketing of immediate and efficient meals. McDonald's has 'rationalized' the notion of the restaurant. Moreover, it has reproduced this process on a global scale. Never mind the arches; McDonald's is the arch modern institution.

Rizter compellingly demonstrates that the principles of fast-food preparation have appeared in a variety of institutions that have nothing to do with fast food per se. We now have drive-through banks and pharmacies. It is possible to be examined and fitted for eyeglasses, or to have one's photos developed, in an hour. These cultural trends indicate the importance placed on such qualities as immediacy, calculability and efficiency. Business management and

---

39. Vandervelde 2003: 19.
40. Rizter 1993: 1. See also Shenk 1996.

marketing techniques have made inroads into the church too. The desire to meet felt needs, or to be 'seeker-sensitive', is a euphemism for 'let the market decide'.

Yet another symptom of modern culture's influence in the evangelical church is the trend towards specialization. As I have indicated, the project of the Enlightenment was to apply instrumental reason – technique – to more and more areas of life. 'How to' books are the paradigmatic literary genre of modernity. The result: increasing specialization. Whereas 'Renaissance man' refers to the generalist who knows a little about everything, his modern counterpart is typically a specialist who knows everything about a little. With increasing specialization comes the problem of fragmentation. This is as much a problem in the pastoral ministry as it is in theological seminaries. With regard to theological education, the most debilitating consequence has been the divide between biblical studies and theology, each of which is a distinct profession and each of which has its many sub-specialities. Similarly, in the church there are now many different kinds of specialist pastors (e.g. preaching, counselling, youth, adult).

T. S. Eliot eloquently states the case against specialization:

Where is the wisdom we have lost in knowledge?
Where is the knowledge we have lost in information?[41]

Neither mastering techniques nor manipulating information can effectively address the human condition. Take, for example, the phenomenon of dieting. There are hundreds of books, methods, techniques, products, aids and support groups to help people lose weight. Yet there are also more overweight people than ever, at least in the modern West. As Richard Watson argues in *The Philosopher's Diet*, we do not need rocket science to know that the way to lose weight is to 'eat less'.[42] To be truly effective, however, we need to change our lifestyle. We need to reorder the desires of our heart (and not only the heart). But this means acquiring virtue,

41. Choruses from 'The Rock'.
42. Watson 1998: 8.

forming character – spiritual formation. Unfortunately, there are no quick and easy techniques for that! People buy diet books in order to maintain the illusion that they can change themselves through self-therapy. Evangelical churches should know better: real personal change requires more than will power, drugs or techniques. Genuine change requires a work of the Holy Spirit.

Too many specialists spoil the holy broth. Yet it is easier to dispense practical advice than it is to cultivate wisdom. Specialization creates the illusion that life is under our control by dividing life up into manageable dimensions. And speaking of management, that is another symptom of the extent to which the church has borrowed from secular culture. Some pastors joke (only it is too near the truth to be funny) that they would have been better prepared for their ministry had they obtained an MBA rather than an M.Div. degree.

What is the nature of evangelical church ministry? Specifically, what model should we use when thinking about the pastor? The Victorian pastor really was a 'master' of divinity, trained in the biblical languages, the intellectual of the community. Common models for the modern pastor are the therapist and the manager. When churches are modelled after business, however, pastors must needs become managers: of personnel, of finances, of programmes. And this brings us back to the McDonaldization of the church. According to George Hunsberger, the church in modernity has become a 'vendor of religious services and goods'.[43] Local churches become retail outlets or franchises of the denominational brand, and the denomination becomes the corporate headquarters. And the congregation becomes the customer, whose needs are always right.

The gospel of success

Well, why not? Evangelical churches have grown into megachurches, and it is a truism that church growth is good. But is it? Everything depends on the *kind* of growth. There is a kind of growth or gain with which the Scriptures are distinctly unimpressed:

---

43. Hunsberger 1996a: 337–338.

'For what will it profit a man, if he gains the whole world and for-
feits his life?' (Matt. 16:26). The operative concept here is profit.
The church must beware of buying into worldly understandings of
success. What is success? For McDonald's, the answer is easy: it is
profits and dividends, billions buying burgers. Ought the church use
the same kind of reckoning: 'over 1 billion seated'? This is a pragmatic definition of success, where success is defined in terms of
what works, what sells, what attracts people to church, what appears
to meet people's needs. What if we gain the whole world but forfeit
our life – the integrity, the fundamental truth and power, of the
gospel? Woe is me if I preach McGospel!

Revisioning the church: ecclesiology as first theology?

Whereas instrumental reason is a hallmark of modernity, tradi-
tion-based rationality is the postmodern watchword. The
philosopher Alasdair MacIntyre contends that all reasoning takes
place within the framework of some tradition or other. MacIntyre
defines tradition as a 'socially embodied argument' about how best
to interpret a formative text. The new respect accorded to tradition in postmodernity has put a premium on the related notions of
'community' and 'practice'. A practice is a form of co-operative
human activity that is directed to some good end, but not necessarily to a 'product'.[44] The most telling criticism of the notion of
individual autonomy has therefore come, interestingly enough,
from philosophy.

Biblical scholars and theologians have been quick to jump
aboard the communitarian bandwagon, so much so that the postmodern turn might well be turned the 'turn to communal
practice'. Much more could, of course, be said about the postmodern condition and its significance for the church.[45] I wish to
focus, however, on the way in which the turn to communal practice has set the stage for one of the most remarkable theological

---

44. MacIntyre 1984: 187; cf. Kelsey 1992: 118.
45. See Vanhoozer 2003a: ch. 1.

comebacks, alongside trinitarian theology, of the twentieth century. The doctrine of the church has, in the last decade or so, moved to the forefront of theological research and writing, primarily among non-evangelicals – so much so that ecclesiology has effectively displaced the doctrine of revelation as 'first theology'.[46]

John Milbank: inhabiting the City of God

John Milbank, the founder of the Radical Orthodoxy movement that embraces a number of theologians connected to Cambridge University, contends that theology is first and foremost ecclesiology.[47] The church is first and foremost a new practice: a new language game and a new form of life. Needless to say, Milbank has no sympathy for the notion that Christianity concerns the relation of individuals to God. The City of God is just that: a real *polis* or society, complete with a distinctive politics, a set of concrete practices that demonstrate a wholly new form of social organization and power (e.g. charity rather than self-love). Theology is, for Milbank, the grammar of the church: the exposition of ecclesial practice. Church practice thus becomes the primary text, theology the commentary. The meaning of the gospel is unintelligible, he claims, apart from its concrete embodiment in human practices such as forgiving, sharing, peacemaking and so forth. Theology is itself a social science, the science of the *societas* of Christ. The church, then, is the socially embodied argument that displays the very meaning of the story of Jesus.

Stanley Hauerwas: church as alien nation

Evangelicals are not used to being criticized by 'liberals' for not taking their faith seriously enough. Stanley Hauerwas hardly qualifies as a modern liberal, but he is no evangelical either, largely because he thinks evangelicals have not taken the church seriously enough. Hauerwas wants the church to become more sectarian than it has been; he worries that the church, especially its evangelical segment, has lost both its saltiness and its peculiarity. The issue

---

46. For a fuller elaboration of 'first theology', see Vanhoozer 2002a: ch. 1.

47. See esp. Milbank 1990: ch. 12.

is not whether the church should be 'in' or 'of' the world; the church need not worry about *whether* to be in the world: 'The church's only concern is *how* to be in the world'.[48] Evangelicals are mistaken, Hauerwas believes, in thinking that they can be biblical without hearkening to tradition and without undergoing the discipline of being members of the visible church. 'Outside the church, there is no (good) interpretation,' Hauerwas might well say.

Hauerwas worries that evangelicals, particularly in North America, bring their democracy to church. The majority rules. And those who don't like what the majority decides – about worship styles, about Sunday school and the like can vote with their feet and leave the First Presbyterian church and try the Second (or Third): 'Evangelicalism cannot help but be susceptible to a market economy to try to attract people on the grounds that "we have what you've been looking for."'[49] The alternative, says Hauerwas, is to recover the practice of discipleship, where new converts are apprentices to masters. One learns to pray the way one learns to lay bricks: by doing it with someone who has more experience and skill. The church thus becomes the key to forming Christian virtues, habits and character. So Hauerwas might also say: 'Outside the church there is no sanctification.' The church's vocation is to preserve its distinct identity, and hence to resist the pressure of becoming like its surrounding liberal democratic individualist culture. The church's calling is to be the kind of community that displays habits and virtues formed by the story of Jesus.

John Yoder: practising the politics of Jesus

Evangelicals are also unaccustomed to other Christians taking Jesus more seriously than they do, but Yoder may well be a case in point. John Howard Yoder wants a church that practices the politics of Jesus – a community of disciples that live the way Jesus lived. Yoder distinguishes this kind of church – a confessing

---

48. Hauerwas & Willimon 1989: 43.
49. Comment made by Hauerwas in an interview with Clapp (1998).

church – from its activist and conversionist counterparts.[50] Activist churches want to build a better society: more peace, more justice. However, this is simply a glorified policy of giving unto Caesar what is Caesar's (viz. the state's). Conversionist churches – including many evangelical bodies – work for inner change in individuals. Consequently, they have no alternative social theory or practice to offer the world.

Milbank, Hauerwas and Yoder himself subscribe to the third or 'confessing' type of church. The church, on this view, is a community of disciples that seek to display a kind of social life that the world cannot manufacture: a community where people tell the truth, keep their promises, bear one another's burdens, forgive those who offend them, and love their enemies.[51] The church is a community on and of the way – the way of Jesus Christ. Its principal concern is with fidelity, not efficiency, though at the same time its goal is to be an effective witness by being a visible community of faith. In particular, Yoder believes that the church is called to be a people that practises non-violence, again following the example of Jesus.

Because witnessing to the truth and walking in its pacific way occasions hostility from the unbelieving world (the darkness does not comprehend the light), the church will have to suffer. The cross, says Hauerwas, 'is a sign of what happens when one takes God's account of reality more seriously than Caesar's'.[52] And for Yoder, the political task of the church is to be a community of disciples that follow the way of Jesus, right up onto the cross.

The Center for Catholic and Evangelical Theology: church practice as a work of the Spirit

Perhaps the most sophisticated apology for giving ecclesiology theological pride of place is Reinhard Hütter's *Suffering Divine*

---

50. Yoder 1969.

51. For an excellent introduction to Yoder's ecclesiology, see Cartwright 1998. The book also contains a number of Yoder's most important writings on the church.

52. Hauerwas & Willimon 1989: 47.

Things: Theology as Church Practice.[53] Hütter, like many evangelicals, sees a certain danger in the idea that the meaning of 'God' is a function of how the community lives. The danger is postmodern constructivism, where 'God' is simply a social (perhaps ideological) projection. Hütter's solution is not to abandon the notion of communal practice, but rather to relate it to the work of the Holy Spirit. The core practices of the church are not 'poetic' but 'pathic': not the result of the church's creative imagination but rather the result of the church undergoing the Spirit's work.

Hütter dedicated his book to The Center for Catholic and Evangelical Theology, the body responsible for producing *Pro Ecclesia.* Theologians associated with this Center, and with its co-founders Robert Jenson and Carl Braaten, have recently produced a manifesto of sorts, again arguing for the priority of the church in Christian theology and Christian life. The common denominator linking these theologians is the assumption that knowing and experiencing God 'is inseparable from participating in a particular community and its practices – a participation which is the work of God's Holy Spirit'.[54]

The notion that knowledge is embedded in communal practice is a familiar postmodern theme. The tie between the Holy Spirit and the church, however, adds an important new dimension to the theme of community. According to Hütter, a theologically adequate description of the church and its tradition must move beyond sociology and ethnography to discuss the economy of the Holy Spirit, whose work the church is. The church does not construct its identity so much as *receive* it. The saint is a person who has not simply been socialized, but *sanctified,* into a set of new practices. Hütter speaks of the church as 'the public face of the Holy Spirit'[55] and, more controversially perhaps, of the Spirit as the 'hypostasis' of the church.[56]

---

53. Hütter 2000. A shorter and more accessible version of his argument may be found in Buckley & Yeago 2001: 23–47.
54. Buckley & Yeago 2001: 1.
55. Hütter 2000: 158.
56. Ibid.: 119.

Tradition, on this account, is not a merely human invention but a way of participating in the work of the Spirit. Hütter resists the idea that the Spirit ordinarily works with individuals in a direct and interior fashion. On the contrary, he argues that the way in which God ordinarily forms his people is by the Spirit working in and through the church. Even the knowledge of God, the goal of theology, arises only when Christians participate in the core practices of the church – baptism, the Lord's Supper, reading Scripture, communal prayer, hospitality – practices that are not simply cultural, but pneumatological. The church is therefore the place where we come to know God and to grow in the knowledge of God. This thesis represents a considerable challenge to the traditional evangelical understanding of the immediacy of our relation to God. Yet, according to these authors, one cannot be truly evangelical – grounded and guided in and by the gospel – outside the catholic church.

Stanley Grenz: the church as community of God

Some evangelicals are listening. Stanley Grenz, for instance, believes that evangelicalism must be communitarian in order to be compelling to postmoderns. For Grenz, the church is both formally and materially central. Formally, the church is central because theology is the articulation of the community's 'mosaic of beliefs'. Materially, the church is central because God's whole purpose in salvation is to form a new people. The conclusion to the story of salvation is, in a word, community. Community, Grenz states, is theology's 'integrative motif'.

Grenz accepts the postmodern critique of modern individualism and of Enlightenment rationality. He also accepts the new communitarian understanding of personhood. Persons are not self-standing or autonomous; rather, the self is shaped by its relationships. The self is not self-constituting but constituted – shaped – by and in community. Character development and spiritual formation, for example, are unthinkable apart from the self's social relationships.

Grenz is not so much capitulating to as correlating with postmodern sensibilities. For example, he describes postmodernity as a 'turn to relationships' but he also points out that 'the overarching focus of the biblical narrative is the person-in-relationship'.[57] The church is a community created by the Holy Spirit who uses the biblical narrative to form Christian identity. Grenz also contends that, because God is three-persons-in-relationship, the only way we can realize the *imago Dei* in humanity is to form a community of persons-in-loving-relationship: the church. The church, then, is the community of God, not only because it has been created by the triune God, but because the church shares in the triune community itself.[58]

Is the church basic? Sic et non

Is the church *basic*? This is the obvious question that follows from assigning so many important roles – epistemological, ethical, theological – to the church, and Grenz is right to pose and wrestle with it. On the one hand, Grenz replies 'No': what is basic is faith's saving encounter with the triune God. Yet, when forced to choose between the alternative foundationalist approaches of conservatism (the Bible is basic to theology) and liberalism (experience is basic to theology), Grenz opts for the non-foundational basicality of the church.[59] Without the church, there would be no life of faith on which to reflect, no theology. Now it is one thing to acknowledge the church – as a community of inquiry – to be a necessary condition (basic) for doing theology. It is an altogether different matter, however, to suggest that the community is a basis of authority. The locus of authority is precisely the issue to which the renaissance of ecclesiology which we have just surveyed gives rise.

Yoder suggests that for many cases of moral and doctrinal decision-making, authority is to be found not in the inspiredness of Scripture, nor in an episcopal magisterium, nor in individual experience, but rather in the gathered community: 'it has seemed good to the Holy Spirit and to us' (Acts 15:28). It is not that the community displaces the canon, but that the Spirit guides the community

---

57. Grenz & Franke 2001: 215.
58. Ibid.: 228; cf. Volf 1998.
59. Ibid.: 233–234.

about what Scripture means for new historical situations. Hence Yoder is able to speak of 'The Hermeneutics of Peoplehood'.[60]

Hauerwas takes this principle to the extreme. He argues that people cannot even read the Bible correctly unless they are already part of the community of God. The hearing of the word does not lead people to church, but participating in church enables people to hear the word. Clearly, on Hauerwas's view the church is indeed basic. We know what Scripture means first and foremost by attending to the lives of the saints – to those whose lives exemplify faithful witness. The other way we learn about the gospel is through the church's liturgy, its ritual enactment. Hauerwas's point is that the community is prior to understanding the word or Scripture. Commenting on the Sermon on the Mount, he says 'The Sermon does not generate an ethic of non-violence, but rather a community of non-violence is necessary if the Sermon is to be read rightly.'[61]

At this point one must ask the question: is it possible to be too ecclesiological, too focused on community? If the church is basic in the sense of an authoritative touchstone for Christian faith and life, how can its practices ever be challenged or corrected by Scripture? If the community is basic, how can it ever be converted? While there is much in these theologians for evangelicals to ponder and perhaps accept, it may be that evangelicals also have something to contribute to the contemporary discussion.[62] As we have seen, to be evangelical is to insist upon the priority of God's word and God's act over the faith, response, or experiences of

---

60. Yoder1984: 15–45.

61. Hauerwas 1993: 72.

62. Contemporary theologians are presently divided over ecclesiology, with the optimists holding a slight advantage over the pessimists. This section has surveyed the leading optimists. Among the pessimists, the most prominent is Radner, who argues (1998) that the disunity of the church is a measure of its incomprehension of Scripture, and an index of the absence of the Spirit of unity and truth. The church is divided, as were the southern and northern kingdoms of Israel, during which the people had to endure the Comforter's absence. See also Reno 2002.

men and women and, I would add, over the faith, response, or experiences of *communities*. Scripture is replete with examples of communities – Israel, the Pharisees, the disciples – that got it wrong, that misunderstood God and what God was doing. Neither does it take much effort to find examples of bad practice in the history of the church. Yet Scripture and church history also contain examples of the transforming power of the word when accompanied by the ear- and heart-opening Spirit.

The evangelical heritage: the nature and function of the church

It was precisely the reality of unfaithful practices in the church that led the Reformers to develop criteria of the true church: the faithful preaching of the word and administration of the sacraments. Let us call these the two 'evangelical marks', for each is a form of proclaiming the gospel, verbally (preaching) and visually (sacraments). At the same time, the Reformers insisted that the word of the gospel was ineffective apart from the Spirit of the gospel.[63] Word and Spirit go together, and the church is their proper home, the context in which they most fully produce their salvific effects. It is the gospel that gathers the people of God; for as the Spirit enables its reception, Christ incorporates its hearers into his body.

My contention, then, is that evangelicals throughout church history (I use the term 'evangelical' broadly, with an emphasis on its theological rather than sociological scope) have always known, at least tacitly, that the church is 'analytic' in, an implication of, the gospel itself. The church does not contain the word and Spirit but is constituted by word and Spirit. According to the Augsburg Confession: 'The Church is the assembly of saints in which the gospel is taught purely and administered rightly.' In short: the

---

63. By 'word' I mean the content of the gospel as attested in Scripture, and by 'Spirit' I mean the minister of the gospel, the Holy Spirit – the word's empowering presence and attestation.

indispensability of the church follows from its Spirit-empowered ministry of the gospel in word and sacrament.

The church cannot be adequately understood unless one gives an appropriately 'thick description', one that goes beyond the human categories of sociology, even beyond the notion of 'community practices'. To describe all that the church is, one must have recourse to properly theological categories. For the church is, in the final analysis, a *theological* community. That is the broad claim I wish to make in this section. I do so by advancing four claims about the church as a 'people of the gospel'. The first two pertain to the nature of the church, the second pair to its function.[64]

1. The church is a theme of the gospel.
2. The church is a result of the gospel.
3. The church is an embodiment of the gospel.
4. The church is an agent of the gospel.

A theological community

'But you are a chosen race, a royal priesthood, a holy nation, God's own people' (1 Pet. 2:9).

What makes the church a peculiar people is its peculiar relation to God. No other human assembly is called and formed by God as is the church. Sociological categories alone cannot describe the church in its fullness; by themselves they offer only thin descriptions of the church's reality. In the words of John Webster:

> there can be no doctrine of God without a doctrine of the church, for according to the Christian confession God *is* the one who manifests who he is in the economy of his saving work in which he assembles a people for himself . . . [and] there can be no doctrine of the church which is not wholly referred to the doctrine of God, in whose being and action alone the church has its being and action.[65]

It is both interesting and ironic that it is mainline Protestants, not evangelicals, who have begun to attribute the current malaise

---

64. I have adapted these four points from Meeking & Stott 1986: 65–69.
65. Webster 2001a: 195.

in the church to the loss of the church's identity as a theological community. In a recent collection of essays entitled *Reading the Bible in Faith*, a number of pastors, largely non-evangelical, call for a recovery of theology in the church. To be precise, they are calling for more pastor-theologians who define their vocation in terms of proclaiming, explicating and applying the word of God:

> The church is often assisted but never renewed by such things as management skills, goal-setting processes, reorganization, public relations, or conflict management. The church waits more faithfully for the gift of new life when it recovers its identity as a theological community and attends to those sources . . . which are the promised means by which God creates, sustains, and preserves the church.[66]

Why are not more evangelicals saying such things?

The fact of the matter is that many of our church members have been formed as much if not more by culture than by church. The average Christian in the West spends more time watching television than reading the Bible; he or she is thus exposed to – even bombarded by – messages that promote the gospels of pluralism, consumerism, materialism, relativism and the like. Despite all the Bible study guides and computer aids that are now available, previous generations of evangelicals probably enjoyed a higher standard of biblical literacy. Evangelicals need to recapture a passion for biblical formation: a desire to be formed, reformed and transformed by the truth and power of the gospel. Evangelicals need to recover the sense that their basic identity is not sexually or culturally determined, nor primarily a matter of race or ethnicity, but rather an identity that is theologically determined: 'in Christ'.

The church is a theme of the gospel
The good news about what God is doing in the world concerns not simply individuals, but a people: 'The message of the Bible . . . is that God is at work to bring into being a people under his rule'.[67]

---

66. Lazareth & Alston 2001: x.
67. Millar 2000: 684.

The Lausanne Covenant says that the church stands 'at the very center of God's cosmic purposes'.[68] As early as Genesis 12, God promises Abraham to make his children into a 'great nation'. God is not a soul-winner but a former of persons-in-relation. Both Israel and the church are 'chosen races' – chosen not simply to enjoy special privileges but to undertake special responsibilities, namely, to proclaim and to display the covenant of grace (a 'holy nation'). To be holy is to be 'set apart', and Israel was charged with being distinct from the other nations by holding fast to the worship of God and to the observance of God's law.

The situation with the church is somewhat different, but no less theological or God-centered. The church is a sign that the kingdom or reign of God has dawned: God's Spirit has been given to his people in a unique and intimate way. The coming of the kingdom is, of course, the realization of Israel's messianic hopes. The church is thus 'an important element in the good news'.[69] For what Jesus accomplished on the cross brings reconciliation not only between God and sinners, but also social reconciliation among human groups that were previously estranged. That is why the New Testament makes such a point of stressing that the gospel was for Gentiles as well as Jews. The church thus has a genuine place in the economy of salvation as the first-fruits of a still-to-be-gathered kingdom community.

The church is a result of the gospel
The church by nature is a theological community; its relation to God is a *sine qua non* of its very *esse* or being: 'the church is ingredient within the divine economy of salvation, which is the mystery of God made manifest in Jesus Christ and now operative in the power of his Spirit'.[70] The church is the result of the oft-repeated covenant promise: 'I will . . . be your God and you shall be my people' (Lev. 26.12). According to George Vandervelde, 'The church comes to be as a result of the triune God's plan to dwell

---

68. Cited in Vandervelde 2003: 7.
69. So Meeking & Stott 1986: 68.
70. Webster 2001a: 195.

with, among, and in the community of those created as his icons.'[71] Accordingly, ecclesiology is 'the systematic reflection on the shape which this dwelling of God takes in the community of Christ that journeys between Pentecost and *parousia*'.[72]

(1) A 'work of the Trinity'. The gospel is the good news that through Jesus Christ, God had made good on his covenant promises to be our God and to make us, sinners though we be, his people. The gospel is the good news that the righteous God has made possible a way of fellowshipping with those who were unrighteous, and a way of sanctifying the unrighteous through the very act of fellowshipping. Thus, *neither the church nor the gospel can be rightly understood apart from the persons and work of the triune God.*

To be evangelical is to be trinitarian, for apart from acknowledging the deity of Father, Son and Spirit, it is not possible to preserve the integrity of the gospel message of salvation by grace through faith in Christ. The gospel is intelligible only in light of the doctrine of the Trinity: life with God is possible only because of the reconciling work of the Son and the regenerating work of the Spirit who unites us with and makes us alive in Christ. Similarly, to be part of the church is to be united to the Son, and hence to one another, in the Spirit. *The church is, in essence, the work of the triune God*: 'The church is therefore the people of God and the assembly of Christ because it is the fellowship of the Spirit.'[73] It follows that the church is like no other earthly society; for it is the Spirit who ultimately creates and sustains the body by giving it life, light and liberty in Christ.

(2) A 'creature of the gospel'. How can one recognize the presence and work of the triune God in a human assembly? How can we identify where the church actually is? The short answer, I submit, is by the presence, practice and power of the gospel. The church has been called a 'creature of the Word'.[74] Yet Calvin identified *two* identifying marks of the genuine church: the faithful

---

71. Vandervelde 2003: 10.

72. Ibid.: 10.

73. Clowney 1995: 51.

74. So Schwöbel 1989: 122.

preaching of the word and the faithful administration and reception of the sacraments. And neither mark is really effective without the work of the Spirit, who uses verbal and visual signs as means of grace, means by which to draw the church into the reality of the living Christ.

Hence wherever the gospel is truly heard and seen, and responded to, there is the church! The church, we might say, is a creature of the gospel, a community of word and Spirit. For how did the church come to be a people 'in Christ'? Lesslie Newbigin answers that we are incorporated into Christ in three ways: by hearing the gospel, by participating in the sacramental practices of baptism and the Lord's Supper, and by receiving and abiding in the Holy Spirit.[75] To be a people of the gospel is to have entered the strange new world of the Bible, where the story of Israel and Jesus Christ become our framework for making sense of reality. To be a people of the gospel is also to have entered the strange new world of the Holy Spirit, that divine quickening that ministers the word and makes it a reality in our lives.

The book of Acts depicts the origins of the church. Ecclesiology begins with a Big Bang, with the preaching of the word and the outpouring of the Spirit. This Big Bang marks the birthday of the church, the beginning of a new reality within the old, an eschatological reality that anticipates God's final purpose for creation. The gifts of word, sacrament and Spirit enable a local church to be a real anticipation of the eschatological gathering of the entire people of God.[76] Each local congregation is thus 'the full expression in that place of the one true heavenly church',[77] the first-fruits of the eschatological *ekklēsia*.

A missionary community

'*The church is. The church does what it is. The church organizes what it does*'.[78] All our thinking about church structure and church programmes

---

75. Newbigin 1953: 30.
76. So Volf 1998: 141.
77. Tinker 2002: 139.
78. Van Gelder 2000: 37.

must reflect our understanding of what the church essentially *is*. What is the church? A people created by the Spirit to live as a missionary community.[79] As the Spirit continues and participates in the mission or sending of the Son, so the church continues and participates in the mission or sending of the Spirit. With regard to its nature, the church is the people of God, but with regard to its function, the church is a people who, precisely because they are *of* God, are *for* the world. *The church thus has an ongoing role in the drama or economy of redemption and has been given the dignity of missionary causality.*

The church is an embodiment of the gospel

As a community of the gospel, the church must display a shape of life that corresponds to the gospel. In the first place, the gathered community celebrates the God of the gospel, seeking both to appreciate more deeply and to respond appropriately to what God has done in Christ. The church thus embodies the gospel – the good news and the people's joyful response – in its worship.

How should people who celebrate the gospel actually live? The people of the gospel must be a 'community that makes present the obedient Lord who underwent death for us'.[80] The gospel is the announcement of the coming of the kingdom of God in the person and work of Jesus Christ; accordingly, *the people of the gospel must live in such a way as to display the dawning of the redemptive reign of God*. In relation to the world, then, the church is a community not simply of the converted but of the subversive: for any community that takes its bearings from the gospel will be a community that engages in counter-cultural practices, as did its Lord. Chief among these practices is forgiveness, an effect of the reconciling power of the gospel. The church embodies the gospel only to the extent that it is a community of reconciliation, a community that anticipates the future of God's new creation in which people of every race and social status will fellowship together. The church is a seed from the future, the first-fruits of an eschatological harvest, a downpayment on the kingdom of God.

---

79. Van Gelder 2000: 25.
80. Meeking & Stott 1986: 67.

The church is an agent of the gospel

'Mission' is usually understood as something that churches support which takes place somewhere else, usually far away, by professionals known as missionaries. I have argued, however, that the church is a theological community, the result of the missionary activity of the triune God. The church is also a community that has been given the privilege and responsibility of participating in God's missionary activity. *Mission is simply the initiative of Word and Spirit to incorporate people into the life of the triune God.* 'Mission cannot be something separate from or added to the essence of the Church. The essential nature of the local congregation is, in and of itself, mission.'[81] In this sense, then, all members of the church are to be missionaries.

We respond to Jesus' great commission, and thus participate in the mission of the Spirit, not simply by proclaiming the gospel but by making disciples, by forming people in the practices of the gospel: worshipping, celebrating, comforting, forgiving. Of course, the church needs not only to evangelize but to catechize. Catechesis names the process 'by which the new believer is conformed to Christ in body, mind, and spirit and made ready to become a disciple'.[82] Evangelicals desperately need to recover this sense of the church as a theological community, one whose mission is determined by her prior commissioning, and by the prior missions of Son and Spirit.

The evangelical imperative: 'become what you are in Christ'

John Leith asks an excellent question: what does the church have to say and do that sets it apart from all other human institutions? He directs his query to his own Presbyterian church, and argues compellingly that the prime cause of decline in the mainline Protestant churches is the loss of theological integrity and competent preaching. The answer to the current malaise is what Leith

---

81. Van Engen 1991: 70.
82. Wells 2003.

calls 'the Reformed imperative', namely, to minister the word: 'The only skill the preacher has – or the church, for that matter – which is not found with greater excellence somewhere else, is theology, in particular, the skill to interpret and apply the Word of God in sermon, teaching, and pastoral care.'[83]

The present essay asks a similar question: what distinct thing must the evangelical church say, do, and be? My answer – call it the 'evangelical imperative' – is that we must proclaim and practise the gospel. *When the church embraces and embodies the gospel, it corresponds to what is ultimately real and confronts the world with reality.* Further, only in so far as it ministers the gospel will the church display the four traditional attributes: one, holy, catholic, apostolic.[84] In Roman Catholic ecclesiology, the four marks are descriptions of a visible society, namely, the institution of the Roman Catholic Church. For Luther, the marks are attributes of the invisible church, which for him meant reality as it is hidden 'in Christ'. Charles van Engen sees the four marks of the church as adverbs rather than adjectives in order to bring them to bear as much on the ongoing mission of the church as on its invisible nature. The four marks thus describe the ministry of the church as unifying, sanctifying, reconciling and proclaiming.[85]

The church is both a sociological and a spiritual entity. On the one hand, it is in the world; more importantly, it is also 'in Christ'. The best way to understand these two aspects is to acknowledge the eschatological nature of the church: as a creation of Spirit, the church is both a sign and a catalyst of the future consummation of God's final kingdom purpose. In the meantime, the church exists between the times. Hence our mandate: to become (in fact) what we are (in Christ).

I propose that we view the four traditional marks of the church eschatologically, naming what is both already (viz. invisibly) the case and not yet fully (viz. visibly) the case. Thus understood, the

---

83. Leith 1988: 22.

84. These four features were defined by the Nicene Creed at the Council of Constantinople 'I believe one holy catholic and apostolic church'.

85. van Engen 1991: 66.

marks are both gifts and tasks – hinges between the doctrinal 'is' and the ethical 'ought'. As in Paul's letters, the flow of the argument is from what is already the case 'in Christ' to what therefore must be the case 'in Christians'. Hence the Spirit's message to the churches is: 'Become what you already are in Christ.' The gospel proclaims what is the case 'in Christ'; yet in order to grow up into the fullness of Christ, the church must attend to this evangelical imperative with all its heart, mind, soul and strength.

'One'

On the one hand, the unity of the church is a *fait accompli:* 'There is one body and one Spirit' (Eph. 4:4). Yet Paul also encourages the Ephesians to maintain the 'unity of the Spirit' (Eph. 4:3). Church unity is both gift and task. Becoming what we are, in this case, means learning how to manifest visibly what is already invisibly the case.

One 'in Christ'

Evangelicals have typically not invested much energy in efforts to display visible unity between churches and between denominations. Evangelicals direct their energy to evangelism, largely through parachurch organizations. The truth of the gospel ranks higher in the evangelical order of priorities than does visible church unity. It may be time, however, to rethink our priorities.

As we have seen, the church is both a theme and a creature of the gospel. There is no contradiction between the desire to maintain the integrity of the gospel and the desire to achieve the unity of the church. Indeed, the one – the integrity of the gospel – may actually *require* the other. Ephraim Radner argues that the truth of the gospel becomes obscured by the all-too-obvious reality of a divided church.[86] Similarly, Geoffrey Wainwright's insight represents a standing challenge to all people of the gospel: 'Spiritual unity and visible unity are not truly alternatives: the alternative to visible unity is visible *dis*unity, and that is a witness against the gospel.'[87]

---

86. So Radner 1999: 364–365.
87. Wainwright 1983: 4.

· In short, evangelicals must revisit the issue of church unity for the sake of the integrity of the gospel. The evangelical imperative states: become what you are in Christ. Clearly, the church is one. That is the gift. Tom Oden states the accompanying task: 'The third millennium faces the task of once again practically embodying the unity that we already have juridically in Christ.'[88] Interestingly, Hans Küng, a Roman Catholic theologian, declares that 'The standard for unity must be the Gospel of Jesus Christ.'[89] In other words, the gospel is the criterion and judge of what counts as the true church, not vice versa.

The eschatological imagination

I argued earlier that evangelical ecclesiology typically focuses on the invisible church to the detriment or neglect of the visible church. Reversing these polarities would hardly represent a solution. What we need is a way of keeping both aspects of the church – the theological/spiritual/invisible and the human/sociological/visible – in mind at all times. The way forward, I submit, is for evangelicals to recover the eschatological imagination.

The evangelical church lacks imagination. The imagination should not be confused with fantasy and fiction. It is rather the ability to grasp things together, to see connections that are not apparent to the senses. By eschatological imagination, I mean the ability to see what is not (yet) there, the ability to see creation as it is being transformed and brought into conformity with Christ. The eschatological imagination helps us to see the visible church in terms of the already-not yet tension. Thanks to the imagination, we are able to envisage what the visible church is becoming.

Without the eschatological imagination, it is impossible to appreciate what is going on in baptism and the Lord's Supper. These symbolic actions are not simply rehearsals of past events; they are also events that incorporate us into the story of Jesus and of his followers. For it is not enough to assent intellectually to the events of Jesus' life; we must *identify with* them. Baptism and the

---

88. Oden 1992: 307.
89. Küng 1968: 291.

Lord's Supper thus become the framework through which we
interpret and seek to understand our daily life. We have died with
Christ to the old order and we have been raised with him to a new
order of life. Baptism is our point of entry into Christian fellowship and the Lord's Supper is a way of cementing the fellowship
we have in Christ. There is probably no more social activity than
sharing a meal. Those who share the Lord's Supper have 'communion': an experience of union with their Lord, and with one
another. Participating in the life and worship of the church is
perhaps the best way to shape our imaginations so that they will
see the world (and the church!) in biblical terms rather than in
terms of the prevailing secular theories of the day (e.g. naturalism,
materialism, utilitarianism).

Empirical reality alone – present divisions between churches,
for instance – should not define us. Our real identity as Christians
is hid 'in Christ'. Our true identity is eschatological: we are new
creatures in Christ, and hence we must become what we are. The
same is true of the church: we are one in Christ, hence we must
become what we are. Empirical reality lags behind its eschatological counterpart; this lag is the groaning of creation. So, too, the
church groans for the unity that Christ has already won.

'Holy'

The gospel is holy because it is 'set apart' from all other words:
there is no other gospel (Gal. 1:6). Similarly, the church is holy
because it is a communion of saints, set apart precisely because it
takes its bearings from, and bears witness to, the gospel.

The church is a worshipping community

The church is holy not because each of its members has reached a
state of moral perfection (recall the tension between the 'already'
and the 'not yet') but because what it is and what it does sets it
apart from every other human institution. To worship God is to
remember the rock from which we were hewn. In worship the
church both gives God his due and reinforces its own identity as
children and servants of God. Worship recalls us to ourselves
precisely by directing us to the gracious initiatives of God.

The church is a working community

The church not only celebrates but continues God's work. The church's vocational holiness – its distinct calling – is to participate in the missions of the Son and the Spirit to the world. The church is to be a missional community known for its works of love. 'The church, the band of Christ's disciples, is the community of those who have taken up the call of God to work on His behalf in His cause of renewing human existence.'[90]

'Catholic'

To speak of the 'catholic' church is to speak of the church as a whole: the church universal, composed of people 'from every nation, from all tribes and peoples and tongues' (Rev. 7:9). In this sense, 'catholic' is (ironically enough) the polar opposite of 'parochial'. Even more ironic is the tendency of evangelicals to be more 'parochial' – narrow-minded, concerned with only their own affairs – than Roman Catholics. The catholicity of the church is ultimately rooted in the catholicity of the gospel itself. The gospel is a message for all kinds and races of people and, as Lamin Sanneh point out, it is eminently translatable into all times and places.[91]

The church embraces all times and places: the great tradition

One way in which the evangelical church denies catholicity is by being monocultural, focused only on the present context, the here and now. The gospel is not served by cultural myopia. Evangelicals need to recover the idea that the local church is a representative of the whole church. The church is Christ's, and twenty-first-century Western evangelicals need to be reintroduced to their long-lost brothers and sisters of former times and distant places. Local congregations must recover a sense of their place in the larger Christian tradition. For tradition, in the best sense, is simply the story of how the gospel has worked itself out in particular places and times among other members of God's family. Church

---

90. Wolterstorff 1997: 197.
91. Sanneh 1989: 214. See also Satari 1996.

tradition is not an authority over Scripture, to be sure, yet to the extent that evangelicals neglect tradition, they neglect an important resource for the present.[92]

The church embraces all kinds: diversity

Monoculturalism is not simply a matter of ignoring the past but also of ignoring the 'other'. Edmund Clowney writes: 'Racism also denies catholicity.'[93] It has been said that the most segregated event in North America is the eleven o'clock Sunday morning worship hour.[94] The church growth movement, based on the principle of 'homogenous people groups', is another example of denying catholicity.[95] To be sure, it may be more comfortable to worship with those who share one's own socio-economic class and colour of skin, but where in the Bible does it say that worship is about feeling comfortable?

The Greek word for reconciliation, *katallagē*, is composed of two Greek words that may be roughly translated '*contra* otherness'. This is a vivid image of reconciliation: to reconcile is to remove the barriers that impede fellowship. The good news of salvation is that God has reconciled sinners in Christ; the apostle Paul depicts the church's ministry of the gospel as a 'ministry of reconciliation' (2 Cor. 5:18). One of the most striking New Testament examples of the catholicity of the church is found in Acts 15, in which the Jerusalem council decided that Gentile Christians did *not* have to become like them (e.g. circumcised). The mystery of cosmic reconciliation finds a preliminary historical proof in the reality of Jews and Greeks gathered round the Lord's table.

The success of the evangelical church in the twenty-first century may well turn on a similar issue. Can we embrace others without

---

92. Bloesch (2002: 30) correctly notes that some evangelicals are abandoning the authority of Scripture for the authority of tradition. Yet it is possible to attend to tradition while still preserving the gospel as the final criterion and authority with the potential to correct and reform tradition.

93. Clowney 1995: 97.

94. See Emerson & Smith 2000.

95. So Clowney 1995: 97.

making them like ourselves? This is the challenge for the evangelical church in what Philip Jenkins has called the 'next Christendom', namely, the advent of global Christianity.[96] Will Christians in the West feel more affinities with their brothers and sisters in Africa, Asia and South America or with other American and Europeans, whether Christian or not, who share their culture and socio-economic status? The catholicity of the gospel demands that our churches be inclusive of those whose ethnic and socio-economic identities may be other than our own: 'the mode in which God is present among the faithful is irreducibly multicultural'.[97] Evangelicals, precisely because of their commitment to the catholicity of the gospel, should be striving for a future that will realize what we might call the 'heterogeneous people group' principle.

'Apostolic'

The fundamental meaning of 'apostolic' has to do with being *sent* (*apostellō* = to send out) to *say* what one has been told. The authority of the apostles does not derive from their being religious geniuses, as Kierkegaard rightly points out, but rather from the content of their testimony: 'that . . . which we have heard, which we have seen' (1 John 1:1). To be apostolic is to be sent on a mission of testimony. The church displays apostolicity to the extent that it corresponds to the apostolic gospel.

A missionary community

The apostle is a missionary with a message. The Reformers were less interested in the question of apostolic succession as a principle of church government than they were with the notion of a 'succession of truth'.[98] The evangelical church is apostolic, then, both because it affirms the apostolic teaching and because it too has been sent into the world. As the Son and Spirit were sent (*missio* = missions or sendings) so, too, the church is sent in the name of the Son and in the power of the Spirit.

---

96. Jenkins 2002.
97. Brownson 1996: 236.
98. Paul Avis, cited in Tinker 1991: 26.

An interpretative community

Apostolic and evangelical succession are thus twin principles: 'the continuing and unadulterated proclamation of the gospel of the risen Christ'.[99] Effective witness involves more than a wooden repetition of biblical statements, however. The gospel must be translated, appropriated and contextualized in order for its meaning and truth truly to be proclaimed in new historical and cultural situations. The church fulfils its apostolic mandate, therefore, when it proclaims 'no other gospel', though this sameness may often have to be expressed in and through new forms. In this regard, evangelicals must continue to put a premium on expository preaching. The church is the place to hear God's word, not the latest human fad or technique. Focusing on the latter all too often gives rise to *impository* preaching!

Conclusion: the theatre of the gospel

To preserve the apostolic message, one must do more than proclaim it. Biblical interpretation demands discipleship and spirituality, work and prayer. A robust interpretation of the gospel must not only be proclaimed but lived. The church must be the place not only where the gospel is heard, but the place where it is seen. For the meaning of the gospel can ultimately be learned only through the testimony of those who understand its length and breadth, its ground and its grammar – by those who not only listen to but *live along* the gospel. Evangelicals must put feet – and legs, and arms – on the gospel for the sake of our effective witness.

The church exists where the Holy Spirit efficaciously ministers the word: where the gospel is heard, received and responded to. The church exists when people take their bearings from the gospel and seek again and again to ensure that their way of life corresponds to the gospel in a way that communicates to the culture. The church thus becomes the theatre of the gospel, the stage on which the Christian world-view takes concrete form. This vision of the

99. Moltmann 1977: 359.

church also responds to Leander Keck's call for a new apologetics that would 'present the Christian faith and its tradition as an intelligible and plausible construal of reality'.[100] Robert Webber sees the task of the evangelical church in similar terms: 'The challenge in a postmodern world is to be the presence of a transcendent reality here on earth.'[101] Such is the aim of the worship, witness and wisdom of the church: to represent a form of life that manifests a world- and life-view informed and transformed by the gospel. The church is the theatre of the gospel: that place where a distinct view of the world – as loved by the triune God – is remembered, celebrated, encouraged, and most of all, lived and performed.

The company of the gospel

To sum up. I have argued that the individualist emphasis in evangelicalism owes more to modern culture than to biblical faith. To be an evangelical is not simply to be a saved individual; rather, it is to be part of what God is doing to renew his created order. Evangelicals must recover the doctrine and the practice of the church. The integrity of the gospel demands no less. At its best, evangelicalism names the tradition that continually reflects on exactly what it means to be a people of the gospel.[102] The visible church matters because it is a concrete sign of the emerging eschatological reality inaugurated by Jesus: a community of reconciliation. I also argued that we must recover a latent theme in the evangelical heritage, namely, the notion that the church is an already/not yet instantiation of the gospel message.

The church, I submit, is the *company of the gospel*. A 'company' is, in the first instance, an assembly. The church is that assembly that

---

100. Keck 1993: 105.

101. Webber 1999: 83.

102. Cf. Tanner's argument (1997) that Christian identity is defined not in terms of a fixed list of qualities or beliefs, but in terms of the ongoing task of determining what it means to be a true disciple. Similarly, evangelical identity may be viewed not in terms of an agreement about the final content of the gospel, but in terms of a shared conviction of its truth and a shared commitment to discover and be ruled by its meaning.

keeps company with the gospel. Wayne Booth agrees with the proverbial wisdom that a person is known by the company one keeps, and this includes the books one reads.[103] Second, the church is a company that displays the gospel in its corporate life, particularly in baptism and the Lord's Supper. The latter practice is particularly significant given the etymology of the term 'companion' (*com* + *panis* = with bread). The church is a company of the gospel because it shares a view of God (a theology) and table fellowship (an ethic). Finally, the church is a company in the theatrical sense: a troupe of singers, speakers and actors. This, I submit, is the best way to envisage the church as a missionary congregation.[104]

A performing company

'For I think that God has exhibited us apostles . . . like men sentenced to death' (1 Cor. 4:9).

The church is the performance of the gospel word in the power of the gospel Spirit. We must be followers of Jesus Christ in all our speech and action, players whose lives display the cruciform shape of the love of God. It is precisely as a company of the gospel that the church can be a hermeneutic of the gospel:

> Interpretation may be so institutionalized in schools and done by learned men and women that it has become over-identified with ideas and written commentaries. Interpretation is meaning, and meaning can be said. But more basically, biblical meaning is done . . . the most authentic Christian biblical interpretation is human enactments of God-informed life. . . . Interpretation, then, in its final form, is God-formed human practice. What we do as the people of God is our interpretation of the Bible.[105]

---

103. Booth 1988.

104. See Hunsberger 1996b: 14.

105. Scott 1995: 144–145. The task of theology is to criticize and improve Christian performance. In this regard, evangelicals would do well to recover the practice of catechism: teaching and training the disciple to correspond in thinking and in living to the Word of God.

The playerhood of all believers

Evangelicals embrace the Reformation principle of the priesthood of all believers. Each member of the church has the privilege and responsibility of reading and interpreting the Bible. But the most adequate form of biblical interpretation, as we have just seen, is a shape of life lived in community. The Roman Catholic theologian Hans Urs von Balthasar only slightly exaggerates when he says that the lives of the saints are themselves interpretations of the gospel, more true and more convincing than all exegesis. From an evangelical perspective, however, all believers are saints: set apart by God for his service. It follows that we should affirm the 'playerhood of all believers'.

Every member of the church is a player: a Spirit-endowed agent with a role to play, a gift to contribute. Evangelicals must resist the idea that the congregation is only an audience watching the actors on stage (e.g. in the pulpit, around the altar). On the contrary, the whole people of the gospel are players. Every church member has been incorporated into the play of the gospel by grace through faith, through the combined initiatives of Word and Spirit.[106]

The church is not to put on a circus but rather *Christus*: the way, truth and life of Jesus Christ. For the church is not a place where the Christian life is a 'put on' or sham (this way hypocrisy lies) but rather a place where Christ is 'put on', a place where members are clothed in Christ's righteousness. Being clothed with Christ – being incorporated into his body, following his way – is something that cannot simply be 'put on' in the sense of pretence. Only the Spirit can create actors whose speech and lives display the mind of Christ. The church is that 'sharing together in a storied life of obedience and service to and with Christ'.[107]

---

106. Historically, this greater role accorded the laity has been a significant contrast between evangelical and Roman Catholic ecclesiologies, though after Vatican II this difference has become less pronounced.

107. McClendon 1986: 28.

Playing and praying both text and table

Evangelical faith and life is essentially the interpretation of the gospel of Jesus Christ. I believe that there is no more important task for the church than putting on Christ and performing the gospel. Woe to us if we do not perform the gospel. Yes, some of our performances may include elements of improvisation, but these will always be governed by two fixed elements: the biblical text as authoritative script; the communion table as set piece. Indeed, the vocation of the church is to perform the text and the table in new contexts. The Spirit gives us all the props and prompts we need: 'The Holy Spirit brings the remembered word of Scripture to life and transforms the anticipated hope of the kingdom into action.'[108]

It is not enough to assent intellectually to the text; even the demons do that (Jas. 2:19). People of the gospel must not only assent to Scripture but indwell it. The gospel must be our touchstone for reality, truth, goodness and beauty. Of all Christians, evangelicals should be concerned to perform the gospel from which the movement takes its name. 'Cheap inerrancy' – the profession without the practice of biblical truth – helps no one. We must rather do the truth, and this means, among other things, doing church.

Evangelicals need to put the Eucharist back into the Lord's Supper. For *eucharistō* means 'I give thanks', and this should be the theme of the evangelical's whole life. The church gathers together to thank God for the gift of Jesus Christ. Thanksgiving (*eucharistō* = I give thanks) is the proper response to the gospel (*euangelion* = good news). The bread and the wine that we share together are both memory of the play's climax and rehearsal for the play's conclusion. It is a key scene, and it must affect our interpretation of all other scenes.

Living along the text and the table is a matter of solemn play. Our evangelical performances show forth the meaning of the gospel 'in the language of our times but in contradistinction to the spirit of the times'.[109] A church that plays and prays Scripture will resist accommodation to culture, to scripts other than the gospel.

---

108. Wells 2003.

109. Bloesch 2002: 274.

To be a confessing church is to witness to the truth of the way of Jesus Christ with our lips, our limbs, our logic and our lives. The church's vocation is to show forth true humanity, the *imago Dei* as displayed paradigmatically in Christ: 'The dire need today is for a faithful church rather than a successful church, a church under the cross rather than a church that has accommodated to the culture.'[110]

Directing the company

'*The church is. The church does what it is. The church organizes what it does.*'[111] To this point little has been said about how the church organizes or orders what it does. If every believer is a player in the company of the gospel, what exactly is the role of those who oversee the church's ministry? Two preliminary points are especially relevant to note in this context. First, not all performances of the gospel are equal – hence the need for critics. The apostle Paul critcized the way in which the Corinthians observed the Lord's Supper, declaring it 'unworthy' (1 Cor. 11:27) and going so far as to say that the Corinthians were actually playing not the gospel but some other scene (1 Cor. 11:20). Second, a disciplined church is itself an aspect of the gospel. This latter point requires further clarification.

The gospel is the good news that Christ has set the captives free – free from the bondage of sin, meaninglessness and death: 'For freedom Christ has set us free' (Gal. 5:1). The company of the gospel is thus a company of the liberated. Christian freedom, however, should not be confused with its modern and postmodern counterfeits. Christian liberty is neither autonomous individualism nor an indeterminate 'anything goes': 'The church's disorder is now celebrated as the freedom and creativity of a new paradigm of unhindered self-assertion.'[112] On the contrary, church order is to a large extent a matter of disciplining human pride and the lust for power. Ephraim Radner points to the example of the apostle Paul, who agreed not to work in fields in which others were already labouring (Rom. 15:20) in order not to 'boast beyond limit'

---

110. Bloesch 2002: 280.

111. Van Gelder 2000: 37.

112. Radner 2001: 227.

(2 Cor. 10:13–16). Church order is a further extension of the church's commitment to follow in Jesus' way: the way of servant-hood and humility. The form of Christian freedom and leadership alike ultimately derives from the example of Jesus.

Churches can go 'out of order'. Some so-called 'independent' churches (and not only the independent!) deny their catholicity by going their own way, for example, by rejecting the doctrine of the Trinity as the dross of human tradition. Such churches err in thinking that they can simply choose for themselves, much like heretics, what to believe and how to live. These undisciplined churches become easy prey to the cultural snares and ideological wolves of the day.

The company of the gospel needs discipline and direction in order faithfully to perform the Scriptures. Historically, the church has availed itself of two such sources, each summoned into being by the gospel. The first is the Nicene Creed, which is both a summary of the gospel – its presuppositions, affirmations and implications – and a 'fence around the gospel' that prevents subse-quent misinterpretation. The creed is 'a public and binding indication of the gospel',[113] and thus serves as a rule for correct per-formance. The second instrument of discipline and direction is the episcopacy: 'A ministry of oversight is a necessary implication of the church's confession of the gospel.'[114] It is the role of the elder or overseer or pastor or bishop to ensure the integrity of the church's gospel witness.[115] Those who oversee the church's witness lead first

---

113. Webster 2001b: 123. Note that the authors of this collection believe that they can achieve something like 'mere' Christianity on the basis of 'Nicene' Christianity.

114. Webster 2001a: 192.

115. By episcopacy, I mean to emphasize the ministry of 'oversight'. Whether the overseer is a bishop (*episkopos*) or an elder (*presbyteros*) is a relatively secondary matter, especially in light of the interchangeability of the two terms in the New Testament (cf. Acts 20:17, 28; Titus 1:5–7). What does matter, however, is that the church acknowledge the role of leader-servants who have a special responsibility for preserving the integrity of the gospel: its preaching, celebration and performance.

and foremost by example, submitting themselves to the gospel's claims and demands. Yet the overseers also have a responsibility for disciplining the community by directing their performance, so that everything that is said and done in the community corresponds to the truth of the gospel.

A parable of the kingdom

According to George Hunsberger, the church's mission is 'to represent the reign of God'.[116] In everything that it does, the church is to be a sign that the kingdom of God has come in Christ and in his Spirit. 'The Church is a prophet and priest that points to a king.'[117] *The church is to show the world the new – new creation, new covenant, new life, new being – as it exists in Christ.* This is one way to realize Newbigin's call for the church to exhibit a different 'plausibility structure' than that shared by the surrounding society.

The kingdom of God is wherever God's will reigns. It would be presumptuous simply to equate the visible church – even the evangelical wing of it! – with the kingdom of God. As we have seen, the visible church is not yet spotless. Nevertheless, the visible church is charged with displaying God's kingdom. To the extent that the church displays kingdom politics, it becomes a theatre of the gospel. Note that this theatrical model of the church takes up Hauerwas's and Yoder's call to the church to be a counterculture while at the same time preserving the traditional evangelical emphasis on word (the authoritative script) and Spirit (the energizing power).

This, then, is the highest vocation of the evangelical church: *to be a parable of the kingdom.*[118] As in Jesus' parables, the church should be a picture of 'the extraordinary in the ordinary', a model of love that surpasses the mundane economies of give and take.

---

116. Hunsberger 1996b: 15.

117. Wells 2003.

118. I believe the model of 'parable' better captures the church's eschatological nature than the model of sacrament, which is often found in Roman Catholic ecclesiologies, as well as in some evangelical treatments (e.g. Webber 1999: 91).

For the church lives out of a different economy: the economy of the triune God who imparts the riches of Christ to his people through the gifts of the Holy Spirit. The church's shape of life together should be so compelling and distinct that it subverts secular notions of society.

No other human society can be a parable of the kingdom of God, for no other society is charged with witnessing to the resurrection nor empowered by the Spirit of the risen Christ to do so. It is because of the resurrection that the church's performance is true. 'Truthful human action is action which is in conformity with the reality which is established in the resurrection of Jesus from the dead.'[119] *The church's special task is thus to witness to the reality of the resurrection.* Each church member has a part in this performance – things to say, things to do – and each is equipped for this role by the Spirit.

What the church has to say and do is no empty play. On the contrary, the company of the gospel engages in play that is both solemn and joyful. The church commemorates and celebrates the story of Jesus Christ, not only the best of all words that can be heard but also the truest. For when the people of the gospel worship in spirit and truth, they witness to a transcendent, glorious reality: to the new emerging from the old, to the holy in the humdrum. In so doing, the church gives Christian form and substance to what would otherwise be empty joy and hollow hope. The company of the gospel gathering together has nothing to do with corporate wish fulfilment; that is the province of *secular* culture. No, the church as parable of the kingdom is not the stuff that dreams are made of, but rather a glimpse, and taste, of truth. The church is a living mission statement, a communal display of the supreme evangelical truth that God is already/not yet with us. In a world that is passing away, the special vocation of the people of the gospel is to live in such a way that shows they are in touch with reality, with that eschatological fullness of the real in Christ.

---

119. Webster 2001a: 224.

Bibliography

Akers, John, John H. Armstrong and John D. Woodbridge (eds.) (2000), *This We Believe: The Good News of Jesus Christ for the World*, Grand Rapids: Zondervan.

Bellah, Robert N. (ed.) (1986), *Habits of the Heart: Individualism and Commitment in American Life*, New York: Harper & Row.

Bloesch, Donald G. (1983), *The Future of Evangelical Christianity*, Garden City, NY: Doubleday.

Booth, Wayne (1988), *The Company We Keep: An Ethics of Fiction*, Berkeley: University of California Press.

Boyd, Gregory and Paul Eddy (2002), *Across the Spectrum: Understanding Issues in Evangelical Theology*, Grand Rapids: Baker.

Brownson, James (1996) 'Speaking the Truth in Love', in Hunsberger & Van Gelder 1996: 228–259.

Buckley, James J. and David S. Yeago (2001), *Knowing the Triune God: The Work of the Spirit in the Practices of the Church*, Grand Rapids: Eerdmans.

Cartwright, Michael G. (1998), 'Radical Reform, Radical Catholicity: John Howard Yoder's Vision of the Faithful Church', in John Howard Yoder, *The Royal Priesthood: Essays Ecclesiological and Ecumenical*, 1–49, Scottdale, PA: Herald Press.

Clapp, Rodney (1998), interview with Stanley Hauerwas, *Books and Culture* (Nov./Dec.): 18.

Clowney, Edmund P. (1995), *The Church*, Downers Grove: IVP.

Dawn, Marva J. (1995), *Reaching Out without Dumbing Down: A Theology of Worship for the Turn-of-the-Century Culture*, Grand Rapids: Eerdmans.

Emerson, Michael O. and Christian Smith (2000), *Divided by Faith: Evangelical Religion and the Problem of Race in America*, New York: Oxford University Press.

Grenz, Stanley J. (1993), *Revisioning Evangelical Theology*, Downers Grove: IVP.

—— (2000), 'Articulating the Christian Belief-Mosaic', in John G. Stackhouse (ed.), *Evangelical Futures: A Conversation on Theological Method*, 107–136, Grand Rapids: Baker/Leicester: IVP.

—— (2000), *Renewing the Center: Evangelical Theology in a Post-Theological Era*, Grand Rapids: Baker.

—— (2002) 'Concerns of a Pietist with a Ph.D.', *Wesleyan Theological Journal* 37: 58–76.

Grenz, Stanley J. and Jonathan Franke (2001), *Beyond Foundationalism: Shaping Theology in a Postmodern Context*, Louisville, KY: Westminster/John Knox Press.

Gundry, Robert H. (2002), *Jesus the Word According to John the Sectarian*, Grand Rapids: Eerdmans.

Hauerwas, Stanley J. (1993), *Unleashing the Scriptures: Freeing the Bible from Captivity to America*, Nashville: Abingdon.

Hauerwas, Stanley and Samuel Wells (eds.) (2003) *The Blackwell Companion to Christian Ethics*, Oxford: Blackwell.

Hauerwas, Stanley and William H. Willimon (1989), *Resident Aliens: Life in the Christian Colony*, Nashville: Abingdon.

Hunsberger, George R. (1996a), 'Sizing up the Shape of the Church', in Hunsberger & Van Gelder 1996: 333–346.

—— (1996b), 'The Newbigin Gauntlet: Developing a Domestic Missiology for North America', in Hunsberger & Van Gelder 1996: 3–25.

Hunsberger, George R. and Craig Van Gelder (eds.) (1996), *The Church Between Gospel and Culture: The Emerging Mission in North America*, Grand Rapids: Eerdmans.

Hütter, Reinhard (2000), *Suffering Divine Things: Theology as Church Practice*, Grand Rapids: Eerdmans, 2000.

—— (2001), 'The Church', in Buckley & Yeago 2001: 23–47.

Jenkins, Philip (2002), *The Next Christendom: The Coming of Global Christianity*, Oxford: Oxford University Press.

Keck, Leander (1993), *The Church Confident*, Nashville: Abingdon.

Kelsey, David (1992), *To Understand God Truly: What's Theological about a Theological School*, Louisville, KY: Westminster/John Knox Press.

Küng, Hans (1968), *The Church*, Tunbridge Wells: Search Press.

Lazareth, William and Wallace Alston (2001), 'Introduction', *Reading the Bible in Faith: Theological Voices from the Pastorate*, Grand Rapids: Eerdmans.

Leith, John H. (1988), *The Reformed Imperative: What the Church Has to Say that No One Else Can Say*, Philadelphia: Westminster Press.

MacIntyre, Alasdair (1984), *After Virtue: A Study in Moral Theory* 2nd ed., Notre Dame: University of Notre Dame Press.

Marsden, George (1991), *Understanding Fundamentalism and Evangelicalism*, Grand Rapids: Eerdmans.

McClendon, James (1986), *Ethics: Systematic Theology*, vol. 1, Nashville: Abingdon.

Meeking, Basil and John Stott (eds.) (1986), *The Evangelical–Roman Catholic Dialogue on Mission 1977–1984*, Grand Rapids: Eerdmans.

Milbank, John (1990), *Theology and Social Theory: Beyond Secular Reason*, Oxford: Blackwell.

Millar, J. G. (2000), 'The People of God', in T. Desmond Alexander and Brian S. Rosner (eds.), *New Dictionary of Biblical Theology*, 684–687, Leicester: IVP.

Mohler, R. Albert (1990), 'Carl F. H. Henry', in Timothy George and David S. Dockery (eds.), *Baptist Theologians*, 518–538, Nashville: Broadman & Holman.

Moltmann, Jürgen (1977), *The Church in the Power of the Spirit*, London: SCM Press.

Mouw, Richard J. (2001), *He Shines in All That's Fair: Culture and Common Grace*, Grand Rapids: Eerdmans.

Newbigin, Lesslie (1953), *The Household of God: Lectures on the Nature of the Church*, London: SCM Press.

Oden, Thomas (1992), *Life in the Spirit*, vol. 3 of *Systematic Theology*, San Francisco: HarperCollins.

Radner, Ephraim (1998), *The End of the Church: A Pneumatology of Christian Division in the West*, Grand Rapids: Eerdmans.

—— (1999), 'The Absence of the Comforter: Scripture and the Divided Church', in Christopher Seitz and Kathryn Greene-McCreight (eds.), *Theological Exegesis: Essays in Honor of Brevard S. Childs*, 355–394, Grand Rapids: Eerdmans.

—— (2001), 'To Desire Rightly: The Force of the Creed in its Canonical Context', in Seitz 2001: 213–228.

Ramm, Bernard (2000), *The Evangelical Heritage: A Study in Historical Theology*, Grand Rapids: Baker.

Reno, R. R. (2002), *In the Ruins of the Church*, Grand Rapids: Brazos.

Rizter, George (1993), *The McDonaldization of Society: An Investigation into the Changing Character of Contemporary Social Life*, Thousand Oaks, CA: Pine Forge Press.

Roxburgh, Alan J. (1996), 'Pastoral Role in the Missionary Congregation', in Hunsberger & Van Gelder 1996: 319–332.

Sanneh, Lamin (1989) *Translating the Message: The Missionary Impact on Culture*, Maryknoll, NY: Orbis.

Satari, Paul Russ (1996), '"Translatability" in the Missional Approach of Lamin Sanneh', in Hunsberger & Van Gelder 1996: 270–283.

Schwöbel, Christoph (1989), 'The Creature of the Word: Recovering the Ecclesiology of the Reformers', in Colin E. Gunton and D. W. Hardy (eds.), *On Being the Church: Essays on the Christian Community*, 110–155, Edinburgh: T. & T. Clark.

Scott, David (1995), 'Speaking to Form: Trinitarian-Performative Scripture Reading', *Anglican Theological Review* 77: 137–150.

Seitz, Christopher R. (ed.) (2001), *Nicene Christianity: The Future for a New Ecumenism*, Grand Rapids: Brazos.

Shenk, Wilbert R. (1996), 'The Culture of Modernity as a Missionary Challenge', in Hunsberger & Van Gelder 1996: 69–78.

Tanner, Kathryn (1997), *Theories of Culture: A New Agenda for Theology*, Minneapolis: Augsburg.

Tinker, Melvin (1991) 'Towards an Evangelical Ecclesiology (Part One)', *Churchman* 105: 18–29.

—— (2002), 'Refining the Reformers: A Theological Response to "The Anglican Understanding of Church"', *Churchman* 116: 149.

Turner, James (1985), *Without God, Without Creed: The Origins of Unbelief in America*, Baltimore: Johns Hopkins University Press.

Van Engen, Charles (1991), *God's Missionary People: Rethinking the Purpose of the Local Church*, Grand Rapids: Baker.

Van Gelder, Craig (2000), *The Essence of the Church: A Community Created by the Spirit*, Grand Rapids: Baker.

Vandervelde, George (1999), 'Ecclesiology in the Breach: Evangelical Soundings', *Evangelical Review of Theology* 23: 29–51.

—— (2003), 'The Challenge of Evangelical Ecclesiology', *Evangelical Review of Theology* 27: 4–26.

Vanhoozer, Kevin J. (2002a), *First Theology: God, Scripture, and Hermeneutics*, Leicester: IVP.

—— (2002b), 'Worship at the Well: From Dogmatics to Doxology (and Back Again)', *Trinity Journal* 23: 3–16.

—— (2003a), 'Theology and the Condition of Postmodernity: A Report on Knowledge (of God)', in Kevin J. Vanhoozer (ed.), *The Cambridge Companion to Postmodern Theology*, ch. 1, Cambridge: Cambridge University Press.

—— (2003b), 'Praising God in Song: Beauty and the Arts', in Hauerwas & Wells 2003: ch. 5.

Volf, Miroslav (1998), *After Our Likeness: The Church as the Image of the Trinity*, Grand Rapids: Eerdmans.

Wainwright, Geoffrey (1983), *The Ecumenical Movement: Crisis and Opportunity for the Church*, Grand Rapids: Eerdmans.

Watson, Richard (1998), *The Philosopher's Diet*, Boston: Nonpareil.

Webber, Robert E. (1999), *Ancient-Future Faith: Rethinking Evangelicalism for a Postmodern World*, Grand Rapids: Baker.

Webster, John B. (2001a), *Word and Church: Essays in Christian Dogmatics*, Edinburgh: T. & T. Clark.

—— (2001b), 'Confession and Confessions', in Seitz 2001: 119–131.

Wells, David (1998), 'Introduction: The Word in the World', in John H. Armstrong, *The Compromised Church: The Present Evangelical Crisis*, 19–34, Wheaton: Crossway.

Wells, Samuel (2003), 'The Gift of the Church and the Gifts God Gives it', in Hauwerwas & Wells 2003: ch. 2.

Wolterstorff, Nicholas (1997), *Art in Action: Toward a Christian Aesthetic*, Carlisle: Solway.

Yoder, John Howard (1969), 'A People in the World: Theological Interpretation', in James Leo Garrett, Jr (ed.), *The Concept of the Believer's Church*, 252–293, Scottdale, PA: Herald Press.

—— (1984), *The Priestly Kingdom: Social Ethics as Gospel*, Notre Dame: University of Notre Dame Press.

Recommended reading

Bloesch, Donald, *The Church*, Downers Grove: IVP, 2002.

Buckley, James J. and David S. Yeago (eds.), *Knowing the Triune God: The Work of the Spirit in the Practices of the Church*, Grand Rapids: Eerdmans, 2001.

Clapp, Rodney, *A Peculiar People: The Church As Culture in a Post-Christian Society*, Downers Grove: IVP, 1996.

Clowney, Edmund P., *The Church*, Leicester, IVP, 1995.

Dawn, Marva J., *Reaching Out without Dumbing Down: A Theology of Worship for the Turn-of-the-Century Culture*, Grand Rapids: Eerdmans, 1995.

Hunsberger, George R. and Craig Van Gelder (eds.), *The Church between Gospel and Culture: The Emerging Mission in North America*, Grand Rapids: Eerdmans, 1996.

Käkkäinen, Veli-Matti, *An Introduction to Ecclesiology: Ecumenical, Historical and Global Perspectives*, Downers Grove: IVP, 2002.

Tinker, Melvin, 'Towards an Evangelical Ecclesiology (Part One)',
    Churchman 105 (1991), pp. 18–29.
Van Gelder, Craig, *The Essence of the Church: A Community Created by the Spirit*,
    Grand Rapids: Baker, 2000.
Vandervelde, George, 'Ecclesiology in the Breach: Evangelical Soundings',
    Evangelical Review of Theology 23 (1999), pp. 29–51.
Volf, Miroslav, *After Our Likeness: The Church as the Image of the Trinity*, Grand
    Rapids: Eerdmans, 1998.
Webster, John B., *Word and Church: Essays in Christian Dogmatics*, Edinburgh:
    T. & T. Clark, 2001.

3. EVANGELICALISM AND BIBLICAL INTERPRETATION

I. Howard Marshall

Over the past couple of decades I have encountered several post-graduate students who wished to do research in the area of 'hermeneutics'. This fact is one symptom of where we are in New Testament research at the present time.[1] Sometimes it has seemed to me that they were not sure just exactly what they really wanted to do, whether to discuss broad principles of interpretation or to attempt some fresh approach to a biblical passage or theme. And that again is symptomatic of the present situation of uncertainty about the whole general area. Biblical interpretation, once perhaps almost taken for granted, has come to the fore as a disputed topic that demands scholarly attention. The current state of discussion is helpfully summarized in two solid Dictionaries and a 'Companion'.[2]

---

1. Galloping professional narrowness will force me to write this essay primarily about the New Testament rather than the Bible as a whole, but what I have to say will hopefully represent the position regarding evangelical biblical studies generally.

2. Coggins 1990; Hayes 1999; Barton 1998.

It is not surprising that within this context there has been fresh attention to it within that branch of Christian faith and scholarship called 'evangelical'.

Three levels of approach

Our survey may be conveniently carried out on three levels, although these cannot be separated sharply from one another:

1. The level of general hermeneutics, which asks what is going on in interpretation in general and then in biblical interpretation in particular. Clearly it is important to investigate hermeneutics at this level. Let me mention just two of the vital questions that arise here. First, there is the question of whether texts can have 'meaning' in themselves, meaning that is objectively there, so to speak, or whether meaning is somehow created afresh through the interaction between the reader and the text, so that texts in themselves have no fixed meaning; clearly this has considerable implications for our understanding of biblical authority.[3] Second, there is the question of how language 'works'[4] and the implications of this for recognizing what is actually going on in biblical texts and in our reading of them.[5] However, largely out of comparative ignorance of this area and also because it is perhaps less immediately fruitful for the nitty gritty of biblical interpretation than the other two levels of study, I propose to leave it rather to one side in this essay.
2. The level of exegesis. Here we consider the various methods and tools that may be used in approaching a text so as to understand it in its own time.

---

3. Vanhoozer 1998.
4. One example of this would be the question of what a Lexicon or Dictionary or New Testament Greek should provide and how it should be organized.
5. See especially Bartholomew, Greene & Möller 2001.

3. The level of application, where we raise the question of whether and how an ancient text can have something to say to the contemporary reader.

The development of evangelical scholarship

It is probably true to say that until comparatively recently evangelicals, like biblical scholars and preachers generally, did not recognize that there were problems in these three areas. Nevertheless, there was a growing awareness of the need for discussion. A single example must suffice. We were no doubt influenced by the mood of the times when the New Testament study group of the Tyndale Fellowship devoted its meeting in 1973 to the topic and discussed a set of papers which eventually were published in 1977 under the title *New Testament Interpretation: Essays on Principles and Methods*. The book was intended to be a comprehensive introductory textbook for theological students. In his essay on 'Approaches to New Testament exegesis' in this book R. P. Martin commended what he termed 'the grammatico-historical method'. He contrasted it with what he called 'the dogmatic approach' and 'the impressionistic approach'; the former of these was where Scripture was seen as a series of theological proof-texts, often interpreted in the light of later ecclesiastical statements, while the latter worked more with the 'blessed thoughts' that a passage of Scripture excited in the minds of the readers. It is fair to say that at a popular level these kinds of interpretation were often used. By contrast, the 'grammatico-historical method' takes seriously the fact that the Bible is a book from a particular historical setting and consists of words in the original languages; genuine interpretation must take account of the setting and attempt to understand the text using all possible resources that will explain the wording. Scripture must be understood on its own terms.[6]

In commending the '*grammatico*-historical method', Martin was probably at the same time distancing himself from the so-called

---

6. Marshall 1977: 220–251.

'historical-*critical* method' that was the dominant approach in biblical scholarship. The two terms sound very similar, and the latter method would have used the tools of the former. However, as formulated by scholars such as E. Troeltsch, the historical-critical method was based on a denial of the supernatural and attempted to understand the biblical text as simply a human, fallible collection of documents. As a consequence historical criticism in the broad sense was viewed with disfavour by evangelicals; they believed that its presuppositions were invalid and that therefore its conclusions must be false, and so they were tempted to reject it lock, stock and barrel. Evangelicals were also wary of a method which seemed to thrive on discovering errors and contradictions in the Bible and building theories upon them. It was also spiritually barren because it seemed to be more concerned with exploring how texts came into existence rather than with elucidating their theological significance. To cite a favourite example, the documentary theory of the Pentateuch was regarded with disfavour because: (a) It denied the Mosaic authorship of Genesis (which was assumed to be asserted in the Bible; e.g. John 1:45); (b) To a considerable extent it based the dissection of the narrative into sections from different sources on the exposure of discrepancies and contradictions between different texts; (c) It tended to ignore the divine authority of the text. Recent criticism of it has also claimed that in principle the method could not bring out the message of the Bible for today and was spiritually barren. Yet a great deal of biblical study was conducted in this manner.

Faced by the prevalence of this approach, evangelicals reacted in two ways:

1. There were scholars who attempted to deal with such problems by taking on the critics on their own ground, producing reasoned refutations of their theories and framing better ones.[7]
2. Probably the majority took refuge in their belief in scriptural infallibility and claimed, that whatever critics might say, the

---

7. Among such might be mentioned G. C. Aalders, O. T. Allis and J. G. Machen.

biblical statements about authorship or prophecy were by definition historically infallible. Many interpreters, therefore, simply ignored the 'higher critics' (as they called them) and their conclusions. There was a consequent distrust of scholarship of any kind. For a long time there was very little serious evangelical scholarship, and evangelical candidates for ministry were sometimes encouraged by their elders not to take theological degrees lest they should be infected with higher criticism and lose their faith.

As for actual interpretation of the text, evangelical scholars followed the practices of the time. Essentially exegesis was carried on perfectly properly by linguistic and syntactical study to discover what the text was saying. Background information was drawn upon to explain it. There was, however, a tendency to spend most of the time in elucidating the details of the text verse by verse rather than to look at larger units of text and their total thrust.

It was assumed that the text would speak to the modern reader more or less as it stood. There was, therefore, little need for 'interpretation' in the sense of reapplying the text to different circumstances or translating it to make it intelligible to people who did not stand in the original situation. For the most part it could be assumed that there was little or no difference between the original readers and the contemporary readers.

We thus have a situation in which – despite the exceptions already noted – there was little or no scholarship, evangelicalism was largely defensive, and hermeneutics was not seen as a problem.

But then came several books, such as the symposium just mentioned. What has caused the change? Over the past fifty years or so there has been a remarkable growth in the industry of biblical scholarship on all sides, and in particular there has been a tremendous interest in 'hermeneutics' or 'interpretation' in the broadest sense by scholars of all persuasions. There have also been some welcome shifts in scholarship. There has been a recognition that the biblical books are theological documents and that one of the main aims, if not the main aim, of interpretation should be to elucidate their theology. A number of major series of commentaries have made this their explicit aim. At the same time, there has been a recognition that texts should be studied in their own right as literary entities. This has led to a concentration on the texts in their final forms and to a lessening of interest in how they came to be. For example, earlier studies of Matthew and Luke tended to look at them redactionally, asking how the authors had used their sources. Now, however, the current impasse in solving the synoptic problem has led to a shift to asking how the Evangelists have told their stories, and narrative criticism and discourse analysis have tended to replace source criticism and redaction criticism.[8] These developments mean that biblical scholarship in general is concentrating on areas that are more congenial to evangelicals.

We are inevitably influenced by our context, and the development of evangelical biblical scholarship over this period must be understood at least to some extent against this broader background of a more positive approach.

There is a recognition that the methods of critical study can be used without acceptance of anti-religious presuppositions that rule out the possibility of the supernatural from the start. It is possible to do grammatico-historical study without accepting the starting-point laid down by Troeltsch.[9] Over against the sceptical 'historical-critical method' may be placed the approach of 'believing criticism'.[10]

However, there is a still a problematic area here. The trouble with historical study is that it may lead to conclusions that

---

8. It is important to stress that the older disciplines have certainly not disappeared from attention; they remain important but other disciplines tend to be at the centre of attention.

9. See Abraham 1982.

10. Wright 1980: 97 mentions J. K. Mozley as using this term to describe a rather wider range of scholarship. (I am grateful for the reference to an unpublished thesis by S. P. Dray.) I use the term for an approach that recognizes that the manner of the human composition of the biblical books is a proper subject for investigation by scholars who also believe in their divine origin and inspiration.

investigators do not want to believe or that go against the beliefs of
their constituency. Some scholars want to start from a position
which rules out the possibility of what they would regard as error
in Scripture. Therefore any method which might find errors is
ruled out as inappropriate in principle. Clearly a lot hangs on what
one understands as error. There is something of a polarization
among evangelicals as a result. At one end we have a rejection of
critical methods by scholars like Robert Thomas who rejects redaction criticism of the Gospels because it leads to the conclusion that
we do not have word-for-word transcripts of what Jesus said in the
Gospels. At the other end we have scholars who accept that the
Evangelists have edited the material that came to them in various
ways.

But even so, the situation is complex. It all hinges on what
is regarded as 'error'. Proponents of redaction criticism would
insist that, if the Gospels do not give us the actual words of Jesus
(admittedly translated into Greek!), this does not constitute an
error but is an accepted way of summarizing or paraphrasing
the words of a speaker. Yet we have the differences between
D. A. Carson and R. H. Gundry, both 'inerrantists', one of whom
understands the Gospel of Matthew to be historical and the other
of whom sees it as largely 'midrash'. The result is that within evangelicalism there is a very wide range of views on such issues as
historicity (Is the book of Jonah a historical account or a parable?),
sources (Was Isaiah of Jerusalem the source of all the prophecies
in the book of Isaiah or have several sources been combined in it?)
and authorship (Did Paul write the Pastoral Epistles or are they the
work of a later author or authors?). In theory an 'inerrantist' could
accept the latter alternatives in each of these three cases, if they fell
within accepted conventions of writing, but in practice some
would have great difficulty with all three.

Now there is nothing new about this diversity. In the 1940s there
took place the creation of the Tyndale Fellowship, which was a
serious attempt to develop an evangelical scholarship which could
face up to the challenges of biblical criticism honestly and fairly.
Writing in 1947 one of its leading founder members, F. F. Bruce,
contrasted the then attitude of the Roman Catholic Church, which
fettered its scholars, to that of the Tyndale Fellowship:

In such critical *cruces*, for example, as the codification of the pentateuch, the composition of Isaiah, the date of Daniel, the sources of the Gospels, or the authenticity of the Pastoral Epistles, each of us is free to hold and proclaim the conclusions to which all the available evidence points. Any research worthy of the name, we take it for granted, must necessarily be unfettered.[11]

It must be admitted that Bruce's statement represented the ideal rather than what was always the reality. Evangelical publishers, in particular, have not always been willing to publish views which were out of tune with their own ideas or those of their constituency – out of the very real fear that they would lose their clientele. One may compare the reaction to proposed revisions in the New International Version by those who feared that it would give support to egalitarian views of the place of women in the home and the ministry which led to the American Bible Society retracting from its intentions.[12] It is evident that the problems of pressure by people with clout on publishers, and censorship by publishers themselves, have not gone away.

Evangelical scholars have both welcomed and forwarded the developments in general hermeneutics (level 1 above) that have been taking place in recent years. Some of the most important contributions to the discussion in this area have been made by R. Lundin, A. C. Thiselton and K. Vanhoozer, and these have attracted wide attention. A wider discussion, led by Craig Bartholomew and involving scholars from a variety of theological stables, is taking place in the 'Scripture and Hermeneutics Seminar'; at the time of

---

11. Bruce 1947: 58f. In a footnote Bruce noted how the *Evangelical Quarterly* had carried contributions which expressed different views on the common authorship of the Gospel of John and the Revelation by George Beasley-Murray and himself.

12. The solution, worthy of Solomon, is to continue to publish the unrevised NIV to satisfy one part of the constituency and to publish a revised version under a different name for the benefit of the remainder of it (Today's New International Version; presumably this was not meant to imply that those sticking to the older version have embraced yesterday's version?).

writing three volumes of papers and responses have appeared.[13]

With regard to methods of study (level 2 above), it is interesting to compare two textbooks for students coming out of the evangelical stable. The book which I myself edited twenty-five years ago covered *inter alia* the following issues: semantics; introduction (authorship, readership, date, etc.); religious background; historical criticism; source criticism; form criticism; tradition history; redaction criticism; genre;[14] and use of the OT. Exegesis was covered by an article which looked at two difficult passages and explored how one goes about understanding them, and a further article on exposition looked at the same passages and how one draws significance out of them for today. All of these approaches were recognized as legitimate, necessary and valuable for understanding the text.

Over against this we may place the much more recent book *Hearing the New Testament: Strategies for Interpretation*, edited by Joel Green, with its list of topics: traditio-historical criticism*; historical criticism and social-scientific perspectives; the relevance of extra-canonical Jewish texts; the relevance of Greco-Roman literature and culture; textual criticism; modern linguistics*; discourse analysis; genre analysis*; the use of the OT*; narrative criticism; rhetorical criticism; the reader in NT interpretation; feminist hermeneutics; reading the NT in canonical context.[15] Two things are impressive.

The first is the number of approaches to New Testament study which were only beginning to be heard of in 1977 or which had not developed sufficiently far to be thought worthy of mention.[16] Thus, while there has always been recognition of the need to study

---

13. Bartholomew, Greene & Möller 2000; Bartholomew, Greene & Möller 2001; Bartholomew, Chaplin, Song & Walters 2002. The Seminar is under the auspices of the School of Humanities, University of Gloucestershire, and the British and Foreign Bible Society.

14. This was covered in Martin's chapter (see note 6 above) which explored the different types of material in the letters.

15. In this list I have asterisked the topics that are common to both volumes to indicate the degree of overlap between them.

16. One culpable omission in the 1977 book was textual criticism.

the Jewish and non-Jewish texts of the period in order to shed fuller light on the New Testament, new tools, such as computerised texts and search procedures, and new discoveries (e.g. the availability of the full corpus of the Dead Sea Scrolls) have revolutionized this area. But there are also new types of analysis of the text, such as discourse analysis, rhetorical criticism and reader-response criticism, which have come to the fore and made us ask new questions of the text.

The second point is not simply that evangelical scholars have taken up these approaches but that in a a number of cases they have made important contributions to their development. Representative of the more traditional approaches is the outstanding work of B. M. Metzger in establishing the text of the Greek New Testament. The pioneer work of E. A. Judge in developing a social-scientific approach to the New Testament is widely esteemed. Several of the contributors to Green's symposium are making their mark as front-runners in new approaches.

Thus, at the level of exegesis of the text, evangelical scholars are playing an important role in the development and the application of methods of study.

To some extent there has been a rapprochement between scholars of a more conservative and a more liberal bent in much recent study. This has taken place because the study of biblical texts has tended to be conducted on the level of texts as literary objects rather than on the level of texts as witnesses to historical events, and this type of study does not raise the questions of historicity, sources and so on that were a major battleground in the past. There is, of course, a danger in conducting literary study apart from historical study in that the temptation may be to explain the texts purely on the literary level: it is easy to explain, say, Luke's portrayal of women in the early church in terms of his particular motivation rather than to recognize that he was constrained by the historical phenomena that he was describing. Evangelicals have an important role to play here in stressing the relation of the texts to the historical events that underlie them. There can also be the danger of ignoring the historical questions and sticking to less controversial issues. At present, for example, much less attention is being paid to the questions of the sources of the books of the Old Testament and preference is being given to study of the books as completed wholes (however they may have reached that state). This emphasis on the final form of the text is certainly to be welcomed. But the question of history cannot be sidestepped for ever.

The application of the text

Possibly the most important issue to be considered is that of the application of the text (level 3 above). How do we read and appropriate ancient texts in the contemporary world?

For a typical answer we may turn to J. I. Packer. In an essay entitled 'Understanding the Bible: Evangelical Hermeneutics', originally published in 1990,[17] he begins by stressing the distinctive character of evangelical hermeneutics on the basis that: 'evangelicals say that they should listen to Holy Scripture, and finally let its teaching guide them, however much reordering of their prior ideas and intentions this may involve, and however sharply it may set them at odds with the mind-set of their peers and their times' (150). He then states four principles that govern their interpretation:

1. 'Biblical passages must be taken to mean *what their human authors were consciously expressing*'. For what the human authors say is what God says (153).
2. 'The *coherence, harmony and veracity* of all biblical teaching must be taken as our working hypothesis in interpretation' (155).
3. 'Interpretation involves *synthesizing* what the various biblical passages teach, so that each item taught finds its proper place and significance in the *organism* of revelation as a whole.' Under this heading Packer comments that progressive revelation 'is not an evolutionary process of growing spiritual discernment through which cruder notions come to be left behind', but rather 'earlier revelation became the foundation for later revelation' (155f.).
4. *The response for which the text calls* must be made explicit. Here the crucial procedure appears:

---

17. Packer 1999: 147–160.

So, just as it is possible to identify in all the books of Scripture universal and abiding truths about the will, work and ways of God, it is equally possible to find in every one of them universal and abiding principles of loyalty and devotion to the holy, gracious Creator; and then to detach these from the particular situations to which, and the cultural frames within which, the books apply them, and to reapply them to ourselves in the places, circumstances, and conditions of our own lives today. Rational application of this kind, acknowledging but transcending cultural differences between the Bible worlds and ours, is the stock-in-trade of the evangelical pulpit, and the recognized goal of the evangelical discipline of personal meditation on the written text . . . Evangelicals do not find their models of interpretation in the 'critical' commentaries of the last century and a half, which stop short at offering historical explanations of the text and have no applicatory angle at all; they find them, rather, in the from-faith-to-faith expository styles of . . . older writers . . . who concerned themselves with what Scripture means as God's word to their own readers, as well as with what it meant as religious instruction for the readership originally addressed, and whose supreme skill lay in making appropriate applications of the material that they exegeted by grammatico-historical means. (157)

Similar statements might have been taken from several sources,[18] for what Packer says here is representative of an agreed position.

---

18. In a popular magazine we find this:

> To apply most New Testament commands, we need to understand the original situation. If the situation is identical or comparable to our own situation, then we can apply the command directly to our lives.
>
> If not, then we need to discover the principle behind the command and apply it to comparable situations that we face.
>
> With some New Testament commands we don't need to find general principles for the specific situations. Rather, we need to find specific situations for the general principles. {e.g. applying love command}
>
> The list is virtually endless. But we haven't applied the commands of Scripture until we have thought about what we could do, ask God for wisdom and guidance, and then act on His guidance (Kuhatscheck 2001).

He makes a distinction between what we may call statements of doctrine and principles of response to God. The former, it seems, are accepted as they stand. However, it is recognized that the forms in which the latter are presented may be shaped by particular situations ('Go to the great city of Nineveh and preach against it', Jonah 1:2)[19] and cultural frameworks ('Let people and animals be covered with sackcloth. Let everyone call urgently on God', Jonah 3:8), and we are required to detach the principles of response to God's message and then make a rational reapplication of them to ourselves in our situation and cultural setting.

We thus have a hermeneutical procedure that commands fairly wide assent and is common practice. It does not, however, always lead to the same results even among interpreters who may be presumed to be living in much the same kind of setting. Fifty years ago there was virtual agreement among evangelicals in confining the ordained ministry and church leadership to men, but today there is no longer such agreement. The practice of apartheid, which was based on a particular understanding of the teaching of Scripture by Christians who professed to be 'Reformed', has been recognized as incompatible with scriptural teaching. On matters of doctrine there are important questions regarding the nature of justice and judgment and consequently regarding the understanding of the atonement.[20] Whereas evangelicals tended to adopt in practice a supersessionist understanding of certain gifts of the Spirit (especially speaking in tongues, prophecy and healing), there has been a revival of these gifts in charismatic congregations accompanied by a reappraisal of the doctrine of the Holy Spirit. There is a continuing debate on the nature of the final judgment on unbelievers; this is concerned both with whether persons may be finally saved although they never heard the gospel and also with whether the final judgment entails conscious, eternal

---

19. Biblical quotations in this chapter are from the NIVI.
20. The question concerns the nature of human punishment, whether it should be retributive as well as deterrent and reformatory. How is it related to the divine judgment upon sin, and should the latter be understood as primarily retributive? See Marshall 2001.

torment.[21] This debate stands alongside the fact that the final judgment occupies a much less central place in preaching than used to be the case. Problems also arise where teaching is given, particularly in the Old Testament, which seems more like 'cruder notions' to be abandoned rather than 'the foundation for later revelation': the divine approval (expressed or tacit) of genocide in certain situations is the obvious and worrying example.

A further set of problems arise where the Christian is called upon to deal with contemporary issues to which there is nothing closely analogous in Scripture (or in the ancient world generally): these are typically issues raised by modern scientific and medical technology, such as questions of fertilization, contraception, genetic modification, and termination of life. How is Scripture to be utilized in these areas?[22]

And yet another area arises with more general issues of human life where Christians would campaign against slavery or unrepresentative government, although these are not questioned in Scripture and people are apparently encouraged to live obediently within such social and political frameworks and are never encouraged to campaign towards fundamental changes in the structures of society and the state (the principle of obeying 'God rather than human beings' [Acts 5:29] appears to apply only where human authorities forbid Christian witness). How do Christians justify civil rights movements, peaceful protests and so on?

There is thus a broad range of questions where adoption of the 'method' does not necessarily lead to unanimity in interpretation. Problems arise at the levels of exegesis of individual texts, constructing a synthesis or harmony of biblical teaching, and making a rational application of the biblical teaching. It is not surprising, therefore, that evangelicals (like other Christians) are examining afresh the ways in which we can appropriate the message of Scripture for ourselves, or, better, to find out how we can tell what

---

21. Some biblical texts may suggest ongoing torment (Mark 9:48; Rev. 20:10, 15), whereas others may suggest complete destruction (2 Thess. 1:9; Jas. 4:12). See the presentation of different points of view in Hilborn 2000.

22. See, for example, Jones 2001; Bruce 2001.

God is telling us to believe and do in Scripture. Moreover, these problems are concerned not just with the application of principles but also in some case with the status of the principles themselves.

Evangelicals are generally clear that they cannot go down the path of classical 'liberalism', by which is to be understood the peeling off of those aspects of Christian faith and ethics which are unacceptable to modern, or, as we must now presumably go on to say, 'postmodern' people. It is recognized that such trimming of the faith subjects the Bible to the changing, arbitrary shifts of contemporary opinion and rests on no firm principles.

A better-based approach would include the recognition that to some extent the contemporary secular mind is shaped by principles that are ultimately inspired by the Christian message or are in harmony with it.[23] In such cases, if minds nurtured on the gospel come to conclusions which seem to clash with scriptural teaching, then this establishes a case for reconsideration of whether we have correctly identified the latter. Note particularly that 'reconsideration' is not the same thing as 'rejection' or 'rewriting'. It is nothing more than an amber light that signifies that something may be wrong somewhere. It is equally possible that the problem may lie with the contemporary mind. In other words, instead of the modern culture and world-view dictating the jettisoning of something in Scripture, the existence of a clash serves as an indicator that there is a problem that needs a solution. Thus the modern so-called scientific world-view that denies the possibility of miracles cannot be allowed to call the shots, and a Christian world-view based on Scripture will rightly recognize that here it is the modern world-view that is defective and needs to be revised.

We thus have to look for some principled way of dealing with such matters, and it is here that the debate will centre for some time to come.

Over against the position so well sketched by Packer let me now

---

23. For example, the recognition of human beings as persons with an inherent worth and dignity and therefore not mere 'things' or disposable objects may ultimately rest upon the biblical doctrine of creation in the image of God or at least be in harmony with it.

place an alternative approach that has been developed by R. B. Hays. That Hays stands very close to evangelicalism is evidenced by the fact that D. J. Moo (1999: 272), though critical, could say that he agreed with the vast majority of what Hays said in the book.[24] Broadly speaking, Hays claims that we must carry out four tasks that sound to me rather like Packer's four principles: read the text carefully (descriptive), place the text in its canonical context (synthetic), relate it to our situation (hermeneutical) and live it out (pragmatic). He then faces the problem that not all the biblical witnesses speak with the same voice.[25] He attempts to solve it by looking for what he calls 'focal images' in the NT and finds these in: the Christian community of discipleship; Jesus' death as the paradigm of faithfulness to God; and the church as the community of the resurrection in a not-yet-redeemed world. His procedure is then to read the texts in the light of these three images. He also argues that NT texts may be expressed in different modes: rules, principles, paradigms and symbolic world, and they have different sorts of authority. In this connection he stresses the paradigmatic authority of the NT as the story of God's redemptive action. Working with these principles he is able to situate the texts within their canonical context and to see how they generate trajectories; for example, it may be legitimate to expand the possible exceptions in the NT to the 'no divorce' rule, 'thereby extending a hermeneutical trajectory that we see within the New Testament itself' (Hays 1997: 370).

Two points emerge from this very brief (and inadequate) summary. First, Hays is attempting to put some flesh on the bare bones of 'understanding Scripture within the context of Scripture'; he is insisting that texts must not be read on their own but in

---

24. Hays 1996. Hays' book was considered sufficiently important by the Institute for Biblical Research to be the subject of a session at its conference in 2000, where he responded to sympathetically critical evaluations of it by D. J. Moo and J. Gundry-Volf.

25. The problem for evangelicals is that Hays appears to find some irreconcilable contradictions within Scripture and is then forced to jettison some scriptural teaching. When does diversity become contradiction?

the light of their proper context which is Scripture as a whole, and that means for him Scripture as seen through the lenses of the nature of the Christian community, the paradigm of the cross, and the nature of the new creation. Such a procedure may relativize the teaching of some texts.

Second, Hays is recognizing that when Scripture is read in this way, its authoritative direction for today may not be identical with the surface teaching of individual texts but may go beyond them. Thus he would allow that the scriptural exceptions to 'no divorce' should be extended to include divorce in cases of domestic abuse with the possibility of subsequent remarriage to another spouse.[26]

The importance of this treatment is that here we have an example of a Christian who takes the authority of Scripture seriously wrestling with the problem of the ethical teaching in Scripture and attempting to find what we may regard as scriptural principles for moving from the text to its application. Confronted by texts given in particular situations and cultural frameworks, we need to find a scriptural basis for interpreting them rather than being told by a secular world what we may and may not accept. Hays' model is intricate, but it may well be that one of the strong temptations of evangelicals is over-simplification: the preacher wants to be able to say 'The Bible says' in as direct and simple a way as possible, whereas the truth is sometimes rather more complex than a single, short statement.

Following this pattern we have a better basis for recognizing what material in Scripture is situational or cultural and what are the basic patterns of Christian belief and behaviour that come to expression in it.

More contentious is the problem of how far we can work with trajectories in doctrinal teaching. Examples of this cannot avoid being controversial. One must suffice. We have in Scripture various pictures of the final state of unbelievers as one of unending fire with the possible implication of continuing torment

---

26. Cf. Instone-Brewer 2003. More problematic are cases where extending the trajectory may be thought to lead to acting in a way that is opposite to the surface level of scriptural teaching.

accompanied by weeping and gnashing of teeth.[27] Many Christians have considerable difficulty with this description in view of the biblical picture of a God who is both just and gracious and in view of the recognition that practising torment is totally incompatible with Christian behaviour: they will ask whether it is ethical for God to do this when it is unethical for his people to do so.

Faced by this dilemma, we may make various responses.

1. We accept the biblical teaching at what we take to be its face value and affirm that, however repugnant modern people may find it, God will indeed punish the ungodly for ever.
2. We may be moved to re-examine the biblical texts and conclude that our exegesis was mistaken and that they do not teach what they appear to teach. There are (in my view) certainly some texts which seem to speak of eternal destruction (i.e. once destroyed a thing remains destroyed, not that it is perpetually being destroyed); maybe the same is true of the other texts.
3. We may claim that the biblical writers expressed the fact of judgment using the imagery that was available to them, although we now recognize that it may give a wrong picture of God, but that in the light of the gospel we must recognize that these images give a partial insight into the truth. They do convey the fact that God's judgment on sin is total and severe, but God is not a torturer; the pictures of exclusion from the heavenly city and the remorse felt by those who realize that they are excluded are primary.

Again, interpretation of Scripture in this way opens up a context for dealing with problems never envisaged in Scripture. They will be solved not by searching (in vain?) for analogous situations or proof-texts but by the development of a total understanding of humanity as God's creation and (potentially) as his re-creation

---

27. Somebody once put the question to a hell-fire preacher: 'But what about those who have lost all their teeth?', to which the preacher replied 'Teeth will be supplied'.

which will provide the framework within which we must work at our contemporary problems.

Where evangelicals may have difficulties with this kind of approach is when it suggests that we can move beyond Scripture or that some scriptural texts no longer apply literally. Probably all of us accept these possibilities tacitly: we do not practise genocide on other peoples who might cause us to fall away from our faith; less extremely we follow Paul in not taking the initiative in putting away unbelieving spouses rather than Nehemiah in so doing; although we are not sure whether the apostolic decree in Acts 15:20, 29 was ever revoked, we don't insist on eating only kosher meat; although Paul appointed leaders called 'bishops' in his churches (Phil. 1:1; 1 Tim. 3:1–7; Titus 1:5–9), many of us don't do so, and we don't have special church care for widows (1 Tim. 5:3–16), nor do we give elders who preach and teach double honour (1 Tim. 5:17). Some of these examples may be situational or cultural, but not all of them. Nevertheless, we tend to be tacit about what we are doing rather than to recognize it openly. We need to consider whether a biblical case can be made for 'going beyond Scripture'.[28]

One of the most welcome features of biblical study at the present time is the growing recognition on all sides that the task of the biblical commentator is not completed until the question of the application of the text to the contemporary reader is faced. In the 1950s we saw the first of the Tyndale Commentaries, concerning which the General Editor wrote: 'The commentaries will be primarily exegetical and only secondarily homiletic, though it is hoped that both student and preacher will find them informative and suggestive.' At that time the need for sound exegesis was rightly recognized. Since that time the same publisher[29] has promoted two

---

28. Important contributions in the realm of ethical development that go beyond the teaching of Scripture but remain in accord with Scripture have been made by Longenecker 1984; Swartley 1983; and Webb 2001.

29. The Tyndale Commentaries were produced by the UK Inter-Varsity Press under its 'Tyndale Press' imprint. The same press is responsible for the BST series, but the IVPNTCS is produced by its independent North American partner, InterVarsity Press.

series. From the UK side has come 'The Bible Speaks Today' and from the North American side 'The IVP New Testament Commentary Series'. In both of these series there is a determined attempt to wed exegesis to contemporary application. Maybe the evangelical press was behind the times in this respect, for already in the 1950s the Abingdon Press was producing *The Interpreter's Bible*, in which pairs of scholars worked together to produce the exegesis and exposition for each biblical book.[30] But now we have something of a growth industry. Outstanding in the wider world of scholarship is the series 'Interpretation: A Bible Commentary for Teaching and Preaching' (Westminster/John Knox Press). Alongside it must now be placed 'The NIV Application Commentary Series' (Zondervan), in which each pericope of the text is discussed under three heads: Original Meaning; Bridging Contexts; and Contemporary Significance. A forthcoming series (the Two Horizons) will consider the relationship between the biblical texts and systematic theology.

Conclusion

Especially in the later part of my essay I have been deliberately raising issues where evangelicals are divided. These divisions extend to the scholars and not just to the pastors or believers generally. This lack of consensus is probably where we are at in regard to biblical interpretation.

Let me put it this way. We have in effect mentioned three areas:

1. The general area of hermeneutics: the question of what interpretation is, how it ought to be practised and how it ought not to be practised. This is a question that is wider than biblical interpretation. Evangelicals have already been caught up in the contemporary discussion of it and the challenge to them is to

---

30. The result was not entirely satisfactory, since the exegesis and exposition were not always in tune with each other, and the amount of space available was perhaps too limited.

play a significant part in it. An important question is whether the acceptance of the Bible as Scripture affects the nature of interpretation.

2. The area of biblical studies in the sense of understanding the biblical texts in their own time. Here two things are happening. The first is that, after a lengthy period of comparative (but never total) neglect of scholarship, many, but not all, evangelicals have returned to a recognition of the need for a believing criticism which employs all possible means that can shed light on the text. The second is that, we have identified the ways in which various new approaches and tools have been recognized to be both legitimate and essential in understanding the text more adequately. A continuing task must be the evaluation of such approaches to ensure that we do not lapse unawares into unbelieving criticism.[31]

3. There is a growing recognition of the need to face the hermeneutical problem in the narrower sense in which this phrase is sometimes used, that is, the principles by which we move from the biblical text to its contemporary message and the actual task of working out its message in the light of these principles. It may well be true to say that as a result of the welcome developments in this area, today's church is much better equipped with the means for understanding and applying God's Word than it was during the earlier part of the twentieth century. Yet there remains much land to be possessed, and in particular there is an urgent need to consider the problem of how Christian doctrine and systematic theology can be developed in a way that is wholly biblical and yet recognizes that 'the Lord hath yet more light and truth to break forth from his holy Word'.[32]

---

31. There are some obvious examples of 'deconstruction' which hardly seem compatible with an acceptance of the Bible as Scripture and indeed seem to be bent on its destruction.

32. The quotation is from the Puritan pastor John Robinson (d. 1625).

Bibliography

Abraham, W. J. (1982), *Divine Revelation and the Limits of Historical Criticism*, Oxford: Oxford University Press.

Bartholomew, C. G., J. Chaplin, R. Song and A. Wolters (eds.) (2002), *A Royal Priesthood? The Use of the Bible Ethically and Politically: A Dialogue with Oliver O'Donovan*, Grand Rapids: Zondervan; Carlisle: Paternoster Press.

Bartholomew, C. G., C. Greene and K. Möller (eds.) (2000), *Renewing Biblical Interpretation*, Grand Rapids: Zondervan; Carlisle: Paternoster Press.

Bartholomew, C. G. , C. Greene and K. Möller (eds.) (2001), *After Pentecost: Language and Biblical Interpretation*, Grand Rapids: Zondervan; Carlisle: Paternoster Press.

Barton, J. (ed.) (1988), *The Cambridge Companion to Biblical Interpretation*, Cambridge: Cambridge University Press.

Bleicher, J. (1980), *Contemporary Hermeneutics: Hermeneutics as Method, Philosophy and Critique*, London: Kegan Paul.

Bruce D. and D. Horrocks (eds.) (2001), *Modifying Creation? GM Crops and Foods: A Christian Perspective*, Carlisle: Paternoster Press.

Bruce, F. F. (1947), 'The Tyndale Fellowship for Biblical Research', *Evangelical Quarterly* 19: 52–61.

Coggins, R. J. and J. L. Houlden (eds.) (1990), *A Dictionary of Biblical Interpretation*, Philadelphia: Trinity Press International; London: SCM Press.

Gundry-Volf, J. (1999), 'Putting the *Moral Vision of the New Testament* into Focus: A Review', *Bulletin for Biblical Research* 9: 277–287.

Hayes, J. H. (ed.) (1999), *Dictionary of Biblical Interpretation*, 2 vols, Nashville: Abingdon.

Hays, R. B. (1996), *The Moral Vision of the New Testament: Community, Cross, New Creation*, New York: HarperCollins, 1996; Edinburgh: T. & T. Clark, 1997.

—— (1999), 'The Gospel, Narrative and Culture: A Response to Douglas J. Moo and Judith Gundry-Volf', *Bulletin for Biblical Research* 9: 289–296.

Hilborn, D. (et al.) (2000), *The Nature of Hell: A Report by the Evangelical Alliance Commission on Unity and Truth among Evangelicals*, Carlisle: Paternoster Press.

Instone-Brewer, D. (2003), *Divorce and Remarriage in the Church: Biblical Solutions for Pastoral Realities*, Carlisle: Paternoster Press.

Jones, G. (2001), *Clones: The Clowns of Technology?*, Carlisle: Paternoster Press.

Kuhatscheck, J. (2001), 'Applying Scripture', *Decision* 42.9: 47.

Ladd, G. E. (1967), *The New Testament and Criticism*, London: Hodder & Stoughton.

Longenecker, R. N. (1984), *New Testament Social Ethics for Today*, Grand Rapids: Eerdmans.

Lundin, R., A. C. Thiselton and C. Walhout (1985), *The Responsibility of Hermeneutics*, Grand Rapids: Eerdmans; Exeter: Paternoster Press.

Marshall, C. D. (2001), *Beyond Retribution: A New Testament Vision for Justice, Crime and Punishment*, Grand Rapids: Eerdmans.

Marshall, I. H. (ed.) (1977), *New Testament Interpretation: Essays on Principles and Methods*, repr. Exeter: Paternoster Press.

Moo, D. J. (1999), 'A Review of Richard B. Hays, *The Moral Vision of the New Testament*', *Bulletin for Biblical Research* 9: 271–276.

Packer, J. I. (1999), *Honouring the Written Word of God: The Collected Shorter Writings of J. I. Packer Volume 3*, Carlisle: Paternoster Press.

Swartley, W. M. (1983), *Slavery, Sabbath, War and Women: Case Issues in Biblical Interpretation*, Waterloo: Herald.

Wright, D. F. (1980), 'Soundings in the Doctrine of Scripture in British Evangelicalism in the First Half of the Twentieth Century', *Tyndale Bulletin* 31: 87–106.

Recommended reading

Bauckham, R., *Scripture and Authority Today*, Cambridge: Grove Books, 1999.

Bray, G., *Biblical Interpretation Past and Present*, Leicester: Apollos, 1996.

Carson, D. A. (ed.), *Biblical Interpretation and the Church: Text and Context*, Grand Rapids: Baker; Exeter: Paternoster Press, 1984.

Dray, S. P., 'From Consensus to Chaos: An Historical Analysis of Evangelical Interpretation of 1 Timothy 2:8–15 from 1945 to 2001', unpublished thesis, University of Wales, 2002.

Fee, G. D., *New Testament Exegesis: A Handbook for Students and Pastors*, Louisville: Westminster/John Knox Press (originally published 1983), 1993.

Fee, G. D. and D. Stuart, *How to Read the Bible for all its Worth*, Grand Rapids: Zondervan; London: Scripture Union, 1982.

Green, J. (ed.), *Hearing the New Testament: Strategies for Interpretation*, Grand Rapids: Eerdmans; Carlisle: Paternoster Press, 1995.

Green, J. B. and M. Turner (eds.), *Between Two Horizons: Spanning New Testament Studies and Systematic Theology*, Grand Rapids: Eerdmans, 2000.

Hayes, J. H. and C. R. Holladay, *Biblical Exegesis: A Beginner's Handbook*, Atlanta: John Knox; London: SCM Press, 1982.

Kaiser, W. C. and M. Silva, *An Introduction to Biblical Hermeneutics: The Search for Meaning*, Grand Rapids: Zondervan, 1994.

Klein, W., C. Blomberg and R. L. Hubbard, Jr, *Introduction to Biblical Interpretation*, Dallas: Word, 1993.

Lundin, R. (ed.), *Disciplining Hermeneutics: Interpretation in Christian Perspective*, Grand Rapids: Eerdmans; Leicester: Apollos, 1997.

Maier, G., *Biblische Hermeneutik*, Wuppertal: Brockhaus, 1990.

McKim, D. K. (ed.), *Historical Handbook of Major Biblical Interpreters*, Downers Grove and Leicester: IVP, 1998.

Morgan, R. with J. Barton, *Biblical Interpretation*, Oxford: Oxford University Press, 1988.

Osborne, G. R., *The Hermeneutical Spiral: A Comprehensive Introduction to Biblical Interpretation*, Downers Grove: IVP, 1991.

Satterthwaite, P. E. and D. F. Wright (eds.), *A Pathway into the Holy Scripture*, Grand Rapids: Eerdmans, 1994.

Silva, M. (ed.), *Foundations of Contemporary Interpretation*, Grand Rapids: Zondervan; Leicester: Apollos, 1997.

Thiselton, A. C., *The Two Horizons: New Testament Hermeneutics and Philosophical Description with Special Reference to Heidegger, Bultmann, Gadamer and Wittgenstein*, Exeter: Paternoster Press, 1980.

—— (1992), *New Horizons in Hermeneutics*, Grand Rapids: Zondervan.

Thomas, R., 'The Hermeneutics of Evangelical Redaction Criticism', *Journal of the Evangelical Theological Society* 29 (1986), 447–459.

Vanhoozer, K. J., *Is There a Meaning in This Text?*, Grand Rapids: Zondervan, 1998.

Webb, William J., *Slaves, Women and Homosexuals: Exploring the Hermeneutics of Cultural Analysis*, Downers Grove: IVP, 2001.

4. EVANGELICALISM AND BIBLICAL THEOLOGY

Graeme Goldsworthy

The simplest description of biblical theology that I have come across is, 'The study of the Bible in its own terms to discover what it is all about'.[1] This statement of Donald Robinson's indicates something of the straightforward, common-sense approach that is characteristic of evangelical approaches to the Bible. Biblical theology naturally appeals to the evangelical mindset because of the inherent confidence that the Bible is God's word written, and written so that ordinary mortals can understand it. Yet, a moment's reflection will lead us to the realization that not all Christians share this conviction and that there is always the need to be ready to defend it. Since the arguments frequently come from more philosophically oriented views of the Bible, it is incumbent on us evangelicals to understand something of the more intellectual, even philosophical bases for our convictions. To that end I will ask the reader's indulgence when we investigate the viability of an evangelical biblical theology. This should not dent

---

1. Robinson 1997: 7.

our enthusiasm for biblical theology; rather it should encourage it as we see the firmer grounds for pursuing such a discipline. My own experience of over thirty years of teaching biblical theology in theological colleges and in local church ministry has convinced me of a couple of things. First, that there is a great need when teaching the Bible to help people to see something of the one grand plan of God's revelation. Second, that ordinary Christians of all ages become more enthusiastic for study of the Bible once they begin to glimpse its overall unity and coherence.

We should not see the subjects represented by each chapter in this volume as separate concerns that contribute to a greater or lesser degree to a central theme, which in this case is, 'the futures of evangelicalism'. Evangelicalism, by definition, implies an integration of all theological disciplines. This means that none can be satisfactorily dealt with in complete isolation from the others. This integration is a corollary of the fact that evangelicalism is, at least in theory, the expression of the principle of *sola scriptura* (the Bible alone). It is a theological position rather than a sociological or cultural one, and thus biblical theology is a key aspect of its identity. Consequently, in this chapter I will attempt to point out some of the ways in which a truly evangelical biblical theology can contribute to the future integration of Christian thought.

Defining biblical theology

Biblical theology is a discipline that has proved elusive when it comes to precise definition. We need some consensus about definition and a set of working criteria so that we can examine the essence of biblical theology conceptually rather than simply deal with a name. The viability of biblical theology is strengthened if it can be shown to have deep and venerable roots in the history of the church's use of the Bible. It is even stronger if it can be shown to be, not merely about the Bible, but actually required by the Bible. We can approach the description of biblical theology both positively and negatively. Thus, in 1787 J. P. Gabler indicated the distinctions between his understanding of systematic and biblical theology.[2] Quite simply, biblical theology is not systematics. Gabler also set some positive parameters for biblical theology: it is descriptive of the biblical data, not philosophically reflective of the abiding truth that must be distilled from these data. Doing biblical theology was a way of separating the purely historically conditioned material, which can be discarded, from the concepts of permanent value. It was a way of enabling the systematician to meet new philosophical challenges and prevailing theological uncertainty.

By the end of the twentieth century much discussion and much sorting out had taken place. Some quite recent works have persisted in addressing the theology of one or other Testament according to doctrinal categories,[3] but generally there has been a movement away from this. In America a whole movement waxed and waned only to be reborn and to join with a much larger movement from other parts of the world, mostly Britain and Europe.[4] A substantial body of literature now exists, mainly from the second half of the twentieth century and beyond. Overall, there is a continuum of evaluations of biblical theology ranging from the most positive to the most negative. There are those who maintain that there is a unified theological stance in the canon of Scripture that, though containing a variety of perspectives, is still perceptible in its unity. Others propose a multiplex approach, and maintain that there is no single theology, but only theologies. Others go still further to challenge the viability of the discipline by rejecting its main presuppositions.

Despite this apparent lack of coherence, there are some key areas of majority agreement that enable us with some justification to use the term 'biblical theology' and to expect that we are largely understood.

---

2. Sandys-Wunsch & Eldredge 1980; Balla 1997; Adam 1995; Knierim, 1995; Stuckenbruck 1999.
3. For example, Jacob 1958; Heinisch 1955; Payne 1962; Richardson 1958.
4. See Smart 1961, chs 8 and 9: 'The Death and Rebirth of Biblical Theology'.

1. There is the general acceptance that when we speak of biblical theology we mean more than a theology that is biblical (as opposed to unbiblical or heretical), even though this confusion still exists among those unfamiliar with the technical use of the term.

2. Biblical theology, in the technical sense, now has come to refer to a way of dealing with the Bible that endeavours to be descriptive of its theological content. It is concerned with understanding the theology contained in the various documents of the canon of Scripture. It may go further to ask how the theology of each book or corpus relates to the rest of the canon. It also may be pursued at the level of concepts or themes rather than of corpora.[5] It thus gives expression to the need to find the nature of the unity of the canon as well as its diversity. In some way biblical theology will ask what was believed, or was being asserted, by the authors of each document, rather than what should be believed now by the community of believers.

3. To the degree that biblical theology looks at the historical contexts of the documents it will face questions of the relationship of the historical truth claims contained in the narrative arc of the canon to what historians believe actually happened. Some aspects of the biblical story – but indeed not all – can be readily related to the extra-biblical historical evidence and thus, with some degree of accuracy, be dated.

Biblical theologians, then, find themselves concerned with a whole range of questions. These include:

- the relationship of the theologically oriented biblical history to 'actual history'
- the theological perspectives of individual texts, books, and corpora, as well as theological themes that may straddle these

---

5. See, for example, Alexander & Rosner 2000, in which the articles are arranged in three sections: the theory and nature of biblical theology; biblical corpora and books; biblical themes.

- the theological relationship of the two Testaments
- the progressive nature of revelation
- the possibility of some kind of unified theology of the whole Bible
- the relationship of what the theology of a text or document meant to its original author and recipients to what it means for us today

Within these broad parameters, biblical theology has been pursued from many different presuppositional bases about the nature and authority of the biblical text. Different notions of authority or inspiration; different theological or philosophical presuppositions; different assessments of the relationship of the Testaments; these all lead to different approaches and emphases in the doing of biblical theology.

Two further points need to be made in this general introduction. First, there is the fact that, while the twentieth century has seen a plethora of theologies of either Testament, almost none of the biblical theologians have attempted to write a biblical theology of the whole Bible.[6] For many this fact is simply the result of the need for division of labour and specialization. The Bible is regarded as simply too big for any one person to be an expert in the totality of the text. It could be argued that the real reason is more a hangover of the Enlightenment rationalism that reduced theology to the history of religions, and thus promoted the notion of the irrelevance to Christian theology of ancient Judaism. The relationship of the Testaments remains a central issue in understanding how biblical theology can be done.[7]

---

6. The early evangelical work of Vos (1948) is curiously incomplete. Vos ignores the former prophets and finishes with the teachings of Jesus, thus omitting the death and resurrection of Jesus and the rest of the New Testament. The most ambitious recent attempt at a comprehensive biblical theology of both Testaments is Childs 1992. Other works include VanGemeren 1988. A briefer introduction is Goldsworthy 1991. Most recently we have the comprehensive evangelical work of Scobie 2002.

7. This is still the case now as it was when commented on by Reventlow 1986.

The second matter relates to the actual procedures for pursuing biblical theology. I refer to the distinction between the synchronic and diachronic methods. This received much publicity when the two major Old Testament Theologies of the twentieth century to come out of Germany, those of Eichrodt and von Rad,[8] were compared. The synchronic approach looked primarily at what happened and was believed at any given point in the formation of the text, and thus made for close analysis of individual texts. In Eichrodt's case it was more an attempt to provide a cross-section of Israel's faith. By contrast, the diachronic approach emphasized the longitudinal 'through time' dimensions and raised the issues of continuity or non-continuity of the various theological expressions. If continuity prevailed, then the result was more of a synthesis of the theology (or theologies) of the several documents and corpora. If discontinuity remained uppermost, the result would be a greater sense of the disparities and even incompatibilities within the canon.

What is an evangelical biblical theology?

History shows us that those who claim the relatively modern label of 'evangelical' represent a fairly broad spectrum of belief.[9] We must attempt a theological definition of evangelical belief. Taking as a working point of departure that evangelicals are those who assign to the Bible the final authority in all matters of faith, we may then strive for the most consistent expression of this. Thus,

---

8. Eichrodt 1961: the English translation was made from the sixth edition of the German, 1959, but the first German edition appeared in 1933; von Rad 1962.

9. Defining evangelicalism is complicated by the tendency, mainly in North America, for many Reformed theologians (who would come under a more general definition of evangelicalism) to eschew the title in order to distinguish themselves from the broader group of American evangelicals that includes fundamentalists of the dispensational variety, and other non-Calvinists.

the nature and authority of Scripture, tradition, and human reason, and the relationships between them, need defining.

Evangelical biblical theology should be consistently biblical by dealing with the unity of the canonical literature within its great diversity. This is because evangelical biblical theology proceeds from a dogmatic construct or, indeed, a series of them.[10] Central to this is the predisposition to regard the Bible as having special authority. Presuppositions may be evaluated according to their degree of internal consistency or self-consistency, along with explanatory power of the world of our experience.[11] From another angle we must reckon with what Calvin refers to as the internal testimony of the Holy Spirit. Either way, we have to recognize that *all* biblical theology begins with some kind of dogmatic-theological framework about the nature of the Bible. Even the atheistic scholar who claims no faith-commitment has, in fact, a theological foundation that assumes the non-existence of a self-revealing and communicating God who is in control of the biblical process.

Evangelical biblical theology is gospel-centred and therefore Christological. I have argued elsewhere that the way into a truly biblical theology is through the One who is declared to be the one mediator between God and man (1 Tim. 2:5).[12] Christology is the basis for understanding the significance of the Old Testament and its relationship to the New Testament. The incarnation is the bridge between this fallen world and the kingdom of God; it is through Christ that we have true knowledge of God himself. Christology is never legitimately Christomonism that focuses on the person and work of Jesus in a way that neglects his role as mediator to bring us to the Father. The early Christological heresies demonstrate the kind of epistemological and theological morasses that occur when both biblical and dogmatic theology are not operating as key dimensions within the hermeneutical spiral.

---

10. See Goldsworthy 1986.

11. Henry (1990) explains the notion of 'self referential incoherence' with regard to the presuppositions of non-Christian beliefs.

12. Goldsworthy 2000b.

The viability of an evangelical biblical theology

Modern evangelicalism has its roots in the Reformation.[13] The Reformation slogan of *sola scriptura*, 'Scripture alone', was bound up with the other 'alones' that the reformers delineated. Here we focus particularly on 'Christ alone' as pointing to the uniqueness of Christ as saviour and Lord. His Lordship stems not only from his exaltation as stated in Acts 2:36, but from the fact that he is the Creator-Word come in the flesh as the source of all grace and truth (John 1:1–14). He affirmed that the authority of the Old Testament was bound up with his unique role to which it testified (John 5:39–46; 10:35). He authorized his apostles to proclaim him as the Saviour with the confidence that his Spirit would lead them into the truth (John 14:6–10, 26; 16:12–15). He linked his Lordship with the fact that his people, his sheep, recognize his voice and follow him (John 10:11–30). On such data as these we have the foundations for a theology of the canon of Scripture, a concept that implies unity. There are a number of concerns about which evangelical biblical theology must make a decision if it is to proceed. These include epistemology, ontology, history and eschatology. The reader who may be wary of some of these technical terms should bear in mind that they are merely shorthand ways of referring to some basic concepts that we use or assume all the time.

Epistemology

The epistemological concern is knowledge: can we know truth in some way, and can we have confidence that we do so know it? Jesus claimed to embody the truth (John 14:6), and Paul understood him to be the source of all wisdom and knowledge (Col. 2:3). These and many other passages in the New Testament indicate that the starting-point for a true knowledge of reality is understood to be the truth as it is in Jesus. When the reformers coined the phrase, 'grace alone', they were repudiating Thomas Aquinas's synthesis of 'nature plus grace' as the equation of

---

13. This is well expressed by Ramm 1973.

truth.[14] Since 'grace alone' was about how salvation came to us, it thus included the salvation of our minds and our ability to know the truth. In fact, any satisfactory view of salvation by grace alone must include the epistemic (knowing) dimension of the renewing of the mind.[15] Scripture is a redemptive word, not merely supplementary information added to that which is available in nature. As a redemptive word it is implicated in 'grace alone' as much as any other aspect of the saving work of God in Christ. Thus, 'grace alone' implies 'Scripture alone', and this, in turn, implies the epistemology that evangelicalism requires. By refusing all forms of synergism[16] in salvation, 'grace alone' embraces an epistemological norm from within a self-authenticating word. In short, Jesus Christ is the epistemological guarantee and the interpretative norm for truth. This knowledge through grace does not stop with Christology, for Christ is the mediator of the knowledge of God. Evangelical theology has always recognized that the ultimate goal is the knowledge and experience of God and his kingdom.

From this we move to the evangelical assessment of Scripture as the one word of the one God about the one way of salvation. Once we acknowledge that salvation is shown in the Bible to be a universal matter of the new creation, and not merely the saving of individual souls, we are bound to say that regeneration and the renewal of the mind have profound epistemological significance.[17] The Bible addresses every fact in the universe in some measure, either by direct reference or by implication. Therein lies the ground for the evangelical assertion of the final authority of Scripture. Some would limit this authority to 'faith' or the 'religious' aspects of life such as ethics and ecclesiology. But while we

---

14. Thomas Aquinas, 1225–74, is regarded as the most significant theologian in the formation of the Catholicism of the Council of Trent and, consequently, of modern Catholicism.

15. Stott 1972.

16. Synergism, literally 'working with', is a term referring to the idea that God has done his part in salvation, and we have to do our part if it is to be effective.

17. See Goldsworthy 2000a: 720.

cannot draw any of the specific data of, say, modern technology and science from the Bible, there is no single datum of these that is not implicated in the biblical view of creation and new creation in Christ. The epistemological question is bound up with the anthropology of the Bible that, in turn, is an aspect of its ontological concerns.

Ontology

To do biblical theology we face the ontological[18] aspects of the world, the Bible, the human reader and interpreter, and the God who is claimed to be Creator of all and ultimate author of the Bible. The evangelical position is usually understood as one that is taken 'from above' or 'from within' the Scriptures. That is, it accepts that the Bible gives an essentially clear revelation of the way things once were, are now, and one day will be. The biblical testimony that points to the ontological status of the Bible as the inspired word of God is rooted and grounded in the creation narrative. God creates humans in his own image and speaks to them a word that structures the hierarchical order of authority in the universe. Reformed (evangelical) theology has always accepted the reality of natural revelation. At the same time, it has rejected the possibility of natural theology in the way Aquinas constructed it, because of our sinful suppression of the truth of God that is revealed in creation. Nevertheless, Calvin referred to the sense of deity; that which gives all people some notions of religion and of right and wrong. It is this that Paul in Romans 1:18 refers to as suppressed but as leaving all men without excuse even, by implication, if they have not heard the gospel.

Again, Calvin expressed the essence of the evangelical position in asserting that the sinful suppression of natural revelation necessitates the special revelation that we have in Scripture.[19] The corruption of sin prevents us from acknowledging the truth in Scripture until we have the regenerative work of the Holy Spirit

---

18. Ontology is concerned with *being*: what things are in themselves.

19. Calvin works out his epistemological stance in the opening chapters of his *Institutes of the Christian Religion*, Calvin, Inst.

and his inner testimony. It is this that prevents the circular argument, 'I know the Bible is the word of God because the Bible tells me so', from being a vicious circle. The biblical doctrine of sin and its lethal effects requires the evangelical understanding of *sola scriptura*, regeneration, and the self-authenticating word of God.

From the perspective of the Enlightenment, which mounted many challenges to the evangelical position, the ontological questions about God are philosophical and historical. That is, biblical theology, if it is theological at all, is merely descriptive of what the ancient Hebrews or the primitive church understood. Enlightenment presuppositions are based on human autonomy and the viability of unaided reason. They take to a logical conclusion the empiricism of Aristotle as employed by Aquinas. Once Aquinas allowed nature to gain a foothold it ended up replacing grace altogether.[20] But, from the evangelical perspective, ontology is at the centre for it relates to the nature of the God that the Bible claims to speak for. As the sovereign Lord of creation, God is the ultimate authority. His word, which we believe the Bible to be, cannot be tested by a higher authority. As Cornelius Van Til has expressed it, to test it by human reason would be like shining a pocket torch on the sun to see if it is real.[21] Evangelical apologetics and theology stand firmly on the ontology of Christian theism.

The ontological questions affecting the pursuit of biblical theology include those relating to the nature of God, Christ, humankind, and the Bible. The obvious question might seem to be about priority or order: which comes first, biblical data or dogmatic formulations about God? But this is only to introduce the hermeneutic spiral which expresses the classic problem of 'the chicken and the egg'. Should we establish the ontological nature of God first? That would be logical since he is before all things. Yet we can only do this on the basis of the truth revealed in the Bible. Furthermore the Bible presents the knowledge of the ontological Trinity

---

20. Schaeffer 1968: ch. 1; see also Van Til 1969: 169–175.
21. Van Til 1948: 37. Van Til goes on to say that we do not thus disparage the light of reason, but only indicate reason's total dependence upon God.

as inseparable from Christology. We see, then, that any distinction between biblical and systematic theology threatens to be simplistic and fragmentary if it tends in the direction of separation.

At the heart of evangelical theism is the Trinity. The 'art' of handling the doctrine of the Trinity is to maintain the equal importance of both the unity of God and his plurality. To do otherwise is to slip into either modalism or tritheism. The former submerges the Trinity into a one-ness (monism) differentiated only by modes of action. The latter separates into three Gods. But the data about God as Trinity are derivative of the speech-acts of God in his word, the most perfect expression of which came in the incarnate Word, Jesus Christ. Our knowledge of Christ, in turn, is derivative of the data of Scripture. The relationship of biblical theology to other disciplines is implicated in this fact of the absolute ontological priority of God and the phenomenological priority of Scripture. To this we add the epistemological priority of the Spirit's regeneration of the mind. We, as believers, know God through Christ whom, in turn, we know through the Scripture. The Scripture, then, has its authority and its nature from its source and its subject. There is a relationship of interdependence between theology, Christology, anthropology and Scripture.

What then do these foci have in common? The very fact of interdependence points to the data about God and about Christ and, then by implication, about all relationships. The trinitarian relationship is in essence unity and plurality, or unity and distinction. As the Chalcedonian definition (AD 451) indicated, unity is asserted without fusion, distinction is asserted without separation.[22] Unity and distinction are equally significant. Thus the relationship of Father to Son and to Holy Spirit is the prior ontological reality that governs the Christological relationship of Jesus' divinity to his humanity. This, then, informs us about the relationship of the Word

---

22. It has been fashionable to criticize the formula of Chalcedon, concerning the two natures of Christ, as essentially Hellenistic. It may have been written in Greek by members of the Eastern church, but the council was truly catholic involving East and West. The perspective of unity–distinction is as Hebraic and as Old Testament as it could ever be!

of God incarnate to the Bible (the word of God inscripturate). From this we have the grounds for determining the relationship of the 'divinity' of the Bible (its ontological relationship to God as his inspired word) to its humanity found in its human authorship and historical context.

The biblical understanding of God, then, is that from all eternity he existed as Father, Son, and Holy Spirit in a relationship of tri-unity, that is, in unity and distinction. The key to the structure of the relationship of God to the creation is ultimately seen in the perfect expression of this relationship, the incarnation of God in Christ. The two natures of Christ are in a unity–distinction relationship, and this characterizes all relationships in the universe.[23] The precise nature of the unity–distinction of each entity to every other entity varies, but the ultimate confusion of the order that God has stamped on his creation is seen when, in any given relationship, unity tends to fusion or distinction to separation.

Since the unity–distinction grid affects our understanding of all relationships, it helps us to understand such things as the way human relationships work in biblical revelation. The ethical dimensions relating to human sexuality, community, Christian love and fellowship, and so on, all show the need to allow for particular aspects of both unity and distinction. We find it in theological dicta such as Luther's description of Christian existence: *simul justus et peccator* (at the same time just and sinner). It underpins the Reformed understanding of the sacraments as *effectual* signs of grace. For the biblical theologian this is vital. It not only illustrates the mutual interdependence of biblical and systematic theology, but also provides the procedural criteria for assessing the relationships within the complexity of the canon of Scripture. The history of interpretation shows, for example, that the relationship of the Testaments, a key issue in biblical theology, has been perceived in a variety of ways that exhibit a continuum from virtual fusion, through unity–distinction, to complete separation.

---

23. Christian trinitarianism thus provided a powerful approach to the age-old philosophical problem of the relationship of the one to the many, of the particular to the general. This is ably discussed in Rushdoony 1978.

The problem of history

The varieties of hermeneutical approaches to the Bible from earliest times express different ways of dealing with the problem of history. Christianity came from an event, or series of events, in time and space that centred upon the person of Jesus of Nazareth.[24] The Gospel accounts of the teaching and ministry of Jesus clearly link them with the past history, as it was perceived, of the Israelite nation and its relationship to the one and only true God. The New Testament presents many testimonies to the links between Jesus and the redemptive history of the Old Testament. Its view of history is discernible in terms of the sovereign purpose of God to redeem a fallen race and creation and to bring them to the goal of the new creation. From the sub-apostolic age to the present time various alien philosophical influences have affected the interpretation of the historic processes from creation to new creation as presented in the canon of Scripture.

Thus, in the early church, Hellenism brought a suspicion of the Old Testament view of God and his actions in history. The solution to this problem was either to allegorize or, in the case of Marcion, to expunge the Old Testament altogether. The early medieval church struggled with multiple possibilities and developed the four-fold interpretative process. Later medievalism, particularly that of Thomas Aquinas, allowed Aristotle's empiricism to colour interpretation. This anticipated the rational-empiricism of Schleiermacher and Troeltsch.[25] The Protestant Reformers endeavoured to restore the biblical philosophy of history, and it is this that modern evangelicalism is heir to. But the Enlightenment of the eighteenth century was to bring an intellectual revolution to Western thought, mainly through the influence of Decartes and Kant. This led to historical empiricism and the classical liberalism that the evangelicals of the late nineteenth and the twentieth centuries either retreated from (fundamentalism) or actively engaged.

---

24. Barnett 1986; 1997; 1999.

25. This comparison between Thomism and the liberalism of the eighteenth and nineteenth centuries is argued by de Senarclens 1963 and Pelikan 1959.

Meanwhile there were other protests against empirical historicism, notably those of Barth, Niebuhr and Bultmann. The influence of existential philosophy caused such theologians to turn their back on the old liberal approach that simply removed anything in the biblical story that claimed to be a supernatural manifestation in history. Bultmann, in particular, aimed to demythologize the New Testament, by which he meant dehistoricize or decode the supernatural elements within it. For him the power of the gospel lay not in the event of Christ as historical event, but in the telling of the story about Christ.

Biblical theology, as a discipline or method of theological investigation, is oriented to biblical history. It thus raises a number of historical questions including the obvious one of the nature of biblical historiography. Biblical scholars have always wrestled with the variety of the biblical documents and the way historical events could be portrayed. Evangelicals have become more accepting of the fact that ancient Hebrew and Christian historiographies present very different faces and operate according to different sets of rules from those we have tended to take for granted because of our belonging to the age of modernism.

Yet the problem is there, and evangelicals are committed to trying to deal with it. A number of mainly neo-orthodox biblical theologians of the *Heilsgeschichte* approach have permitted a wedge to be driven between *Historie*, events as they actually happened, and *Heilsgeschichte*, events as constructed according to authorial faith-commitment. Evangelicalism is rightly suspicious of a dialectic between the Jesus of history and the Jesus of faith. Evangelicals, in adopting the obvious approach of redemptive history as the framework of the biblical narrative, have had to confront and evaluate a range of assessments of the relationship of biblical history to actual events. The evangelical scholar is concerned with the literary question of how historical truth-claims are presented and how we recognize them.

Historical truth-claims, because of the nature of the biblical texts, imply a further relationship with the theological dimension. Questions of inerrancy and infallibility, of inspiration and authority, will never go away. An enduring frustrations for evangelicals is that of how to express adequately the nature of biblical authority.

One promising development, which affects both biblical studies and hermeneutics, has been the application of speech-act theory to the whole question of how God speaks in Scripture.[26] The problem, nevertheless, is to avoid a radical disparity between *Historie* and *Geschichte*.

Evangelicals, then, acknowledge that there are biblical grounds for a Christian philosophy of history. The problem of ancient historiography remains, and the grounds for accepting the historical truth-claims of biblical narratives would seem to be cumulative. But they are also inseparable from the matter of authority which hinges very much upon the recorded biblicism of Jesus and the apostles. Genre analysis still remains relevant to the interpretation of biblical narrative. Yet, when it is looked at in the broad spectrum, the overall claim that the gospel is an event in time and space is unavoidable. Evangelical theology, biblical and dogmatic, asserts the centrality of the historical event of Jesus of Nazareth in his life, death and resurrection. This historicity of the gospel event has been compromised by various perspectives, including Gnostic dualism, the internalizing of grace in Catholicism,[27] the religion of feeling promoted by Schleiermacher[28] and the existentialism of Bultmann.[29] A robust evangelical biblical theology is necessary to prevent these dehistoricizing tendencies from taking hold in

---

26. Evangelicals that have worked on this aspect include Anthony Thiselton, Kevin Vanhoozer and Nicholas Wolterstorff.

27. This is not to imply that conservative Roman Catholics do not accept the historicity of the Gospel records, but only that Catholicism has pushed the once-for-all event into the background of the continual real presence of that event on the altar. The emphasis of grace is similarly moved from the historic event to the present sanctifying of the soul.

28. It could be argued that a religion of feeling also characterizes much modern charismatic religion which, by subjecting the interpretation of Scripture to experience, is more modernist that evangelical.

29. If evangelical 'Jesus in my heart' theology is more Catholic than evangelical, so also the popular evangelical reduction of the gospel to the call for one 'to make your decision for Jesus' is more Bultmannian than evangelical.

popular evangelical piety. It is also necessary to prevent dogmatic theology from becoming a series of lifeless abstractions.

Eschatology as teleological history

The Bible not only contains the record of prophets who spoke in the name of God about the events of the future, it also purports to give us a time line from creation to the new creation at the end of the age. Even the most descriptive and theologically uncommitted approach to biblical theology must come to terms with this biblical view of time and history which asserts that they are totally under the sovereign control of God. Eschatology is teleological (purposive), rather than deterministic, history. It is thus totally at loggerheads with evolutionism. We cannot divorce the biblical problems of history from the biblical claims to give a comprehensive outline of history from creation to new creation. If God is Lord of history and the author of Scripture, there is no inherent problem in recognizing that references to future events may be included in revelation. Nor is this simply a way of assuring the believers about a future life. It is in fact integral to the world-view of the gospel that centres on Jesus as the defining event of all world history. The history of Christian thought shows how easily eschatology can be hijacked and turned into something that virtually replaces the centrality of the gospel.[30] In this way it has become the motivation and power of certain cults and sects.

The future of evangelical biblical theology

In the light of the foregoing discussion, we can attempt now to make some summary comments about the role of biblical theology in shaping the future of evangelicalism. I stated at the outset that evangelicalism's adherence to the dictum of *sola scriptura* was an integrative force that we cannot under any circumstances forgo.

---

30. A timely warning and corrective is provided in König 1989. He argues that the term 'eschatology' reflects the word *eschatos* (last One = Christ), rather than *eschata* (last things).

The four 'alones' of the Reformation provide complementary perspectives on this reality. 'Scripture alone' allows for no external epistemic authority by which to test Scripture's truth claims.[31] 'Faith alone' repudiates all forms of personal synergism that diminish the uniqueness of Christ's person and work as the sole basis of our renewal and acceptance with God. 'Christ alone' shows Christology as the hermeneutic principle by which all facts and events in all space and time are ultimately interpreted, and as the operating power for the restoration of all things. 'Grace alone' focuses on the sovereign working of God through Christ to create, reveal, save and regenerate. These four perspectives are the heart of evangelical epistemology, apologetics, hermeneutics, theology (both biblical and systematic), ethics and Christian living. Biblical theology has the potential for being an integrative force within evangelicalism, but only if there is the will in the academy and the local church to engage the notion of such integration.

The integration of biblical studies

With its Christological focus and dogmatic presuppositions, evangelical biblical theology is well equipped to investigate the nature of theological unity within the diversity of the text. Unity–distinction does not tell us everything about the relationships between the various themes, books, corpora and Testaments. But it does alert us to the need to avoid unity without distinction (fusion), or distinction without unity (separation). The nature of biblical history and literature is also informed by the incarnational paradigm of the relationship of the divine person and action to the human in Jesus Christ. Within the framework of evangelical presuppositions, biblical theology will continue to do the hard work of close reading and exegesis. It will function as a key hermeneutic tool for the translation of the biblical message into contemporary terms that retain the essential truth of the historic gospel. As such, it will continue

---

31. It is important not to confuse this presuppositionalism with fideism. Evidences are not excluded from attesting to the truth of Scripture. But, the criteria for the acceptance of evidences are not objectively self-evident or neutral territory.

to search for ways to deal with the linguistic, literary, and historical analyses that are essential to exegesis.

This concern to overcome some of the existing fragmentation in biblical studies is not a new thing, but much work needs yet to be done. Is it too much to hope that the nineteenth-century academic models of theological curriculum can yet be defossilized and adapted to meet the needs of the twenty-first century? Joel Green and others have helpfully reviewed the desire for interdisciplinary theological studies, and the accompanying problems.[32] I would suggest, however, that interdisciplinarity is perhaps not what we are seeking so much as the development of a comprehensively integrated biblical perspective on the whole task of theological study. If that sounds hopelessly circular, I can only refer the reader to the discussion above of the hermeneutical spiral and the presuppositions of Christian theism. With regard to the academy, we note first that modernism assumed that a reconstructed tradition-history of the text qualified its meaning. Evangelicalism has largely rejected this while seeking to acknowledge the importance of the historical context. But, it has nevertheless asserted that ultimately the divine revelation must explain what is behind the text. In the final analysis, history does not explain the text; the text explains history. A second academic concern is whether the theological curricula always need to be driven by needs of specialization and division of labour. Perhaps they will, but they can also aim to promote a greater sense of the unity of theological understanding. If nothing else, this means a radical revision of the pragmatic succession of biblical disciplines from exegesis to biblical theology and, finally, to dogmatics. Perhaps as a legacy of Gabler's assertion of the dependence of dogmatics on biblical theology, evangelicals have followed suit, and also continue to practise exegesis as if it were a neutral,

---

32. Green & Turner 2000. See Green's essay in this volume, 'Scripture and Theology: Uniting the Two So Long Divided'. One has to wonder why this volume, given its interest in interdisciplinary thinking, should confine itself to New Testament studies and Systematics. The volume is entirely relevant to biblical studies as a whole.

objective, and non-theological exercise.[33] There may not be an overtly Christian way to teach Hebrew and Greek and the processes of exegesis. But, it can at least be acknowledged that the application of human language, analytical skills, intelligence, and reason is a gift of God and an aspect of being made in his image.

The integration of Christian thought and world-view

As we develop an authentically self-conscious evangelical biblical theology we are confronted constantly with the universal claims of God and of his Christ. An extension of the concerns for an integrated theological approach to the Bible is the business of attempting to translate the theology of the Bible into a total world-view.[34] How, then, can biblical theology help in the achievement of an evangelical world-view? Two main ways come to mind. First, there is the constant need for biblical theology to try to express the unifying aspects of biblical revelation, without ignoring the diversities. Given the presuppositions that I have proposed, we can avoid simplistic harmonizations by a recognition that some difficulties may, at least for the present, defeat us, and that we have to hold to the unity as a datum of faith in the unity of God and his purposes. Thus, the biblical 'big picture' of creation to new creation, extended in both directions into eternity, is a coherent framework within which to work.

The second way of moving towards our goal is to be more active in researching the Bible for thematic biblical theologies that enable us to address the concerns of our day more comprehensively. When James Barr burst the bubble of word studies in biblical theology he cleared the way for a more acceptable thematic or conceptual approach.[35] Themes, however, do not always present themselves to us as easily as a concordance-based list of vocables. There are of course the 'big' ones that commend

---

33. The priority of exegesis and biblical theology, upon which the doing of systematics depends, seems to be the emphasis of, for example, Geerhardus Vos and John Murray and others.

34. See the chapter in this volume by Craig Bartholomew.

35. Barr 1961.

themselves as central and uniting concepts, such as the kingdom of God, the law, the people of God, or the covenant. But there are others, that are of vital concern for a comprehensive world-view, but which are not so directly evident. In these cases, biblical theology offers a way of using creative lateral thinking to relate contributing themes that may help us construct a biblical perspective.[36] Whereas in the nineteenth century, evangelicals were socially concerned with such matters as slavery, poverty, child labour, and exploitation of workers and women, now the global village forces us to broaden our concerns to matters such as ecology, environment and conservation, Third World poverty, prostitution and drugs, law and order in society, multiculturalism, child abuse, weapons of mass destruction and terrorism. If, as we believe, the Bible can and must speak to us on such issues, the biblical theologians need to engage in a certain creativity of approach to enable the people of God to understand the mind of God on such matters.

The integration of congregational life and pastoral practice

During fourteen years spent in an Anglican parish in Brisbane as minister for Christian Education, I had opportunity to examine ways of relating biblical theology to the community life of a congregation and to pastoral practice. I became convinced that one of the highest priorities for ministry teams should be to see that everyone who has a leadership role, especially if it involves teaching, should be instructed in basic biblical theology and Christian doctrine. It is irresponsible to recruit people for practical courses in evangelism, Sunday school teaching, pastoral visitation and so on, without requiring them to have a basic understanding of the economy of salvation in the history of redemption, and of the key Christian

---

36. I was recently approached by the Social Issues Executive of the Anglican Diocese of Sydney for a suggested outline of a biblical theology of the family. I proposed an approach, using lateral thinking, considering the possible significance of the themes of creation, image of God, sexuality: male and female, marriage, procreation, covenant, household, father's covenant role, family under the gospel, Christ and his bride.

doctrines.[37] Elsewhere I have suggested a number of ways that biblical theology informs congregational life and practice.[38] Properly taught, biblical theology reinforces the evangelical view of *sola scriptura*, which we so easily take for granted and rarely explain. It enables us to proclaim the historic Jesus in the context of the whole of redemptive history. It thus promotes a high view of the gospel that avoids a human-centred focus and superficiality. It enables the church to understand the dignity and importance of the ministries of the church and to deliver these from mere professionalism. It is the basis for a biblical self-consciousness as the people of God that helps to preserve a congregation from becoming a religious club.

Finally, evangelical biblical theology has enormous potential for demonstrating the nature of our engagement with the world in evangelism and the relief of the needy. It does this by putting the theology of mission into global and eternal perspective both as to its origins and its goals. It is needed to address the pressing issues of contextualization in mission and Bible translation. It will prevent the gross distortions that corrupt the notion of dynamic equivalence by showing that the gospel is Jewish and given to the Jew first (Rom. 1:16–17). Contextualization may change the symbols (language) but dare not change the referents. It is wrong to tell the biblical story as if it happened anywhere other than in the biblical world. Indeed, biblical theology will highlight the universality of the gospel in a way that requires the story *always* to be told of Abraham coming out of Ur, Israel fleeing from Egypt, and Jesus, the Jew, being born in Bethlehem, and crucified under the Roman, Pontius Pilate. Evangelicalism will permit the gospel to be dehistoricized and recontextualized to its peril. It has happened before more than once, and it can happen again. Biblical theology, practised as required by the nature of the Word of God written, is a strong safeguard against that eventuality.

---

37. My book *According to Plan* (Goldsworthy 1991) was worked out as a series of studies in our local church, which I taught to ordinary church members each year for the last five years of my ministry in Brisbane. During a Sunday morning Christian education hour, one of the church elders gave instruction in the Thirty-nine Articles of Religion.

38. Goldsworthy 1992; 1997.

Bibliography

Adam, A. K. M. (1995), *Making Sense of New Testament Theology,* Macon, GA: Mercer University Press.

Alexander, T. D. and B. S. Rosner (eds.), (2000), *New Dictionary of Biblical Theology*, Leicester: IVP.

Balla, P. (1997), *Challenges to New Testament Theology,* Peabody, MA: Hendrickson.

Barnett, P. W. (1986), *Is the New Testament History?* Sydney: Hodder & Stoughton.

———— (1997), *Jesus and the Logic of History*, Leicester: Apollos.

———— (1989), *Jesus and the Rise of Early Christianity*, Downers Grove: IVP.

Barr, J. (1961), *The Semantics of Biblical Language*, London: Oxford University Press.

Calvin, J. (Inst), *Institutes of the Christian Religion* (trans. F. L. Battles, 1960), Library of Christian Classics, vols. XX and XXI, Philadelphia: Westminster Press.

Childs, B. S. (1992), *Biblical Theology of the Old and New Testaments*, London: SCM Press.

de Senarclens, J. (1963), *Heirs of the Reformation*, London: SCM Press.

Eichrodt, W. (1961), *Theology of the Old Testament*, trans. J. A. Baker, London: SCM Press.

Goldsworthy, G. (1986), ‘"Thus says the Lord!" – The Dogmatic Basis of Biblical Theology’, in P. T. O'Brien and D. G. Peterson (eds.), *God Who is Rich in Mercy: Essays Presented to D. B. Knox*, Homebush West: Lancer.

———— (1991), *According to Plan: The Unfolding Revelation of God in the Bible*, Leicester: IVP, 1991; Downers Grove: IVP, 2002.

———— (1992), ‘The Pastoral Application of Biblical Theology’, in D. Peterson and J. Pryor (eds.), *In the Fullness of Time: Biblical Studies in Honour of Archbishop Donald Robinson*, Homebush West: Lancer.

———— (1997), ‘The Pastor as Biblical Theologian’, in R. J. Gibson (ed.), *Interpreting God's Plan: Biblical Theology and the Pastor*, Explorations No. 11, Carlisle: Paternoster Press; Adelaide: Openbook.

———— (2000a), ‘Regeneration’, in Alexander & Rosner 2000.

———— (2000b), *Preaching the Whole Bible as Christian Scripture: The Application of Biblical Theology to Expository Preaching*, Grand Rapids: Ecrdmans; Leicester: IVP.

Green, J. B. and M. Turner (eds.) (2000), *Between Two Horizons: Spanning New Testament Studies and Systematic Theology*, Grand Rapids: Eerdmans.

Heinisch, P. (1955), *Theology of the Old Testament*, ET Collegeville, MN: Liturgical Press (German original 1952).

Henry, C. F. H. (1990), *Toward a Recovery of Christian Belief*, Wheaton: Crossway.

Jacob, E. (1958), *Theology of the Old Testament*, ET London: Hodder & Stoughton (French original 1955).

Knierim, R. P. (1995), 'On Gabler', in *The Task of Old Testament Theology*, Grand Rapids: Eerdmans.

König, A. (1989), *The Eclipse of Christ in Eschatology: Toward a Christ-Centered Approach*, Grand Rapids: Eerdmans.

Payne, J. B. (1962), *The Theology of the Older Testament*, Grand Rapids: Zondervan.

Pelikan, J. (1959), *The Riddle of Catholicism*, New York: Abingdon.

Rad, G. von (1962), *Old Testament Theology*, trans. D. M. G. Stalker, Edinburgh: Oliver & Boyd.

Ramm, B. L. (1973), *The Evangelical Heritage*, Waco: Word Books.

Reventlow, H. G. (1986), *Problems of Biblical Theology in the Twentieth Century*, Philadelphia: Fortress Press.

Richardson, A. (1958), *An Introduction to the Theology of the New Testament*, London: SCM Press.

Robinson, D. W. B. (1997), 'Origins and Unresolved Tensions', in R. J. Gibson (ed.), *Interpreting God's Plan: Biblical Theology and the Pastor*, Carlisle: Paternoster Press; Adelaide: Openbook.

Rushdoony, R. J. (1978), *The One and the Many*, Fairfax, VA: Thoburn Press.

Sandys-Wunsch, J. and L. Eldredge (1980), 'J. P. Gabler and the Distinction between Biblical and Dogmatic Theology', *Scottish Journal of Theology* 33: 133–158.

Schaeffer, F. A. (1968), *Escape From Reason*, Downers Grove: IVP.

Scobie, C. H. H. (2002), *The Ways of Our God: An Approach to Biblical Theology*, Grand Rapids: Eerdmans.

Smart, J. D. (1961), *The Interpretation of Scripture*, Philadelphia: Westminster Press.

Stott, J. R. W. (1972), *Your Mind Matters*, Leicester: IVP.

Stuckenbruck, L. T. (1999), 'Johann Philipp Gabler and the Delineation of Biblical Theology', *Scottish Journal of Theology* 52.2: 139–157.

Van Til, C. (1948), Introduction to B. B. Warfield, *The Inspiration and Authority of the Bible*, Philadelphia: Presbyterian and Reformed.

_____ (1969), *A Christian Theory of Knowledge*, Phillipsburg, NJ: Presbyterian and Reformed.

VanGemeren, W. (1988), *The Progress of Redemption: The Story of Salvation from Creation to the New Jerusalem*, Grand Rapids: Academie.

Vos, G. (1948), *Biblical Theology: Old and New Testaments*, Grand Rapids: Eerdmans.

Recommended reading

Alexander, T. D. and B. S. Rosner (eds.), *New Dictionary of Biblical Theology*, Leicester: IVP, 2000.

Baker, D. L., *Two Testaments, One Bible*, revised and enlarged ed., Leicester: Apollos, 1991.

Dumbrell, W. J., *The Search for Order: Biblical Eschatology in Focus*, Grand Rapids: Baker, 1994.

Gibson, R. J. (ed.), *Interpreting God's Plan: Biblical Theology and the Pastor*, Carlisle: Paternoster Press, 1997.

Goldsworthy, G., *According to Plan*, Leicester: IVP, 1991.

_____, *Preaching the Whole Bible as Christian Scripture: The Application of Biblical Theology to Expository Preaching*, Grand Rapids: Eerdmans; Leicester: IVP, 2000.

Hafemann, S. (ed.), *Biblical Theology: Retrospect and Prospect*, Downers Grove: IVP; Leicester: Apollos, 2002.

Jensen, P. F., *At the Heart of the Universe*, Leicester: IVP, 1994.

Scobie, C. H. H., *The Ways of Our God: An Approach to Biblical Theology*, Grand Rapids: Eerdmans, 2002.

Watson, F., *Text and Truth: Redefining Biblical Theology*, Edinburgh: T. & T. Clark, 1997.

5. FUTURE TRENDS IN MISSION

Christopher Wright

'The people who prefer to dance' – a very short story

There is a tribe in northern Nigeria known as the Gwandara-wara. During the early part of the twentieth century, two attempts were made by Christian missionaries to reach and evangelize this tribe. Both attempts failed. The gospel was not communicated. Nobody came to faith in Christ. No church was planted. In the mid 1980s, a third group of missionaries tried again. This time they were more successful. They were allowed to live among the tribe and cultivate some land. They discovered that the tribe's name means, 'The people who prefer to dance'. From the tribal elders and story-tellers – the guardians of the tribe's identity and history – the missionaries established that this name went right back to the tribe's rejection of Islam in the nineteenth century when, in response to the attempt to convert them to Islam, the tribe had insisted, 'we prefer to dance' – that is, we will not give up our culture of music and dance for a religion which wants to prohibit them.

Reflecting on this new information, the third group of mission-aries came up with a new strategy of evangelism: they would dance the gospel to the 'people who prefer to dance'. So they devised a means of telling the Bible story, including the story of Jesus and the cross, through the medium of African music and dance. The communication gap was bridged. There was a breakthrough of understanding; some believed the gospel and there is now a church of Jesus Christ among the Gwandara-wara.

Who were this third group of missionaries who succeeded where others had failed? They were not white nor Western, neither American nor European. They were in fact Africans, members of the Evangelical Missionary Society of ECWA – the Evangelical Church of West Africa, one of the largest churches in Nigeria and throughout West Africa. The EMS is a fully indigenous Nigerian mission agency, with some 1,000 missionaries serving cross-culturally throughout western Africa.[1]

This is a story which could be repeated myriad times in many other parts of the world. It illustrates at least three things about mission today and in the future. First, God is still keeping his promise to Abraham. Second, mission, like the church itself, is multinational and multidirectional. Third, God is calling for adaptation, creativity, flexibility and hard thinking in mission.

The God who prefers to bless – a very long story

At one level, the conversion of the Gwandara-wara was a tiny footnote in the huge story of Christian mission in the twentieth century. But at another level it was part of a story that goes a lot further back – not merely back to Christ and his command to make disciples of all nations, but right back to Abraham. For it was to Abraham that God made the promise, 'through you all the nations of the earth will be blessed' (Gen. 12:3). This is the foundation of the great biblical dynamic of mission – the mission of God himself to bring blessing to the nations of humanity, in the

---

1. The story is told by Bill Taylor, as reported by the then director of the Evangelical Missionary Society of Nigeria, Dr Panya Baba in Taylor 1994.

context of their fallenness and rebellion so colourfully described in Genesis 3–11. So important was this promise that Paul actually calls it 'the gospel in advance' (Gal. 3:6–8), – for it was indeed good news: God intends to bless the nations. This was God's great manifesto commitment. This was why he called Abraham in the first place, as he reminded himself even as he was on his way to deliver judgment on Sodom and Gomorrah (Gen. 18:18–21). This was why he created Israel – to be a light to the nations. That's why he sent Jesus as the Servant of the LORD, with the task not only of bringing Israel back to himself but also of bringing forth justice to the nations so that his salvation should go to the ends of the earth (Is. 49:6). That's why Jesus could say, when giving his disciples their final lecture in Old Testament hermeneutics, that 'this is what is written': not merely that the messiah would come, suffer, die and rise again, but also that repentance and forgiveness of sins would be preached in his name to all nations (Luke 24:45–48). Mission to the nations, in other words, is as much part of the significance of the Old Testament scriptures as their messianic fulfilment. The words of Jesus here instruct us to 'understand the scriptures' both messianically and missiologicaly.

That's why the apostle Paul believed himself to be the 'apostle to the nations', commissioned to carry forward the Servant's mission (Acts 13:46–47), and to fulfil the priestly role of Israel in bringing God to the nations and bringing the nations to God (Rom. 15:16; cf. Exod. 19:4–6).

So then the biblical gospel only truly is the gospel, the good news God intended it to be, when it is in dynamic action breaking down barriers and crossing borders, bringing the nations into saving contact with Christ. When the Ethiopian eunuch and Cornelius found joy and salvation in Jesus, God was keeping his promise to Abraham. When Paul obeyed the Macedonian call and brought the gospel to Europe, God was keeping his promise to Abraham. When European missionaries took the gospel to other parts of the world, God was keeping his promise to Abraham. When African missionaries crossed the barriers of language, culture and religion to make the gospel meaningful to the Gwandara-wara, God was keeping his promise to Abraham. And when one day people of every nation, tribe, people and language stand before the throne of

God singing the praises of the Lamb (Rev. 7:9–10), God will have kept his promise to Abraham.

The point of this brief lesson in a biblical theology of mission is this. Whatever the trends in mission in the twenty-first century, they will be simply the continuation of a very long story – the story of God's missional engagement with God's world, through God's people, for God's own purpose – the purpose of bringing blessing and redemption to humanity and indeed to his whole creation. We need to see our own concern for mission and mission strategy in this very broad historical and biblical perspective – partly in order to undermine our tendency to consider our own generation wiser or more important than any that went before, and partly to acknowledge that mission is about God's agenda, which may or may not coincide with our own agendas or prognostication.

The fruit of God's promise to Abraham: a multinational church and multidirectional mission

The second thing which the story of the Gwandara-wara illustrates is the extent to which we are privileged to live in a generation in which God's promise to Abraham has borne spectacular fruit. While it is still a challenging reality, of course, that the growth of the church has not yet begun to outstrip the growth of the human population of the planet (Christians are still approximately 31% of the world's population, as they were a century ago, in spite of phenomenal church growth in numerical terms), it is nevertheless a fact that Christians are now to be found in almost every country on earth. 'Repentance and forgiveness of sins' is being preached in nearly all nations. The growth and vigour of the church in Nigeria which itself reached a tribe that Western missionaries had twice failed to reach with the gospel illustrates this fact in just one part of the world.

The growth of the non-Western churches
To those of us who live in the West, where the church has been declining numerically for decades, the growth of the church in the rest of the world is sometimes a surprising revelation. Yet it is unquestionably the most significant phenomenon in the twentieth-century history of Christianity. The idea of Christianity as 'the

Western religion' is a myth or a prejudice, but certainly not the sta-tistical truth.[2] It is now a truly global faith, and the centre of gravity of world Christianity has moved steadily south and east through-out the past hundred years. Whereas in 1900 approximately 90% of all those who would have claimed the name Christian in any form lived in the countries of the north or west (i.e. predominantly Europe and North America, along with Australia and New Zealand), by 1980 it was only 50%. Today it is estimated that at least 75% of the world's Christians live in Africa, Asia and Latin America – that is, outside the West, which is becoming increasingly peripheral to the heartlands of Christianity.

The greatest proportion of this growth has been among evan-gelical churches, and especially among Pentecostal and other charismatic churches and movements. The number of Christians in Independent churches (i.e. outside the mainline and ecumenical denominations) has risen from approximately 3.7 million in 1900 to well over 500 million in 2000. And the fastest growing segment of independent and mainly charismatic evangelicalism is to be found in the non-Western continents. The growth in Latin America in particular has led some to say that Spanish will soon overtake English as the language of world evangelicalism.

More Christians are in Anglican churches on any Sunday in Nigeria than in all the Anglican churches in the UK, Europe, North America and Australia combined. There are more Baptists in the Democratic Republic of the Congo (Zaire) than in Britain. More people worship in Christian churches in mainland China than in the whole of Western Europe. The Assemblies of God have ten times more members in Latin America than in the USA.

---

2. The facts and figures that follow in the rest of this section have been culled from various sources, but mainly: David Barratt's annual table in the *International Bulletin of Missionary Research* (see recently, Barrett 2002), and Johnstone & Mandryk 2001. It is acknowledged that all such statistics have to be treated with care since they reflect differing methods of collec-tion and various criteria of selection. Nevertheless, even allowing for a fairly generous margin of error, the trends they present are unmistakeable and incontrovertible. See also Jenkins 2002.

Of course, one has to say immediately that not all such growth
is healthy growth. Statisticians are good at keeping track of figures
for churches planted, but not so good at keeping check on
churches that die away again, of conversions that never lead to discipleship. Sadly, much growth is growth without depth, without
teaching and without adequate pastoral care, so that young
churches are vulnerable to extremism, lack of balance, doctrinal
error and chronic divisiveness (not unlike the New Testament
church, then). And it is also patchy, and gross numbers are not
necessarily indicative of relative proportions. In Korea for
example, the church grew from two churches in 1900, to 7,000
churches in Seoul alone and a population considered 27%
Christian by 2000 – a century of growth; whereas in a North
African country, the church grew from 30 known national believers in 1998 to some 250 by 2001. Which is greater growth in the
eyes of God?

The growth of non-Western mission

Alongside this phenomenal growth of the non-Western church,
we have to set the growth of non-Western mission. Mission is no
longer (not that it ever really was), 'from the West to the Rest'. It is
from everywhere to everywhere – multinational and multidirectional. The explosive growth of cross-cultural mission agencies
and movements in the continents once (and sadly often still)
regarded as 'mission receiving' contexts has been another major
feature of the second half of the twentieth century of Christian
history. The story of the Gwandara-wara illustrates that too. The
EMS of ECWA is an indigenous Nigerian mission agency supporting some 1,000 mission partners – which makes it large by any
standards.

The statistics are again quite staggering, especially to those whose
minds still flicker with the caricature of 'the missionary' – the white,
pith-helmeted Westerner taking the gospel to grateful 'natives'. The
USA is still the largest exporter of cross-cultural Protestant missionaries (some 60,000). But the second largest is now India, with
44,000. 60% of these are working in India, but in situations that are
decidedly cross-cultural in geography, language, culture and religion. Korea sends approximately the same number of missionaries

as the UK (about 10,000). Brazil sends nearly 5,000; Nigeria close to 4,000; the Philippines nearly 3,000 and the Ukraine some 2,000. The proportions are revealing. North America accounts for about 35% of all Protestant missionaries in the world – but Asia now accounts for some 36%. Africa and Latin America together account for about 11% – the same proportion as Europe. Thus, in total, at present approximately as many missionaries are being sent by the churches of the south and east as by those of the north and west.

75% of world Christians are non-Western. 50% of Protestant Christian missionaries are non-Western.

Challenges to the Western church

What, then, is the challenge to the church in the West as we respond to such facts and trends, and see in them, as we surely must, the sovereign hand of our God? At least two things.

First, there is a need for humility and repentance. Humility certainly befits us in the face of the tragic decline of the church in the West (especially in Europe) – the humility at least to puzzle over the irony that the great bulk of books and programmes and strategies about church growth and world evangelization come from that part of the world where the church, far from being marked by vigorous growth is concerned about its long-term viability in some places. How come that the part of the world where the church is shrinking claims to teach the rest of the world about church growth? And then we have the gall to export these off-the-peg strategies to places where the church could teach us more than we are willing to learn about evangelism.

Repentance would also be an appropriate response to our apathy and indifference, and our surrender to the cultural idolatries that surround us, particularly the idolatries of affluence and arrogance, of noxious ethno-centric pride and a 'natural-born leaders' superiority complex. We in the West, with the embarrassing abundance of financial, technological, literary and institutional resources available to us, tend to look upon the rest of the church as the church of the poor – with varying degrees of compassion or paternalism in our response. What does God see as he surveys the obscenely distorted Body of his Son? Could it be that he is saying to church of the West what he said to the church of Laodicea, 'You say, "I am rich; I have acquired wealth and do not need a thing." But you do not realise that in fact you are wretched, pitiful, poor, blind and naked' (Rev. 3:17)?

Second, there is a need for genuine partnership. Unfortunately, although partnership is something of a vogue word in mission circles, the style and culture of some Western mission agencies is still beset by the ethos of superiority and unilateralism that flows from our material dominance. We still use the metaphors and paradigms of nineteenth- and early twentieth-century mission, implying not only West to the rest, but West knows best. Books on mission strategy published in the West can still talk of 'the home base' and 'the mission field', as if Jesus had never said 'the field is the world'. 'The mission field' is still thought of as 'out there in far off needy countries', when in reality Europe is probably the most challenging and needy 'mission field' on earth at present. We still talk of sending and receiving countries – even when formerly receiving countries now send more than ten times the number of cross-cultural missionaries they receive (as is the case for India). We perpetuate the language of our business-dominated and consumer-obsessed culture, and pepper our mission discourse with goals, strategies and management-speak; or we perpetuate the military metaphors of warfare, targets and conquering strongholds. We need a much more sensitive dialogue with the churches of the majority world and their mission agencies. This means a partnership in spirit – in which we recognize that we are equals in Christ and are called to be properly and critically accountable to one another under him. And a partnership in attitude – in which we show true respect and honour to leaders of churches in the Two-Thirds World, rather than the somewhat paternalistic and politely disguised racist attitudes which still sometimes colour our relations. And a partnership in action – through joint projects and commitments which display a real sharing of resources, mutuality in giving and receiving, and in which both parties are blessed and changed (not just the 'beneficiaries' or 'customers').

Adaptation, creativity, flexibility and hard thinking in mission

The third thing that the story of the Gwandara-wara illustrates is the amazing creativity that mission calls forth. Dance the gospel? It is a fair guess that this is not a response to the communication barrier that would ever have occurred to the first two groups of Western missionaries. It is more likely that they would have mirrored the Islamic reaction and sought to replace dance with the gospel than to marry the two. But the Nigerian missionaries, understanding that this was the cultural medium in which that which mattered most to the tribe was preserved and communicated – that this was the language of the heart and the deepest repository of the tribe's identity – found a way to communicate that which matters most to all human beings, the gospel of God's grace, in that 'language'. Evangelism was not a matter of a few tracts, or the fascinating power of a strange technology presenting Jesus on a movie screen, or of a mass 'crusade' (why are we still using that awful word in contexts of substantial Muslim communities?), or of a translated and franchised Alpha course. Evangelism for the Gwandara-wara was to dance the gospel. The reality and the great challenge of all mission is that while there is only one gospel (because it is essentially the announcement of good news about what happened once and for all in Jesus of Nazareth, his life, death and resurrection), the ways by which it can be lived out, communicated and responded to, are as many and varied as there are people and cultures.

Diversity of methods

Flexibility also demands an increasing diversity of mission methods. There has been a growing trend, for example, to short-term forms of mission. There are some advantages in such programmes: they can be highly educative and motivational for those who engage in them; they can meet immediate practical needs; they are often cheaper and require less 'infrastructure' of support and logistics. But their weaknesses make it unlikely that short-term mission can ever replace longer-term cross-cultural commitment: they are non-incarnational, do not really allow for significant engagement with language and culture, can be somewhat

idealistic and optimistic in expectation, and can even cause problems or damage that have to be picked up by the local church later.

There is also a trend towards more creative tent-making forms
of mission – where people go and work professionally in a cross-
cultural context as Christians and thus support themselves rather
than depending on a mission agency and/or a network of personal friends 'at home'. Apart from having impeccable biblical
precedent in the apostle Paul, such professional employment gives
people more credibility in their local context. The embarrassing
question, 'What are you here for?' is less likely to be asked of
someone doing an obvious and culturally understandable job of
work. A Christian lawyer, working in the Middle East employed by
a local law firm, told me that it gave him three major advantages
over other expatriates in more traditional forms of 'missionary'
activity (though the word is not used): (a) it gave him far more
daily shoulder-rubbing contact with the majority community in the
country; (b) it gave him the significant discipline of doing a worthwhile daily job of work with accountability built in and a
meaningful reason for his presence in the street where he lived;
and (c) his job in itself and the taxes he paid were of benefit to the
host country so he felt that the call to be a blessing and to seek the
welfare of the country where God had placed him was not limited
to evangelistic opportunities alone. There is no reason why far
more Christian professionals should not make the effort of
finding ways of using their skills to earn a living in countries where
their presence can be a great encouragement to local Christians, or
where they can live out the love of Jesus in situations where open
evangelism is impossible. An important provision is that such
work should have integrity – that is, tent-making is not a 'cover' by
which one *pretends* to be doing a job but then spends all one's time
in evangelism. Host countries see through that very quickly and
the consequences, not only for oneself but for others, can be disastrous. As someone has said, 'If you're going to be a tent-maker,
you'd better actually make some tents' – like Paul, then.

Then there is the growing trend for 'Third-agers' going into
cross-cultural mission. This term has come to be applied to men
and women usually in their 50s or above, whose children have
married and left home, who are themselves financially secure and

in good health, and who may be in a position to retire from secular employment and offer themselves for a wide variety of tasks at the request of churches or mission agencies in other lands. Bringing maturity and the wisdom of life-experience, such people can be an invaluable resource – especially in traditional societies where greater respect is given to people of a certain age than to fresh-faced young mission partners with much zeal but not always 'according to knowledge'.

Globalizing sub-cultures

The spread of globalization raises new challenges and opportunities for mission. We need to recognize a whole new category of 'mission field'. Whereas in the past the term usually signified a territorial 'field' – some country or continent, or a people united by some linguistic, religious or geographical cohesion, there is now a growing number of what might be called non-territorial, globalizing subcultures. There is, for example, the global culture of sport. On the one hand there is the proliferation of 'world-cup' kind of events, in which sportsmen and women of many nations compete – along with the whole travelling circus of sports medics, commentators, coaches, journalists, spectators and the like. There is an international culture surrounding such recurring programmes. On the other hand, there is the world of participatory sport from street-kids banging a burst football around, to amateur clubs of every description. It is a 'world' with its own 'language', conventions, heroes, ethics, pastoral needs, tensions, joys, disappointments and ecstasies. It is a world in which and through which the gospel can have almost unlimited access to multitudes of people otherwise quite out of touch with the living witness of any church. But, like other forms of cross-cultural mission, sports ministry also needs relevant and effective training, careful and sensitive strategy and cultural awareness. Recognizing this has led two sports ministry organizations, Christians in Sport and Ambassadors in Sport to enter into a partnership with All Nations Christian College in the UK to offer a qualification in sports ministry and inter-cultural studies – that is, to treat it as a valid form of 'missionary training' for a new kind of 'mission field'. As the twenty-first century progresses, as globalization gathers pace and generates more such global cultures, we are likely to see the need for fresh adaptations of mission strategy to reach them. Already one could add the cultures of global business, of global youth, of the internet, of NGO aid agencies. What will be the equivalent of 'dancing the gospel' to new forms of global human 'tribes'?

Not only flexibility, but agility, will be needed in twenty-first-century mission. Cliché though it is, we live in a world of rapid and accelerating change. Postmodernity calls on its devotees to relish the changing kaleidoscope of culture, to savour the moment and pass on. Some kinds of mission need to be like that. Fortunately God has raised up a generation that is culturally postmodern and comfortable with expressing their long-term commitment to Christ and to his mission through rapidly changing, nimble forms of multiple engagement in different places. We need to be able to respond quickly to new opportunities, move in and if necessary be prepared to move out again. But alongside this need for agile opportunism, there will be still a paradoxical need for patient perseverance. There are places still in the world where, if the gospel is ever to take root, it will take decades of incarnational commitment. Sometimes Christian mission partners in such places may feel like Ezekiel – dumb and bound, unable to speak or witness openly. Yet their very presence, and the actions they perform as men and women who incarnate the grace the Lord Jesus Christ in the midst of poor and suffering people, will eventually lead to the shining of the light of the gospel there. The twenty-first century will still need people of that calibre, people prepared to bury themselves in a country and a culture, like the seed that falls into the ground and dies – eventually to bear abundant fruit, but possibly not for a generation or more. Short-term-ism is no substitute in such contexts.

So, mission calls for adaptation, creativity, flexibility – but also for some hard thinking. That is the task of missiology. Elsewhere I have reflected on what seem to me to be major theological challenges that face evangelical missiology in the twenty-first century.[3]

---

3. Wright 2000. Taylor 2000 is a large and significant book that contains the published papers of the major consultation held in Foz d'Iguassu, Brazil, in October 1999, including the text of the Iguassu Affirmation.

They revolve around three of the distinctive evangelical concerns: for Scripture, Christology and the practical ethics of transformed living.

Theological tasks

First, mission in the twenty-first century will call for a fresh articulation of our doctrine of the *authority of the Bible*. It is one thing to affirm it as a conceptual doctrine, as evangelicals do. But how do we understand and utilize the authority of the Bible in a postmodern world of conflicting authorities or of the denial of all authority? This is a hermeneutical challenge, and fortunately many biblical scholars are increasingly recognizing the missiological dimension of hermeneutics – that is, we must have a way of reading and understanding the Bible that enables, that delivers, that offers dynamic engagement with our own cultures and missional tasks.

Second, mission in the twenty-first century, as in all previous centuries including that of the New Testament itself, will call for a fresh affirmation of the *uniqueness of Jesus Christ* in the context of religious pluralism and other competing claims, or denials. This will be so whether we are still engaged in conflict with the *epistemological* pluralism that characterizes modernity. That is, only that which is scientifically verifiable can claim the status of 'knowledge'; religion and morality come into the separate category of mere belief or opinion and nobody can therefore claim objective truth for any religious affirmation. So, says a modern pluralist, we must allow for possible truth in any or all religions but cannot claim it absolutely for one alone. Or whether we are tackling, as we increasingly must, the *ontological* pluralism of postmodernity. That is, there is no such thing as final, objective or absolute truth in any human endeavour or affirmation – including that of science. So, says a postmodern pluralist, we have only the multiplicity of relative cultural and ideological claims; many 'stories' but no grand metanarrative. Missiology will have to continue to wrestle with presenting the biblical claims regarding the work of God in Christ, its uniqueness and universality, in the context of both kinds of pluralism.

And third, mission in the twenty-first century must not neglect the *ethical dimension*. For what is it that makes the gospel believable and makes mission transformative? Only the reality of changed people and changed communities. This means that we must sustain an integrated and holistic understanding of mission. Sadly, one still encounters those who seem determined to turn the mission clock back to the first half of the twentieth century when evangelicals lost touch with their historical roots and embraced a view of mission as entirely or primarily evangelistic. Theologically, in my view, the case was biblically and convincingly made in the epochal Lausanne Covenant of 1974 and the subsequent series of conferences during the 1980s, that evangelism and social action belong inseparably together as part of the total mission of God's people.[4] God's purpose in the history of his saving work is to bring blessing and wholeness to every part of his whole creation, including every dimension of human life and need. Our mission, therefore, needs to be equally whole and comprehensive. Not evangelism without compassion and social action; not compassion and social action without evangelism. And neither without environmental concern for God's creation entrusted to our care. As in so much else, evangelicals have a regrettable tendency on the one hand to polarize into unbalanced extremes, and on the other hand to have to re-invent the wheel in every generation. Part of the dynamic of this constant attention to our holistic mission in the coming years will be a fresh vision of what it means to be human. We shall have to work harder as evangelicals to articulate that in genuinely biblical terms, not merely in terms of Western individualism, consumerism or scientific reductionism. And as we seek a more biblical understanding of what it means to live and relate in truly human ways as an expression of the gospel itself, we in the West will have a lot to learn from the less impoverished traditions of humanity in community found among Christians in the non-Western world. In this as in so much else, the strength of evangelicalism in the Two-Thirds World will be a major asset to the world church in mission.

---

4. For a full account of the debate and an exposition of the various documents that accompanied it, see Stott 1996.

Bibliography

Barratt, David (2002), *International Bulletin of Missionary Research* 26.1 (January): 22–23.

Jenkins, Philip (2002), *The Next Christendom: The Coming of Global Christianity*, Oxford: Oxford University Press.

Johnstone, Patrick and Jason Mandryck (2001), *Operation World: 21st Century Edition*, Carlisle: Paternoster Press.

Stott, John (ed.) (1996), *Making Christ Known: Historic Mission Documents from the Lausanne Movement 1974–1989*, Carlisle: Paternoster Press.

Taylor, William D. (1994), in John D. Woodbridge (ed.), *Ambassadors for Christ*, 336–347, Chicago: Moody Press.

—— (ed.) (2000), *Global Missiology for the 21st Century: The Iguassu Dialogue*, Grand Rapids: Baker (WEF).

Wright, Chris (2000), 'Christ and the Mosaic of Pluralisms', in Taylor 2000: 71–99.

Recommended reading

Bosch, David J., *Transforming Mission: Paradigm Shifts in Theology of Mission*, Maryknoll: Orbis, 1991.

Goldsmith, Martin, *God on the Move: Growth and Change in the Church Worldwide*, Carlisle: OM Publishing, 1998.

Guthrie, Stan, *Missions in the Third Millennium: 21 Key Trends for the 21st Century*, Carlisle: Paternoster Press, 2000.

Jenkins, Philip, *The Next Christendom: The Coming of Global Christianity*, Oxford: Oxford University Press, 2002.

Moreau, A. Scott (ed.), *Evangelical Dictionary of World Missions*, Grand Rapids: Baker; Carlisle: Paternoster Press, 2000.

Taylor, William D. (ed.), *Global Missiology for the 21st Century: The Iguassu Dialogue*, Grand Rapids: Baker (WEF), 2000.

Winter, Ralph D. and Steven C. Hawthorne, *Perspectives on the World Christian Movement: A Reader*, Pasadena: William Carey Library; Carlisle: Paternoster Press, 3rd ed., 1999.

6. EVANGELICALISM AND ETHICS

Robin Parry

The task of rethinking evangelical theology and praxis is fraught with danger. If we do not do it we find our message increasingly unable to connect with our audience (Christian and not-yet-Christian). We also face the very real danger of possibly fossilizing moral errors as when evangelicals in the past supported slavery and defended it from Scripture as the Christian ethic. If evangelical ethics is fixed and never open to reassessment we are in danger of making an idol of our own interpretations of Scripture. On the other hand, rethinking and rejecting the wisdom of ages past can take us away from the path of holiness in the name of 'relevance'. There is a very real danger that Christian ethical reflection takes its cue from values the 'world' esteems, baptizing them into the church in the name of contextualization. Evangelical ethics must walk the knife-edge of constant reflection and rethinking in the light of experience and reason whilst being true to the tradition and, most crucially of all, to the Bible. We need to avoid both the Scylla of fossilization and the Charybdis of compromise. Evangelical ethics is thus an ongoing, communal project that will never be complete this side of the New Age.

What makes an ethical claim or action evangelical is not whether it is believed, spoken or performed by an evangelical but whether it accords with the evangel, the message of the good news, and whether it is biblical in a more general sense. An evangelical ethic must be one grounded in an evangelical theology.

Evangelical ethics has made advances in recent decades. Perhaps most significant is the recovery since the 1970s of the long obscured place of social ethics in evangelicalism.[1] Whether from an unhealthy individualism or a fear of the liberal 'social gospel' we lost sight of the social ethic of our evangelical roots. The Lausanne Congress in 1974 marked a watershed in the restoration of evangelical social ethics and it is now accepted as central by large sections of the evangelical mainstream. Ongoing evangelical theory and praxis in social ethics is a cause for both encouragement and frustration. However, in this chapter I shall not try to chart the historical development of evangelical ethics (a task I am not in a position to do). Rather, I wish to outline how I see the broad narrative-theological parameters within which evangelical Christians should conduct their ethical reflections, whether the focus be personal or social. My reflections are intended as more normative than descriptive, but they draw on recent work in evangelical ethics. In this way I hope to outline some of the encouraging, current evangelical thinking going on in ethics and some areas for further reflection.

Evangelical ethics and the biblical metanarrative

It is traditional amongst evangelicals to claim that ethical deliberations must take account of the *whole* of the Bible and not simply one's favourite sections. The problem many evangelical books fail to address adequately is how all the different biblical texts relate to each other theologically, and yet this question is of the utmost importance. Evangelicals, at a popular level at any rate, have too

---

1. On the loss and ongoing recovery of evangelical social ethics see Smith 1998.

often been misled by an undeveloped doctrine of inerrancy into reading the Bible as a two-dimensional instruction book from which moral truths can be lifted unproblematically without much concern for canonical contexts.[2] If we are to avoid an *ad hoc* use of biblical texts in ethics we must appreciate the subtleties of their theological interconnections. Christians must, as Tom Wright has argued persuasively, understand the relevance of a particular biblical text by locating both it and their own situation within the grand narrative of creation to new creation.[3] Wright suggests that we imagine the Bible as being akin to a Shakespeare play the last Act of which is unfinished (apart from some sketches from the Playwright on how the story should end). Some actors have the job of putting on the play, but rather than write an 'authorized' penultimate Act they decide to leave it unwritten. Any actors who wish to perform the play must immerse themselves in the story so far, the characters and the sketches for the ending, then they must improvise the missing Act. Their improvisations must not simply reproduce the earlier Acts, but this does not mean that anything goes. Performances may be authentic or inauthentic depending on how faithful they are to the characterization, the story so far and the hints of its ending. This, suggests Wright, is how we ought to think about using the Bible today. The Bible is the story of God's dealings with humanity up until the end of the first century plus hints at the end of the story. We find ourselves having to play out the continuing story in a way faithful to the plotline so far and the ending towards which it hastens. We cannot necessarily just reproduce previous Acts as if nothing has moved on. On the other hand, the biblical story constrains what counts as the faithful performance of a Christian life. I wish to explore this thought as a key to evangelical theological ethics, whether personal or social. But first, a brief reflection on the God–morality connection.

---

2. I hasten to add that I am not claiming that a doctrine of inerrancy *must* be misused in this way.

3. Wright 1992: 139–144.

God and ethics

The most fundamental ontological question about ethics for the
Christian is that of the relationship between God and ethics. This
relationship has been construed in three basic ways. Some, following William of Ockham's divine command ethic, have held
that 'right' is whatever God commands people to do and 'wrong'
is whatever God commands people not to do. Murder is wrong
because God forbids it, but he could just as easily have com-
manded it thus making it our moral obligation. This version of
divine command theory makes God's *will* primary in moral obligation. A contemporary evangelical whose ethical theory bears some
similarities to Ockham's is Roy Clouser.[4] Clouser maintains that
the Being of God is utterly mysterious to humans and cannot be
known, but that God (timelessly) created his own nature as wise
and good. But God did not have to be wise and good – he could
have created his nature otherwise. God is simply *not subject* to any
moral laws as humans are – God *makes* the laws.

Thomas Aquinas represents a different strand in the divine
command tradition. For Aquinas, God's nature is goodness itself
and thus God could only ever command that which is good. God
commanding something makes it a moral obligation, but the
things God can command are 'limited' by his perfect nature. God
could not command someone to torture children for pleasure, for
instance. It would be a mistake to imagine that this theory makes
'good' and 'bad' standards *external* to God to which his commands
must measure up. On the contrary, goodness is God's nature and
if, per impossible, God did not exist, then goodness and badness
would not exist either. This version of divine command ethics
makes God's *nature* primary. Contemporary orthodox Christian
philosophers who defend this view include William Lane Craig,
William Alston and Katherine Rogers.[5] A slightly different take on

---

4. Clouser 1991: 167–195; 1999: 143–151.

5. Craig 1996; Alston 1989: ch. 12 (strictly speaking Alston does not claim to
   defend this view but simply to provide ammunition for those who wish to
   do so); Rogers 2000: ch. 9.

this Thomist model is one which shifts the emphasis from divine *commands* and obedient human *actions* to divine and human *virtues*. Linda Zabzebski, a Catholic philosopher, has defended a model in which the foundations of ethics are the virtues of God.[6] Human virtues are rooted in God's virtues.

A third view takes the Platonic route of seeing goodness, justice and so on as objective standards (Forms) which do not depend on God. God's existence makes no difference to the content of ethics – indeed his commands are only right if they cohere with the standards of rightness. This view might seem out of order for an orthodox Christian. However, it is not as awkward as it seems at first. Wesley Morriston, a contemporary evangelical philosopher who defends this view of ethics, argues that as God is perfectly good, his commands always would be perfectly good and what more does a Christian need to assert?[7] Indeed God, being omniscient, knows moral truths perfectly, so, given our finitude, his communications to us on moral matters are crucial for our guidance. Morriston argues that no important theological claims are lost on his view of ethics.

Obviously evangelical philosophers have, and continue to, disagree on this issue. What is an unquestioned assumption in the biblical texts and a non-negotiable for evangelicals is that God's commands are obligatory for us – all are agreed on *that* point. For myself, I would argue that Christian ethics is rooted in the divine nature and in particular in the love of God. When John says that 'God is love' (1 John 4:8, 16) he seems to be making a claim about God's nature – that God is *essentially* loving. In other words, it is inconceivable that any action of God could be unloving and this, I suggest, includes his expressions of vengeance and wrath.[8] The

---

6. Zabzebski 1998.

7. Morriston n.d.

8. The traditional dichotomy theologians often draw between God's love and his justice increasingly seem to me to be unhelpful. I think that evangelicals ought to explore seriously the possibility that God's acts of just vengeance do not require him to set aside his love (either temporally or eternally). If God's nature is holy love then *all* God's acts are holy, just and loving.

holy love of God is the foundation of all Christian ethics. Indeed, orthodox Christian ethics would see this love as flowing between the persons of the Trinity in self-giving care. This loving community within the divine being is the root of morality and ethics – it is from this holy, loving Being that the creation-structuring commands of Genesis 1 issued. Divine commands, then, ought not be thought of as arbitrary but as motivated by holy love. With that in mind, we turn now to the creation order that was organized by God's decrees.

Act one: creation

The first plot element in the biblical story is creation. When I speak of 'creation' I refer not simply to an event long ago, but to the *ordered totality* of all that has been created by God. This creation-order is not simply the physical structures studied by the natural sciences, but includes a normative order governing how humans *ought to* behave.

The Bible teaches several things which have become central in creation ethics, and it is worth briefly noting them:

1. Creation depends upon God for its existence past and present.
2. Creation is *ordered and structured* by God. It is a cosmos and not a chaos waiting for humanity to bring ethical order. Thus a creation ethic resists any claim that morality is simply a human creation.
3. Creation is *good*. This explains the 'theoretical' Christian rejection of any view that demotes the physicality of created existence to a realm of evil (and thus to be avoided) or to a realm of moral irrelevance (making 'immorality' unimportant). I say that Christian resistance to such dualist ethics has been 'theoretical', because it is quite clear in the history of the church that dualisms which demote the 'physical' and promote the 'spiritual' have crept in and exerted considerable influence. One thinks, for instance, of the tensions generated in patristic attitudes towards sexuality by the biblical desire to

affirm the goodness of marriage and non-biblical view that
sex was a bodily (and thus second rate) act that the most
'spiritual' were somehow above. The evangelical churches still
have their demons to exorcise in this area and our theologians
must continue to help us in this task. That said, there has
been a welcome recovery in recent years of the Reformation
emphasis on the ethical and spiritual significance of so-called
'secular' vocations.[9] Further work is needed here for a
rounded Christian life-ethic.

4. Humans are created in the 'image of God' (Gen. 1:26–28).
   This teaching has long been the ground for Christian emphasis on the importance and value of human life (following
   Gen. 9:6) and that in spite of the fact that the exact meaning
   of the expression has never been agreed upon. At a popular
   level most evangelicals have understood the phrase 'image of
   God' to describe the rational and creative aspects of the
   'soul'. Some more recent evangelical thinkers have seen the
   image in more *functional* terms – humans serve as God's rulers
   over the creation and *in this way* they image God. Such an
   interpretation has more to commend it in terms of the exegesis of Genesis 1. Others have, following Karl Barth, shifted to
   recover a more relational model of the image of God. Being
   in God's image is something we do together in our relationality rather than something we can be as isolated individuals.[10]
   This is just one of many ways in which the communality of
   ethics is being restored in an evangelical theological tradition
   which has overemphasized the place of the isolated individual.
   The nature of the human person has important implications
   for ethics and some creative theological work is going on
   exploring the notion again in the light of current biblical
   research, biology, neurology, psychology, philosophy and

9. For instance, Walsh & Middleton 1984; Stevens 1999.
10. Tom Smail is writing a book exploring the notion of relationality and the
    image of God in trinitarian terms. He thinks that theologians need to
    explore what the image of God means when we image him as Father, as
    Son and as Spirit in our relationships (forthcoming, Paternoster Press).

sociology.[11] The role of narrative is receiving more attention as a crucial element in the identity of a 'person' and this is opening new ways of thinking of the role of biblical narratives in creating Christian self-identity.[12] This focus on the notion of 'person' and its ethical implications will continue for some time to come. Although the outcome of such discussions will not affect the role 'personhood' plays in supporting the value of human beings, it *may* have implications for issues such as embryo research and abortion. On the functional and relational conceptions of the 'image of God' we must say that, at very least, an embryo and a foetus are not fully *functioning* in God's image *yet* and this *could possibly* undermine an important biblical support for the traditional Christian resistance to such practices as abortion. Evangelicals who support functional views of the divine image need to explore this question carefully. Is an embryo in the divine image? Is it *potentially* in the divine image? If the latter, does this potentiality grant it moral status and protection from deliberate harm?[13]

Also grounded in creation order is the human relationship to the natural world (to care for it and bring out its potential) and to animals (authority over the animals for the benefit of the animals). There has been a welcome flowering of evangelical ecological ethics in recent years which places great store on these themes.[14]

---

11. White 1996; Elliot 2001.

12. Philosophers defending a narrative notion of personhood include Paul Ricoeur, Alasdair MacIntyre, Charles Taylor and Richard Kearney. Theologians who have followed suit include Stanley Hauerwas, Vernon White and George Stroup.

13. Philosopher Don Marquis (1997) argues that what makes killing in general wrong is that the person we kill is deprived of the goods of having a 'future like ours'. This, says Marquis, makes abortion wrong even if the foetus is not yet a fully functioning person or even a person at all. A strategy like this could be adopted by the functionalist and the relationalist.

14. For instance, Schaeffer 1970; Osborn 1995; Berry 2000; Bouma-Prediger 2001.

Less ethical reflection has gone on about the issue of animal welfare, but here too there are welcome signs of change.[15] The command to humanity to 'subdue the earth' has been understood by many recent evangelicals to be a 'cultural commission' to develop agriculture, technology, music and so on.[16] This, again, is a needed development of the positive Reformed evaluation of the totality of human created life. The door is now opened to fruitful theological-ethical work to be done on technology in all its manifestations, art, music, work, politics and so on.[17]

The twentieth century has seen a recovery of the influence of Wisdom literature (Proverbs, Job, Ecclesiastes) in Christian ethics and this has played a role in the recovery of creation ethics. Recent evangelical Wisdom scholars have emphasized the importance of wisdom ethics for the church to recover the value of the whole of life lived to the glory of God. [18] Recent work by non-evangelical OT scholars also offers promise for evangelical adaptation. James Barr and John Barton have both detected traces of 'natural law' ethics within OT laws and prophets.[19] The fact that OT laws have many well-known parallels with non-Israelite Ancient Near Eastern laws ought to suggest that God's commands to Moses were not totally unknown prior to Sinai. It is not as if the Israelites thought that murder was OK until they received the Decalogue! Evangelical theologians need to reflect more on the theological import of such parallels for ethics, but I suggest that they simply reinforce the claim that Mosaic laws were linked with natural law.[20]

---

15. See the studies mentioned by Rodd 2001: ch. 16 and the two essays by Richard Bauckham on 'Jesus and Animals' in Linzey & Yamamoto 1998: 33–48, 49–60. See also the essay by S. R. L. Clark on God's covenant with the animals and the response by J. Goldingay in Cartledge & Mills 2001.

16. Walsh & Middleton 1984; Wolters 1996.

17. On work see Stevens 1999. There has been a flowering of recent theology of art, music, politics, etc.

18. Bartholomew 2002; Van Leeuwen 1990.

19. Barton 1998.

20. A connection also made in some OT and Second Temple Jewish literature that linked creation, wisdom and torah.

Christian ethics has long appealed to the order of creation in its ethical reflection. The early fathers adapted Stoic natural law theories and Aquinas modified Aristotle in constructing his own Christian natural law account.[21] After a decline in popularity, natural law ethics is experiencing something of a deserved revival among Christian ethicists.[22] One issue that will continue to divide evangelicals here though is the question of the epistemic access-ibility of this natural law. Can the unregenerate person understand the natural law by the use of reason without needing to appeal to special divine revelation? Aquinas was rather positive on this front, but evangelicals have been much more cautious (indeed some-times downright hostile). The epistemic damage caused by sin needs to be taken seriously, but so too does the fact that there is reasonable cross-cultural and inter-religious agreement on ethical questions. To the Christian, all humans share the divine image and live in the same created order, so one should expect *some* true understanding of that order apart from special revelation.

It is not the case that a 'creation ethic' has been welcomed by all Christians. There is a traditional dichotomy within Christian ethics between a 'creation ethic' grounded in the natural order and a 'kingdom ethic' rooted in Jesus' radical and subversive mission. Some 'kingdom ethicists' dismiss creation ethics as conservative and supportive of the moral status quo. It seems to me that this dichotomy is most unhelpful and urgently needs transcending.[23]

---

21. See Holmes 1997: chs. 4, 6.

22. See, for instance, Porter 1999.

23. How the creation–kingdom dichotomy can be transcended is suggested by Oliver O'Donovan whose *Resurrection and Moral Order* is perhaps one of the most significant works in evangelical ethics to appear in the last fifty years. O'Donovan argues that evangelical ethics must be founded upon the gospel and thus upon the resurrection of Christ from the dead. And the resurrection 'tells us of God's vindication of his creation and so of our created life' (1994: 13). This leads O'Donovan into a rigorous discus-sion of the created order which grounds moral action. Evangelical creation ethics will look to this magnificent work as a primary source for some years to come.

Evangelical ethical theory needs to pay attention to the *whole* biblical plot and to seek a way of integrating it. To set creation against Jesus in order to reject the moral import of the former is a very unhelpful move that will end up misunderstanding Jesus as well as creation. Thus the work of kingdom ethicists like Stanley Hauerwas, although immensely useful for evangelical ethics,[24] cannot be uncritically appropriated because he downplays the significance of creation.

The perennial question of how, apart from special revelation, we can know what the natural law is, remains one of the most problematic aspects of natural law theories and one which requires further attention. It is not simply that humans disagree about what is natural and what is merely cultural, but Christians (evangelicals included) do also. Consider genetic engineering. Is the modification of the genetic structure of plants and animals 'playing God' and violating the structure of creation or is it merely bringing out the potential God has placed within the world? Was God's plan that humanity one day modify creation like this? Is genetic engineering wrong in principle, or only wrong if it is misused, and if the latter, how are we to determine what counts as misuse? The answers to such questions are not immediately obvious and will be the subject of much debate amongst Christians in the coming years.[25] Indeed the biological technologies are going to raise some very serious challenges to the notion of a fixed natural law with its traditional focus on the unchanging nature of different species. With genetic modification, an urgent challenge for the current and next generation of evangelical ethicists is whether humans can redesign their own nature!

To take just one more area of current concern – to what extent are the relations between husbands and wives cultural constructs and to what extent are they 'given' in creation? In previous

---

24. Wells (1998) offers a superb evangelical analysis of the theological ethics of Hauerwas.

25. On the question of genetic modification the recent Evangelical Alliance book brings some sensible reflections (Bruce & Horrocks 2001). On cloning see Jones 2001.

generations it was taken for granted that God's creation order was that a wife be under the authority of her husband. This is now widely questioned within Western evangelicalism and has become one of the major ethical fissures within our communion. My point is that seeing ethics as rooted in creation order does not automatically answer all our ethical questions apart from some practical account of how that natural order is known.

The previous discussion is closely related to one of the most divisive issues within evangelical ethical hermeneutics: that of how we can know which parts of biblical teaching are trans-cultural. Clearly the biblical texts were not written in some hermetically sealed cultural vacuum. One of the great advances in biblical studies over the past hundred years or so is the vast increase in our knowledge of the ancient cultural worlds in which the Bible took shape. We are now better placed than ever to read these texts against their cultural background and the interpretative pay-off has been significant. However, the distancing of the texts in this way has also made them seem more alien to us than they did to previous generations. It is very clear to most evangelicals, whether they be scholars or not, that many aspects of the text reflect the culture of the day and are not of enduring normative ethical value. For instance, the social organization of the Israelite household is not seen as normative by most evangelicals today but as simply a passing, culturally-limited model. But once it is conceded that some parts of the Bible are culturally limited, it becomes less clear how we are to decide which parts are culture-transcending (note: I do not say 'non-cultural' as all of the Bible is 'cultural' in some sense). It seems obvious to us that the command to love is culture-transcending *but on what basis do we make this judgment?* In the debates about the role of women or the status of homosexual relationships, the notion of cultural relativity is increasingly appealed to by some sections of the evangelical community to the horror of other sections. The problem is that those who resort to this method often do so in an ad hoc way.

Those who do provide criteria can often provide far too radical ones. For instance, Charles Kraft seems to suggest that when the teachings of the NT depart from the cultural norms we have culture-transcending teachings, *but when they follow the culture of the day they are probably culturally limited.*[26] This criterion of dissimilarity is far too harsh in that it would make the Jewishness of Christianity incidental to its true nature, thus losing the crucial connections between NT and OT. Also it would rule out belief in God and other such things from the core of Christianity!

A far better approach was that charted by Richard Longenecker in his *New Testament Social Ethics for Today.*[27] Longenecker argued that the ethics of the NT epistles represents the planting of the gospel seed into the social institutions of the Roman world. The gospel seed transformed the institutions in a certain direction, but further growth is to be expected given Galatians 3:28. Thus the early church did not abolish slavery (they were hardly in a position to do so), but they modified the institution in the light of the gospel. Arguably later Christians are legitimated in following this trajectory further and abolishing slavery.

The most stimulating development of this 'Redemptive-Movement' hermeneutical approach to culture and biblical ethics is William Webb's *Slaves, Women and Homosexuals.*[28] Webb provides the most systematic and consistent approach to separating the culturally relative chaff from the culture-transcending wheat I have yet come across. He sets out eighteen criteria, which are consistent with a high view of Scripture, by which to weigh biblical teachings and make wise judgments on their contemporary applicability. This is a very positive step forward for the use of the Bible in contemporary Christian ethics and in my opinion Webb has now placed the ball in the court of those who want to take a different line. This issue will become increasingly prominent in future studies and rightly so.

------

26. Kraft 1990: ch. 9. Kraft does not follow the practice he seems to suggest, for he wants to take Jesus' views on the spirit world (which were typical for his day) as normative for Christians today. It is unclear to me how he can do this when, on his own criteria, Jesus' views on the subject could just be culturally limited.

27. Longenecker 1984.

28. Webb 2001 (see also Adeney 1995).

Act two: the fall

The story of the fall, which is the story of humanity in rebellion against God, focuses our attention on the realism found in Christian ethics. According to Reformed evangelical theology, sin effects every dimension of God's creation order. Not in the sense that the structures of creation are damaged (God in his common grace preserves them), but in the sense that each of those structures is redirected away from God to serve other purposes. Thus sin infects our emotions, desires, our relationships with God, our spouses, our children, our parents, our friends, our neighbours, our environments and other creatures in God's world. Politics, work, religion, art, love, education, economics and every other dimension of human life are distorted by sin.[29] The liberal Christianity of the early twentieth century which reflected the modernist view of the essential goodness of human beings was dashed to pieces upon the rocks of two World Wars, and its occasional revival in television shows such as *Star Trek*[30] represents nothing more than a desperate hope, the falsity of which is continually exposed in ongoing conflicts world-wide and within each human heart. Christian ethics sees the human heart as the root of the ethical problems we face. All human attempts to overcome 'the flesh' – be they ancient asceticism or modern psycho-therapy – will end in failure.

Within Christian ethics this view of sinful human nature has led to the view that human laws are there *primarily* to constrain sin rather than as a means to promote good. So, for instance, we have laws that forbid murder but none that forbid angry thoughts. Thus laws often set a threshold one must not fall beneath, rather than an ideal to which one must aspire. Christians reflecting on contemporary national laws would be well advised to bear this in mind.[31] Reinhold Niebuhr (1902–71) perhaps more than any other

---

29. Wolters 1996; Spykman 1992.
30. The *Star Trek* future is one in which humans have used reason and technology to eradicate crime, war, poverty, illness, greed, etc.
31. Mitchell 1987; Beaumont 2002.

recent Christian ethicist made the fall the centre of his ethical system. He structured his entire social ethic around the idea that the will-to-power must be resisted by restraining evil[32] and came to see the ethics of Jesus as an ideal impossible to realize within human history. Unfortunately Niebuhr saw the struggle with sin as eternal and thus underestimated the power of the cross, the Spirit and the consummation of the new creation in his ethic. Niebuhr does not so much overestimate the power of sin as underestimate the power of the gospel. Nevertheless, he does perhaps alert us to what Christians can expect in this age in an ethic designed for an unregenerate world which remains a prisoner to sin. Exactly what emphasis to give to sin's continued power in our current situation, located as we are between the inauguration of the new creation in Christ's resurrection and its consummation at the parousia, is a matter of dispute amongst evangelicals.

Act three: law

Central to the ethics of God's covenant people Israel was the law given through Moses at Sinai. Evangelicals have always disagreed about the extent to which OT laws are still applicable today. Those of a Lutheran inclination tend to oppose law and gospel and see the law as no longer applicable to the Christian who now lives in the power of the Spirit. The law was only given to bring people to an awareness of their need of God. Those of a more Calvinist inclination see more unity between OT and NT, with the law as a guide of continuing relevance for the Christian. The differences are not as sharp as they seem, for although Luther did not think the Christian was obligated to obey the law, in his actual practice he made much use of OT laws to explain the ethical standards expected of the Christian church. The interpretation of Paul's view on the law plays a key role here and that matter is one of the hottest potatoes dividing evangelical Pauline scholars

---

32. On this interpretation of Niebuhr see Lovatt 2001.

today and it will continue to divide in the short and medium term.[33]

Within contemporary OT scholarship, evangelicals have made major contributions to discussions of the ethics of OT laws.[34] Of special note we could draw attention to the work of Walter Kaiser,[35] Gordon Wenham and Christopher Wright. C. J. H. Wright's paradigmatic model for OT ethics remains the most helpful model for Christian re-appropriation of OT laws.[36] Wright sees Israel-living-under-torah-in-the-land-of-Canaan as a paradigm of what it means to live as the godly humanity on the earth. Thus the laws of Israel reflect God's standards for the nations. The church is eschatological Israel and the laws can still be applied typologically within the church which also lives as a model to the nations of what it means to live in God's world God's way. Complementary approaches have been used by John Goldingay[37] and Richard Bauckham.[38] So OT laws are still a crucial resource for Christian ethics in that they indicate God's standards. However, recent evangelical work has helped nuance this picture. Gordon Wenham has argued that many OT laws do not legislate for the moral ideals, but represent a compromise between the ideals and the reality of fallen humanity.[39] It is

---

33. On the one hand we have the so-called 'new' view of Paul and the law best represented in broadly evangelical circles by James Dunn and Tom Wright. On the other we have modified versions of the more traditional view represented by Peter Stuhlmacher, Donald Carson, Simon Gathercole, Seyoon Kim, Stephen Westerholm, Mark Seifrid et al. Alongside this debate is the classic Reformed debate on the role of the law in guiding Christian ethics (see Bayes 2000 for both historical and biblical exegetical discussion).

34. Cyril Rodd's recent book on OT ethics (2001) frequently interacts with evangelical authors, which is testimony to their importance in this area.

35. Kaiser 1983. Kaiser, however, places too much emphasis on the place of law in OT ethics.

36. C. J. H. Wright 1983; 1995.

37. Goldingay 1990.

38. Bauckham 1989.

39. Wenham 2000: ch. 5.

wrong, maintains Wenham, to imagine that OT laws simply embody the ethics of the Bible writers. To get closer to the ethical ideals one needs to look also at Wisdom literature and especially narratives.

There have been growing signs of a deeper awareness of the narrative context of Israel's laws, but little ethical work has been done exploring these links. Paul Ricoeur thinks that setting Israel's laws in a narrative context will impact both the narrative sections (in the light of the laws) and the law sections (in the light of the narrative).[40] This insight urgently needs following up. What exactly are the *theological* interconnection within OT ethics between creation ethics, law ethics, narrative ethics, prophetic ethics and wisdom ethics? Let me suggest three lines of research I hope will be followed up:

1. Could it be that Wisdom ethics is grounded in creation ethics; that law/covenant ethics are also grounded in creation ethics plus the narrative of Israel; and that prophetic ethics are grounded in law/covenant ethics (and thus creation ethics). Following Dumbrell, I want to see all the OT covenants as sub-sets of a single covenant with creation within which we can locate all of the above.[41] This covenant, of course, is rooted in the love of God. I suspect that the pursuit of this line of thought will lead to a greater theological integration of OT ethics and thus better guide Christian applications of them.

2. The time is ripe for a detailed analysis of the relationship between the narrative ethics of the OT (say 1 Samuel) and OT laws. Some work has been done here[42] but it is an under-researched area.

3. I wonder if an examination of Genesis 1–3 would yield some fruitful answers to our questions. Within these chapters one finds creation ethics, wisdom ethics, prophetic ethics and law

---

40. Ricoeur 1998.
41. Dumbrell 1984.
42. E.g. Millar 1998.

ethics – all the main types of OT ethical literature. If we can clarify how they are related to each other here then, given the placing of Genesis 1–3 at the head of the canon, we could have a model for understanding their relations across the OT and this, too, will better inform Christian use of OT ethics.

Act four: Christ's teaching and ministry

The teaching and example of Christ has always been central to Christian ethics. The key issue for an evangelical ethic is how Jesus' teaching connects with the rest of the canon, for one must not isolate Jesus' teaching from its canonical context. The focus in Jesus' teaching on the kingdom of God alerts us to the fact that his ethics are kingdom ethics,[43] which is to say they are the ethics of the new creation. Jesus' ethic was eschatological, but this should not be taken to imply that it was a radical, unrealistic ethic for a people who expected the end of the world within a generation. It is a radical ethic for the people of God who live in the presence of the in-breaking new creation even in the midst of the 'world'. That describes the church of today as much as the first Jewish believers so the ethic of the twenty-first-century church must be as eschatological as that of the first century. Any evangelical account of Jesus' ethic must see it as having continuing application to Christians, even if it does not set a standard we should expect political policies or legislation to live up to.

The relation of Jesus' ethic to the OT law is a complex and controversial issue[44] and it should be described in terms both of continuity and discontinuity. The developments in the story of salvation-history led the NT writers to see redundancy in certain aspects of the law (e.g. food laws, circumcision, sacrifice) and continuity in others (what we may call moral laws). When Jesus seems to disagree with the law, what he is often doing is following its moral trajectory and developing it further. So the Levitical

---

43. See N. T. Wright 1996.
44. See Moo 1992.

command to love one's neighbour (Lev. 19:18) is affirmed but extended to apply to non-Jews (Matt. 5:43–44), and the Exodus restriction on vengeance to *only an eye* for an eye (Exod. 21:24) is intensified to radical non-retaliation (Matt. 5:38–39). Jesus (Mark 12:28–34 pars), as later Paul (Rom. 13:8–9) and James (2:8–9), saw the law as summed up in the command to love. Jesus operated a hermeneutic of love according to which we judge the continued application of a law on the basis of an understanding that its *raison d'être* was love. Any use of the law which did not demonstrate such love was thus a misapplication. After the utilitarian love ethic of situation ethics in the 1960s many evangelicals felt a need to distance themselves from an ethic that could be boiled down to love. This is a shame, because it seems quite clear that Jesus and the NT writers *did* believe that Christian ethics could be summed up in the command to love. However, what is meant by 'Christian love' cannot be understood apart from the story of creation and redemption told in Scripture. Any universal, generic account of love will be too thin for a robust ethic and this *may* explain the weakness of situation ethics. For ethical living we need a tradition-shaped account of love, and for the Christian the concept of 'love' takes shape as it is stretched across the contours of the story of God's loving covenant with creation, his gracious redemption and provision of the law, his sending Christ to die and be raised, the empowering presence of God in the Spirit and the consequent sweeping up of forgiven sinners within the very life of God himself. 'Love' so understood can serve as the core of Christian ethics and it is encouraging to see evangelicals re-engaging with love in something like the way suggested here.[45] Jesus' ethic is a radical one that subverts ideologies of power and it remains a constant challenge to a church that can so easily slip into accepting the status quo. However, we must not set his kingdom ethic up over

45. For instance, Atwood 1998. Atwood makes the creation covenant, moral rules and love central to his account and once it is seen that love is compatible with moral rules many of the problems with a love ethic dissolve. Grenz (1997) similarly summarizes the content of Christian ethics as 'comprehensive love'.

against a creation ethic as some are wont to do. The very 'kingdom' in question is the rule of God over his creation – it is the restored creation envisaged by the prophets of old.[46] Jesus' ethic does serve as a critique of the *misdirected structures* of God's universe – what the NT refers to as 'the world' – but it is not a critique of those structures themselves. Jesus does not oppose political power but only its misuse, not religion but hypocrisy and legalism, not marriage nor wealth but their idolization, and so on.

Act five: cross

One of the criticisms of creation ethics is that it can be ethically conservative and end up justifying oppression such as slavery or political institutions such as monarchy as part of the natural God-given order. O'Donovan has been criticized for neglecting the centrality of the cross in Christian ethics, and given the cruci-centrism of evangelicalism I think that this criticism needs to be taken very seriously. In the NT the cross seems to relate to ethics in three different ways:

1. The cross is God's victory over human sin and is the basis upon which Christians are set free from the power of sin and liberated for obedience to God (Rom. 6:1–14; Col. 2:8–23).
2. It is a paradigm of the life of the Christian in the present evil age. Like Christ, we will be rejected by the world and suffer for our obedience to God, but we must endure such shame as we await the new age (1 Peter).
3. It becomes a model for power-relations within the church. One of the most stimulating recent evangelical works developing this theme is Graham Tomlin's *The Power of the Cross*. Tomlin examines the practical application of the cross motif in Paul's first letter to the Corinthians, in the work of Luther and in Pascal. He concludes that for these theologians the crucifixion of Jesus was not just a freak event in the way God

---

46. Dumbrell 1984.

deals with humanity but *a revelation of how God acts throughout history*: 'God still works in and through what is to conventional understanding, weak and powerless and apparently irrational rather than through what is strong powerful and reasonable.'[47] True power begins not in the fallen social power-structures of 'the world', but in recognition of one's own powerlessness before God enabling one to surrender power, rights and privileges for the sake of others. Thus the cross becomes a means of unmasking and resisting ideologies which abuse power. It is not that there is anything wrong with power – following Foucault he sees power as inevitable in any social relationships – but power is open to abuse and the cross raises a critique of the way power operates within communities:

> The power which this discourse produces, is power not to dominate or control, but to love, to enable and to release. It is not so much a power over others, but a power to give oneself for others. The truth which it proclaims is not so much a will to power as a will to love. It hold out the vision of a community built not upon relations determined by domination, but relations where power and privilege are at the service of others, rather than serving to divide and oppress.[48]

The power of the cross is a community-building power and 'the theology of the cross can be realised only in community, within the power relations of the social networks operative between members of churches, their leaders, their preachers and their people'.[49] Some theologians share the Marxist fear that a theology of the cross is a theology put out by the powerful to keep the weak in their place by encouraging them to 'take up their cross'. However, the NT always uses the cross as a model for the Christian community *as a whole*. Indeed, as Richard Hays points out, it is the powerful ones who are asked to surrender their 'rights' for the weak and *not vice versa*

---

47. Tomlin 1999: 279.
48. Ibid.: 299.
49. Ibid.: 307.

(Mark 10:42–45; Rom. 15:1–3; 1 Cor. 8:1 – 11:1; Eph. 5:21ff.).[50] The ethical challenge of the cross to churches is to re-examine the power relations within our communities. Do our leaders draw power to themselves and lord it over the people, or do they exercise the power of love, looking out for the needs of others before their own needs?

The cross also becomes foundational for the *way in which* Christians resist evil. For Luther it was right to resist the abusive use of political power by rulers but such resistance must be the non-violent resistance modelled by the cross. For Christians to 'take up the sword' would be to abandon the crucified Lord they claim to serve.[51] Gospel social ethics works by transformation, not revolution.

Acts six, seven, eight: resurrection, the Spirit, and the new creation

What are the implications of the resurrection for evangelical theological ethics? Everything here hangs on the relationship between creation and redemption. We could see at least four different views on this relationship in the history of theology:

- Grace *opposing* nature (nature is bad and redemption is good)
- grace *replaces* nature (i.e. redemption order replaces creation order)
- grace *completes* nature (i.e. nature is good but incomplete without redemption)
- grace *redeems* nature (i.e. redemption is 'creation regained')

The first of these options has always been rejected by orthodox Christians. However, evangelicals have been found to embrace all three of the others and much hangs on our answer. To indicate how to proceed here we need to observe that in the NT the resurrection

---

50. Hays 1997: 197.
51. Tomlin 1999: 300.

of Christ is a foretaste of the New Age – indeed with the resurrection of Christ the New Age has already began. Thus to clarify the connections between creation and redemption we need to clarify the connections between creation and the new creation. What are the continuities and discontinuities between the two movements within the story? The answer seems to be somewhere between the Thomist (view 3) and the Reformational (view 4) views. The new creation is *this* creation renewed (the NT offers no support for the claim that it is a replacement creation that takes the place of the present one which is destined for destruction). Thus new creation is the redemption of *this* created order. But the new creation is not simply a return to Eden. The original creation order was like a seed which needed its potential bringing out and much legitimate development of the created order has taken place in human history. All that has been of value within human culture and history will be taken into the new order (an idea perhaps represented in Rev. 21:22–26). But the discontinuities are deeper than this. Paul is quite emphatic that the bodies which we shall have are not like the ones humanity was originally created with (1 Cor. 15:35–50) and Jesus is clear that the crucial creation ordinance of marriage will no longer be necessary in the kingdom (Matt. 22:29–30; perhaps explaining the positive evaluation of singleness within the realized eschatological life of the Christian church). This indicates that new creation is not simply a return to creation, but also a transformation of it. For myself I prefer to accommodate the discontinuities within the notion of creation order. Thus I tentatively suggest that we should think of marriage as a temporary institution which God always intended should cease at the appointed time in the development of humanity. Similarly, I think that it was always God's intention that the mortal body of Adam should be transformed into an immortal one by partaking of the tree of life.[52] So new creation is a restoration of creation order, but at a later stage in its development.

Returning to the resurrection, we can see that it is God's 'Yes' to

---

52. This requires an interpretation of Genesis 2 – 3 according to which humans were created mortal and only took on immortality if they ate from the tree of life. Not all will feel comfortable with such a view.

his creation. It is the redemption *of* creation (thus the importance of a *bodily* resurrection) and not a redemption *from* creation (as, sadly, many evangelicals have seen it). Oliver O'Donovan brings this out brilliantly in his *Resurrection and Moral Order*. A gospel ethic is a resurrection ethic, which is a renewed creation ethic.

The Spirit is also crucial here. The giving of the Spirit to the people of God was a sign of the presence of the kingdom (Joel 2:28–32), thus Pentecost is proof positive that the New Age had dawned with the resurrection (Acts 2:14–21). The Spirit promised by God in Ezekiel would internalize the laws of God and enable obedience to them (Ezek. 36:25–27), and this obedience-empowering role is one Paul sees the Spirit as playing in the ethical life of the believer.[53] The Spirit of holiness within the believer and the community produces community-building virtues (Gal. 5:22–23). This is realized eschatology. For the Christian community the New Age has begun and the community is called to live in the present age by the values of the age to come as a prophetic witness to the future of the world.

However, all is not quite this straightforward. Across all the NT texts the church is presented as living in a tension between the old and the new ages. The new creation is here and *yet it is still to come*. This tension within the NT between realized and future eschatology raises its ethical head to complicate matters. The Christian life is not presented as instant and easy victory over sin, and the work of the Spirit in us is resisted by the desires of our this-present-age-flesh (Gal. 5).[54] Even a cursory reading of 1 Corinthians will reveal that the church in NT times often fell short of its ethical calling as it does today. The danger of an ethically over-realized eschatology is that it underestimates the shadow cast by human sin over the Christian community. Resisting the desires of the flesh is a *lifelong* struggle, though one that should get easier as good, Spirit-inspired habits are formed. On the other hand, there has been a tendency within some quarters to overestimate the power of sin and to

---

53. See Dunn 2001.

54. The essentially Reformed approach I take to sanctification is not one that all evangelical traditions will accept.

underestimate the power available through the cross and the Spirit to resist it. Victory over sin is a real possibility for the Christian *in the present*. Paul would never support a theology that saw holiness as merely future and that in the meantime we should reconcile ourselves to the fact that we can't help ourselves.[55] So sin may be hard to resist, but the resources are now available for the Christian to resist it. However, the NT is also realistic in seeing the moral transformation of the believer as long term (1 John 1:8–10). The challenge for evangelical theology here is to discern where the balance lies between the now and not-yet and to carefully integrate NT insights on sinful behaviour with insights from psychology and sociobiology on human behaviour and addictions.

In the NT kingdom hope also serves to inspire a church living the cross-shaped life that is the destiny of all who would walk in the ways of the Lord in the midst of a God-rejecting world. In one sense we live resurrected lives, but in another we are the crucified ones who await a better resurrection. Thus the cross is not a phase the church can move beyond in its ethics, but is an ongoing reality.[56]

---

55. In my view, such theologies tend to begin from their experience and then misinterpret Romans 7 in the light of it. But when Romans 7 is read in the context of Romans 6 and 8 it is hard to support such a theology.

56. A word about virtue ethics: Since the early 1980s there has been a major revival of virtue ethics within philosophy and this has spilled over into Christian ethics (Hauerwas & Pinches 1997). Virtue ethics is a diverse family of views but what they share in common is a focus on the primacy of character as opposed to actions and their consequences. Virtue ethics cannot be appropriated uncritically (Bunting 2000) but there are great insights for those who do it wisely. Within the evangelical community one of the most exciting virtue ethicists is Robert C. Roberts who has integrated a focus on virtues and vices in the NT with psychology and philosophy. Roberts' work restores emotions, narrative, psychology and spirituality to their places within evangelical ethics as well as spelling out a clearly Christian account of the virtues (Roberts 1991; 1992; 1995a; 1995b; 1999). Evangelical ethicists of the future need to adjust their work to integrate insights from virtue theory. The fact that this comment comes in a footnote indicates that I have yet to achieve such synthesis myself.

In conclusion, evangelical ethical theory and practice will flow from ongoing reflection on the narrative of creation, fall, redemption and new creation. We ought to aim at thinking ethically with all the elements of the story in their proper place. In the coming decades I would hope that evangelical ethicists continue to refine the theological interconnections in dialogue with historical theologians and biblical scholars. In particular the relationship between creation ethics and kingdom ethics needs detailed exegetical fleshing out if the claims made in this chapter are to be adequately supported. Also the debate on the place of OT laws in Christian ethics will not go away. Recent work by Chris Wright and other evangelical OT scholars has been very helpful in pointing a way forward, but to carry the day it still needs to be more fully integrated into a whole-Bible ethic by more rigorous NT exegetical work. In a nutshell, I would love to see Christian ethicists and biblical scholars working really hard at clarifying the interconnections between the parts of the meta-narrative.

An evangelical ethic will take account of the range of biblical ethical material from law to narrative, from proverb to prophecy. Major advances in appreciation of biblical genres have occurred in evangelical circles, but the implications for contemporary ethical use need further consideration.

I am also keen to see some way of biblically integrating insights from virtue ethics, natural law ethics, divine command ethics and so on. My suspicion is that some philosophical account yet awaits to be thought of which can pull off this wonderful trick and in so doing provide a way of doing justice to biblical creation ethics, law ethics, character ethics and the like.

One of the most important areas for continued work is consideration of the cultural and historical gap between the biblical texts and out own situations. It is here that some of the most thorny issues in the ethical use of Scripture lie. The theological connections outlined in this chapter ought to go some considerable way to guiding the modern Bible reader in proper contemporary use, and in my view recent work by Webb and others points to a constructive way forward, but further work and debates lie ahead. May the Spirit of God grant us love and wisdom in our ongoing negotiation of the Scylla of fossilization and the Charybdis of compromise.

The current evangelical research on the ethics of poverty, international relations, economics, politics, violence, ethnicity, medicine, technology, sexuality, psychiatry, law, business, and so on is encouraging and needs to continue. The claim that a biblical ethic can be a whole-life ethic is a pudding vindicated only in its eating.

Evangelical ethics will grow through a deeper understanding of the theological relationships between the parts of the Bible and it will creatively interact with our contemporary context. It will be an ethic that gives a key role both to moral rules and the importance of character. Most importantly, it will be an ethic rooted and founded in the covenant-God and his love.

Bibliography

Adeney, B. T. (1995), *Strange Virtues: Ethics in a Multi-Cultural World*, Leicester: Apollos.

Alston, W. (1989), 'Some Suggestions for Divine Command Theorists', in W. P. Alston, *Divine Nature and Human Language: Essays in Philosophical Theology*, 253–273, Ithaca: Cornell University Press.

Atwood, D. (1998), *Changing Values: How to Find Moral Truth in Modern Times*, Carlisle: Paternoster Press.

Bartholomew, C. (2002), 'A God is For Life and Not Just for Christmas: The Relevance of God in the Old Testament Wisdom Literature', in P. Helm and C. Trueman (eds.), *The Trustworthiness of God*, 39–57, Grand Rapids: Eerdmans; Leicester: IVP.

Barton, J. (1988), *Ethics and the Old Testament*, London: SCM Press.

Bauckham, R. (1989), *The Bible in Politics: How to Read the Bible Politically*, London: SPCK.

Bayes, J. F. (2000), *The Weakness of the Law: God's Law and the Christian in New Testament Perspective*, Carlisle: Paternoster Press.

Beaumont, P. (ed.) (2002), *Christian Perspectives on the Limits of Law*, Carlisle: Paternoster Press.

Berry, R. J. (ed.) (2000), *The Care of Creation: Focusing Concern and Action*, Leicester: IVP.

Bouma-Prediger, S. (2001), *For the Beauty of the Earth: A Christian Vision for Creation Care*, Grand Rapids: Baker.

Bruce, D. and D. Horrocks (eds.) (2001), *Modifying Creation? GM Crops and Foods: A Christian Perspective*, Carlisle: Paternoster Press.

Bunting, H. (2000), 'Ethics and the Perfect Moral Law', *Tyndale Bulletin* 51.2: 235–260.

Cartledge, M. and D. Mills (eds.) (2001), *Covenant Theology: Contemporary Approaches*, Carlisle: Paternoster Press.

Clouser, R. (1991), *The Myth of Religious Neutrality: An Essay on the Hidden Roles of Religious Belief in Theories*, Indiana: Notre Dame University Press.

—— (1999), *Knowing With the Heart: Religious Experience and Belief in God*, Downers Grove: IVP.

Craig, W. L. (1996), 'The Indispensability of Theological Meta-ethical Foundations for Morality', at http://home.apu.edu/~CTRF/papers/1996_papers/craig.html

Dumbrell, W. J. (1984), *Covenant and Creation: An Old Testament Covenantal Theology*, Exeter: Paternoster Press.

Dunn, J. D. G. (2001), 'Judaism and Christianity: One Covenant or Two?', in Cartledge & Mills 2001: 33–55.

Elliot, M. (2001) (ed.), *The Dynamics of Human Life*, Carlisle: Paternoster Press.

Goldingay, J. (1990), *Approaches to Old Testament Interpretation*, 2nd ed., Leicester: IVP.

Grenz, S. (1997), *The Moral Quest: Foundations of Christian Ethics*, Leicester: Apollos.

Hauerwas, S. and C. Pinches (1997), *Christians among the Virtues: Theological Conversations with Ancient and Modern Ethics*, Indiana: University of Notre Dame Press.

Hays, R. B. (1997), *The Moral Vision of the New Testament: A Contemporary Introduction to New Testament Ethics*, Edinburgh: T. & T. Clark.

Holmes, A. F. (1997), *Fact, Value and God*, Leicester: Apollos.

Jones, G. (2001), *Clones: The Clowns of Technology?* Carlisle: Paternoster Press.

Kaiser, W. (1983), *Toward Old Testament Ethics*, Grand Rapids: Zondervan.

Kraft, C. (1990), *Christianity With Power: Experiencing the Supernatural*, London: Marshall Pickering.

Linzey, A. and D. Yamamoto (1998), *Animals on the Agenda*, London: SCM Press.

Longenecker, R. N. (1984), *New Testament Social Ethics for Today*, Grand Rapids: Eerdmans.

Lovatt, M. F. W. (2001), *Confronting the Will to Power: A Reconsideration of the Theology of Reinhold Niebuhr*, Carlisle: Paternoster Press.

Marquis, D. (1997), 'An Argument that Abortion is Wrong', in H. LaFolette (ed.), *Ethics in Practice: An Anthology*, 91–102, Oxford: Blackwell.

Millar, G. (1998), *Now Choose Life: Theology and Ethics in Deuteronomy*, Leicester: Apollos.

Mitchell, B. (1987), 'Should the Law be Christian?' *The Month* (March): 95–99.

Moo, D. J. (1992), 'Law', in J. B. Green, S. McKnight and I. H. Marshall (eds.), *Dictionary of Jesus and the Gospels*, 450–461, Leicester: IVP.

Morriston, W. (n.d.), 'Must There Be a Standard of Moral Goodness Apart From God?' *Philosophia Christi* 2.3: 475–486, at http://stripe.colorado.edu/~morristo/goodness.html

O'Donovan, O. (1994), *Resurrection and Moral Order: An Outline for Evangelical Ethics*, 2nd ed., Leicester: Apollos.

Osborn, L. (1995), *Guardians of Creation: Nature and Theology in the Christian Life*, Leicester: Apollos.

Porter, J. (1999), *Natural and Divine Law: Reclaiming the Tradition for Christian Ethics*, Grand Rapids: Eerdmans.

Ricoeur, P. (1998), 'Biblical Time', in P. Ricoeur, *Figuring the Sacred: Religion, Narrative and Imagination*, 167–180, Minneapolis: Fortress Press.

Roberts, R. C. (1991), 'Virtues and Rules', *Philosophy and Phenomenological Research* 51.2: 325–343.

—— (1992), 'Emotions Among the Virtues of the Christian Life', *Journal of Religious Ethics* 20.1: 37–68.

—— (1995a), 'Kierkegaard, Wittgenstein and a Method of "Virtue Ethics"', in M. Matustik and M. Westphal (eds.), *Kierkegaard in Post/Modernity*, 142–166, Indiana: Indiana Press.

—— (1995b), 'Character', in D. J. Atkinson and D. H. Field (eds.), *New Dictionary of Christian Ethics and Pastoral Theology*, 65–71, Leicester: IVP.

—— (1999), 'Narrative Ethics', in P. L. Quinn and C. Taliaferro (eds.), *A Companion to the Philosophy of Religion*, 473–480, Oxford: Blackwell.

Rodd, C. (2001), *Glimpses of a Strange Land: Studies in Old Testament Ethics*, Edinburgh: T. & T. Clark.

Rogers, K. A. (2000), *Perfect Being Theology*, Edinburgh: Edinburgh University Press.

Schaeffer, F. (1970), *Pollution and the Death of Man,* Wheaton: Tyndale.

Smith, D. (1998), *Transforming the World? The Social Impact of British Evangelicalism*, Carlisle: Paternoster Press.

Spykman, G. J. (1992), *Reformational Theology: A New Paradigm for Doing Dogmatics*, Grand Rapids: Eerdmans.

Stevens, R. P. (1999), *The Abolition of the Laity: Vocation, Work and Ministry in a Biblical Perspective*, Carlisle: Paternoster Press.

Tomlin, G. (1999), *The Power of the Cross: Theology and the Death of Christ in Paul, Luther and Pascal*, Carlisle: Paternoster Press.

Van Leeuwen, R. (1990), 'Liminality and Worldview in Proverbs 1–9', *Semeia* 50: 111–144.

Walsh, B. and R. Middleton (1984), *The Transforming Vision: Shaping a Christian Worldview*, Downers Grove: IVP.

Webb, W. J. (2001), *Slaves, Women and Homosexuals: Exploring the Hermeneutics of Cultural Analysis*, Downers Grove: IVP.

Wells, S. (1998), *Transforming Fate Into Destiny: The Theological Ethics of Stanley Hauerwas*, Carlisle: Paternoster Press.

Wenham, G. J. (2000), *Story as Torah: Reading the Old Testament Ethically*, Edinburgh: T. & T. Clark.

White, V. (1996), *Paying Attention to People: an Essay on Individualism and Christian Belief*, London: SPCK.

Wolters, A. (1996), *Creation Regained*, Carlisle: Paternoster Press.

Wright, C. J. H. (1983), *Living as the People of God: The Relevance of Old Testament Ethics*, Leicester: IVP.

—— (1995), *Walking in the Ways of the Lord: The Ethical Authority of the Old Testament*, Leicester: Apollos.

Wright, N. T. (1992), *The New Testament and the People of God*, London: SPCK.

—— (1996), *Jesus and the Victory of God*, London: SPCK.

Zabzebski, L. (1998), 'The Virtues of God and the Foundations of Ethics', *Faith and Philosophy* 15.4: 438–453.

7. A CHRISTIAN WORLD-VIEW AND THE FUTURES OF EVANGELICALISM

Craig G. Bartholomew

Introduction

Writing in 1963, in the postscript to his well-known book, *The Christian Mind*, Harry Blamires posed the important question:

> will the Christians of the next fifty years, over against a strengthened secularism, deepen and clarify their Christian commitment in a withdrawn cultivation of personal morality and spirituality . . . Or will the Christians of the next fifty years deepen and clarify their Christian commitment at the intellectual and social levels too, meeting and challenging not only secularism's assault upon personal morality and the life of the soul, but also secularism's truncated and perverted view of the meaning of life and the purpose of the social order?[1]

Blamires posed the question in this way because as he looked around at the church of his day he discerned a real and lamentable

---

1. Blamires 1963: 189.

lack of a Christian mind, or what my title calls a Christian world-view. Blamires begins his book with these stirring words:

> There is no longer a Christian mind. There is still of course, a Christian
> ethic, a Christian practice, and a Christian spirituality . . . But as a
> thinking being, the modern Christian has succumbed to secularisation.
> He accepts religion . . . But he rejects the religious view of life, the view
> which sets all earthly issues within the context of the eternal, the view
> which relates all human problems – social, political, cultural – to the
> doctrinal foundations of the Christian Faith, the view which sees all
> things here below in terms of God's supremacy and earth's
> transitoriness, in terms of Heaven and Hell.[2]

There are still some years to go before the fifty-year time period
that Blamires refers to is up. Nevertheless, his *forward* look provides a useful springboard from which we can look back and ask
how evangelicalism has progressed in terms of the Christian mind
or world-view.[3] Before we do that, it is appropriate to pause and
ask, 'What is a Christian world-view or a Christian mind? And why
is the possession or lack thereof important?'

What is a (Christian) world-view?

The word 'world-view' is an English translation of the German
Weltanschauung, a word coined by the German philosopher Kant.[4]

---

2. Blamires 1963: 3, 4.
3. Some time before Blamires issued his challenge in the UK, Henry (1947)
   had issued a similar challenge to evangelicals in the USA. Henry critiques
   the world-flight pattern of older fundamentalism and encourages evangelicals to 'develop a competent literature in every field of study, on every
   level from the grade school through the university, which adequately presents each subject with its implications from the Christian as well as
   non-Christian points of view . . . Evangelicalism must contend for a fair
   hearing for the Christian mind, among other minds, in secular education.'
   Henry 1947: 70.
4. See Naugle 2002; Wolters 1983.

'World-view' became a common English word only well into the twentieth century as a way of referring to beliefs that underlie and shape all human action and thought. A world-view is thus about how we think about and live in the world. A world-view not only gives us a perspective on how the world is – its *descriptive* function – it also acts as a guide for how the world ought to be and how we ought to live in the world – its *normative* function. A *Christian* world-view is about how, from a Christian perspective, we think about and live in our Father's world.

Within evangelical circles, Francis Schaeffer probably did more than anyone else to waken evangelicals to their faith as a world-view.[5] It was particularly through his writings that I, as a young South African living in the midst of apartheid, began to see how utterly comprehensive is Christian faith. Since Schaeffer, evangelicals have developed the discussion about Christianity and world-view in a variety of ways. An excellent, accessible introduction to Christianity as a world-view and to other major world-views is James Sires' *The Universe Next Door*. Sire defines a world-view as a 'a set of presuppositions (assumptions that may be true, partially true or entirely false) which we hold (consciously or subconsciously, consistently or inconsistently) about the basic makeup of our world'.[6] The point of Sire's title is that within our pluralistic societies there are many different world-views, so that our neighbour may, as it were, be living in a different universe!

Among evangelical groupings, the Dutch neo-Calvinist or Kuyperian tradition has been a particularly fertile one for thinking about faith as a world-view.[7] And within this tradition the most significant book is Al Wolters' *Creation Regained*. Wolters defines a world-view as 'the comprehensive framework of one's basic beliefs about things'.[8] 'Things' is deliberately vague so as to include all that we might hold beliefs about, such as suffering, gender, family life,

---

5. For a recent assessment of Schaeffer's legacy see Hamilton 1997. For Schaeffer and world-view see Naugle 2002: 29–31.

6. Sire 1997: 16.

7. See Heslam 1998.

8. Wolters 1985: 2.

God, and so on. 'Beliefs' indicates that a world-view involves claims to know about the world, claims which are deep convictions (*basic*, i.e. ultimate convictions) and which one would try and defend with arguments if pushed on these issues. 'Framework' alerts us to the unifying and comprehensive nature of a world-view.

An implication of this approach is that part of what it means to be human is to have a world-view – God has made us such that we look at and interpret the world in a particular way and live in the light of this perspective. However, a world-view may not be *conscious*. A world-view is like a pair of glasses; we look through them at the world, and only rarely do we look at the glasses directly. Consequently it is easy to think that one sees the world in an unmediated fashion, until one becomes conscious that our perspective upon the world is always mediated through a world-view. Indeed, James Sire rightly argues that a service Christians can render is to help people become conscious of their world-view. In his writings Sire has developed a series of diagnostic questions that can help to foreground a person's or a community's world-view. These are questions such as the following:

- What is prime reality?
- What is the nature of the world around us?
- What does it mean to be human?
- What happens at death?
- Why is it possible to know anything at all?
- How do we tell what is right and wrong?
- What is history about?[9]

In recent years such an approach has been developed in a variety of ways, evidenced by evangelical exploration of academic disciplines and areas of life such as education, medicine, art, philosophy, psychology, economics and sociology. Among evangelicals world-view analysis has been adopted at a high theoretical and at very practical levels. In the UK, for example, Nick Pollard has used insights from world-view analysis to shape up a pre-evangelistic

---

9. Sire 1997: 17, 18.

approach to great effect among high school students.[10] He tells
the delightful story of one student going home to tell his parents
with great delight that he had discovered that he is an Epicurean
hedonist!

The approach outlined above suggests that a world-view is
central to Christianity. Not all evangelicals agree. However, it does
seem to me that the notion of a world-view is a core issue for
Christianity. The gospel is utterly comprehensive and embraces
the whole of life. This could be argued from a whole variety of
biblical angles, not least the doctrine of creation. Let us briefly
consider, however, the one who is utterly central to Christianity,
Christ.

In 1 Corinthians 12:1–3 Paul starts to instruct the Corinthians
about the issue of spiritual gifts, which was proving so divisive.[11]
To Christians who thought they were experts in this area, Paul tells
them he would not have them ignorant! The irony in 12:1 in this
respect would have been like a slap in the face to the Corinthian
readers.[12] For all their rhetoric about spiritual gifts, they had missed
the fundamental point that *the* mark of the Spirit is not the exercise
of gifts but the confession 'Jesus is Lord.'[13] This is the fundamental
gift of the Spirit to all Christians and the basis of Christian unity.

To ears sensitive to the Old Testament in its early Greek translation,[14] the image of Yahweh as creator and redeemer would come
to mind; Lord (= *kyrios* in Greek) translates *Yahweh*[15] some 6,000
times in the Septuagint.[16] Yahweh, as Exodus 3 and 6 indicate, is

---

10. For his philosophy of evangelism see Pollard 1997.

11. For a thorough overview of the different readings of 1 Cor. 12:1–3 see
    Thiselton 2000.

12. Witherington 1995: 256.

13. Cf. Rom. 10:9. Scholars rightly point out that the confession 'Jesus is Lord'
    was an established confessional formula from very early on, probably used
    at baptisms and in worship more generally. Cf. Cranfield 1979: 527.

14. The Septuagint, which was the early church's Old Testament.

15. The Hebrew Tetragrammaton is nowadays generally translated as 'LORD'.

16. See Cranfield 1979: 529 for the argument that this is the main background
    informing Paul's usage of *kyrios* in this context.

essentially the name of Israel's God as the one who rescues God's people from slavery and brings them to himself.[17] For citizens of the Roman Empire this confession would have had another polemical thrust to it. In the Roman Empire there was ultimately only one who could be called *kyrios*, namely Caesar. No citizen of the Empire would embark on a business initiative or set up a school without asking about Caesars regulations for that part of his Empire. The mark of the Spirit, however, is that one recognizes that there is one way above the Caesars of this world, who is truly *kyrios*.[18] Either way, this confession contains a huge view of Jesus as sovereign over all, over every area of creation. It is this insight that Abraham Kuyper expressed in his well-known statement that 'there is not a square inch of the whole of creation of which Christ does not rightly say, That is mine'. The mark of the Spirit, according to Paul, is that our lives are opened up from their centre to make this confession about Jesus, that he is *kyrios*!

This approach alerts us to three important aspects of a Christian world-view:

- First it is *Christocentric* and therefore it is
- second, utterly *comprehensive* in that it relates to the whole of life, for to be anything less would be to exhibit a deficient Christology. And
- third it is *communal*, for to possess the Spirit and make this marvellous confession is to be part of the body of Christ (cf. 1 Cor. 12:13).

It follows from this that the work of the Spirit in our lives yields a distinctive understanding of the world with Christ at the centre.

---

17. See Exod. 19:3–6.
18. Cranfield (1979: 527, 528) notes that the contrast with the use of *kyrios* as a title of the Roman emperor will have given to this confession a special significance, but that it would not have originated as a response to the confession 'Caesar is Lord.' The contrast with Caesar is clear and has very real public significance. See Wright 2002 for the current rediscovery of just how political Paul is.

This means that exploring how Christianity relates to the whole of life is normal, biblical Christianity and not some fad that a few eccentrics engage in. At heart a Christian world-view indicates that we serve a God who is Lord over all and that as his servants we seek to promote and do his will on earth, as it is done in heaven. Once we pause to reflect on the nature of our God – revealed in Christ – this becomes obvious. The logic is well and humorously captured by Hauerwas and Willimon: 'As one of our Jewish friends says, "Any God who won't tell you what to do with your pots and pans and genitals isn't worth worshiping."'[19]

And why is the possession or lack of a Christian world-view important?

Does a Christian world-view really matter? One meets evangelicals who become impatient with this kind of concern as though it is emphasizing secondary or marginal issues. Hasn't the church got enough to worry about? – dwindling numbers attending mainline churches and the need to make evangelism an absolute priority, the recovery of expository preaching in a day of 'sermonettes' breeding 'Christianettes', discipling Christians to read their Bibles and to witness to their faith in a secular culture, and so on and so forth. Evangelism, preaching and discipleship are all vital, but we betray a malformed or dualistic world-view if we pit these against a Christian world-view.

What gospel are we proclaiming in evangelism if it is not the message of the kingdom, which is about God's reign over all and the consummation of history in a new heavens and a new earth? And what Bible are we preaching if our sermons are not full of the story which moves from Eden to the new Jerusalem, from the garden to the city, from creation through fall, redemption and to final consummation? And what kind of discipleship are we doing if we fail to take every Christian seriously as a full-time servant of Christ, the only difference being where they are called to serve,

---

19. Hauerwas & Willimon 1999: 20.

in medicine, as a homemaker, in politics, economics or in the church?

Evangelism, preaching and discipleship are crucial activities, but our understanding of them will itself be shaped by our world-view. A world-view is a foundational framework and it affects our understanding of central church activities such as evangelism and discipleship – indeed it even influences the way we read the Scriptures.[20] There is thus much at stake in evangelicals appropriating a biblical, Christian world-view. Let me elaborate on just how important it is for Christians to appropriate and embody a Christian world-view.

First, *nothing less than God's glory in his creation is at stake!* In the Lord's Prayer we pray 'hallowed be your name, and your kingdom come – your will be done on earth as it is in heaven.' To hallow is to treat as special, and central to the Lord's Prayer is this petition that God's name, that is, his character, be treated appropriately by all his creatures. 'God's glory' speaks of the content of God's name, of the uniqueness of God, of his character as God, as the infinite Creator who inhabits eternity and is utterly distinct from the creation and creatures in this respect. What would it mean for God's name to be hallowed?

This request is elaborated on in the following request that his kingdom come. The kingdom of God/heaven is the reign or rule of God.[21] What this means is clarified in the words that follow – it would mean that God's will would be done on earth as in heaven. We know that heaven is the place where God's will is done perfectly and here we are given a vision of a world which mirrors that perfection, a world in which God is acknowledged in every area of life as he made it. This, as we know from Genesis, is what God always intended, and in the Lord's Prayer Christians commit themselves to pray and live in the context of this comprehensive, creation-wide perspective.

It is hard to see how Christians can take the Lord's Prayer seriously and neglect a Christian world-view and its implications.

---

20. For a fine example of this see Wolters 1984.
21. For the most through recent study see Wright 1992.

Furthermore, if we operate as though the service of Christ has only to do with church and evangelism narrowly understood, we effectively withdraw Christian involvement from large sectors of life as God has made it, thereby ensuring that God is not hallowed in large sectors of the creation. An example of a theology of withdrawal is the vocational pyramid that has operated in much evangelicalism. Crudely understood, this perspective maintains that if one is really committed to Christ then you become a missionary or a minister. Somewhat less committed and you enter medicine. Business comes further down the pyramid – its main use is to raise money for the church and to fish for souls. Art and sculpture contribute only marginally to church activities and so they come near the bottom of the pyramid. The disastrous effect of this theology has been to discourage Christians from seeing art, politics, economics, psychology and the like as legitimate fields of full-time service of the Lord Christ.

It follows from this, second, that *the well-being of creation is at stake*. Creation flourishes as it fulfils its God-given intentions. In God's good but fallen world the well-being of creation thus depends to a significant extent on the structures of creation being directed in obedience to God rather than in rebellion against God.[22] In our modern, Western democracies with their welfare nets and high standards of living it is too easy to forget the human cost of bad politics and disastrous economics.

The human cost of oppressive racism in apartheid South Africa is a good example of what happens in a society that goes in the wrong direction. Particularly after World War 2, the whole of South African society was increasingly shaped by racism, with the best jobs, wealth and education reserved for the white minority. The disastrous effects of this approach are well documented, not least in literature.[23] The extraordinary thing about apartheid South Africa was that some

---

22. For a helpful discussion on the structure–direction distinction that I make here see Wolters 1985: ch. 5.

23. A wealth of great literature has emerged from the South African experience. For example, for apartheid South Africa read Paton 1948, and for the difficulties of post-apartheid South Africa, Coetzee 2000.

77% of the population described themselves as Christians! Churches were full and massive amounts of evangelism and mission were being done. But we were in serious trouble as a nation:

- Every aspect of society was structured around skin colour.
- Terrible discrimination and oppression was being practised against 'non-whites' in the name of Christ.
- Evangelicals went to their Bible studies and to church. They were devout and energetic Christians but on the whole – apart from some important exceptions such as Michael Cassidy – they could not see that apartheid was a problem from a Christian perspective. Government was appointed by God (Rom. 13) and ours was Christian and gloriously anti-communist.

The Truth and Reconciliation Commission has brought to the surface some of the cost of apartheid to South Africa – death squads, torture, unending pain and darkness, and now the challenges of reconstruction in a country in which Christianity lacks credibility because of its racist past. If only evangelicals had woken up to the fact that Christianity is a world-view and one in which love of one's neighbour is utterly central, who knows what suffering and pain might have been averted? This is not for a moment to suggest that evangelicals are *the* key to setting God's creation right! The story of the church in South Africa is eloquent testimony to the fact that in the main it was Christians of other traditions who really saw the contradiction between apartheid and Christianity. However, if one believes, as I do, that evangelicalism is the closest contemporary expression of biblical Christianity, and if one takes account of the numerical growth of evangelicalism, then it really does matter whether or not evangelicals embody a faith that relates to all of life.

Twentieth-century recovery

Blamires, in his critique referred to at the outset, is not referring to evangelicals in particular, but there can be no doubt that evangelicalism has been deeply infected by this disease of cultivating personal morality and an individualistic spirituality while ignoring or even regarding as unspiritual the intellectual and the social. From one perspective evangelicalism has a great history of social involvement to draw upon: one naturally thinks of Jonathan Edwards, Shaftesbury – of whom Florence Nightingale said that if he was not reforming the lunatic asylums he would be in them! – Wilberforce, Booth, Spurgeon and the like. Nineteenth-century evangelicalism is an important study area in this respect, not only because of these colossal examples but also because it is in this period that the effect of the Enlightenment in Christian thinking really starts to take hold and evangelicalism faces immense intellectual and social challenges. Despite the serious attempts by theologians like James Denney and James Orr[24] – whose works are still eminently worth reading – evangelicalism was not up to this challenge and by the early twentieth century had withdrawn into a pietism of personal spirituality and evangelism far removed from the great social and intellectual movements of the day. David Smith points out just how serious this withdrawal had become:

> as these Scottish theologians were urging the necessity of addressing modern people in intelligible terms, the Cambridge University Christian Union was relying upon an American revivalist whose evangelism was characterized by an emotional sentimentality. As a soloist sang a song with the words, 'Tell Mother I'll be There,' Charles Alexander asked undergraduates to stand if they wished to meet their mothers in heaven . . . The Christian Union had clearly abandoned any attempt to speak the word of God meaningfully in a university permeated by secular thought and a mission which resorted to such frankly subjectivistic techniques was bound to confirm the intelligentsia in their belief that religious faith was irrational and impossible.[25]

It is really only in the second half of the twentieth century that evangelicalism began to recover a Christian mind, and that

---

24. Orr is extremely significant for Christian development of a world-view. See Naugle 2002: 6–13.

25. Smith 1998: 74.

through the labours of evangelicals like Carl Henry (USA), Francis Schaeffer (L'Abri, Switzerland), John Stott (UK), the Lausanne Congress on World Evangelization in 1974, and then through a smorgasbord of subsequent developments. The Lausanne Congress was of particular importance in this respect for worldwide evangelicalism:

> Certainly Lausanne signalled a public shift in mainline evangelical understanding of the relationship between evangelism and social concern. In this it was not original: thinking on this theme had been growing steadily since at least the publication of Carl Henry's *The Uneasy Conscience of Modern Fundamentalism* thirty years before, with its firm declaration that 'There is no room . . . for a gospel that is indifferent to the needs of the total man nor of the global man.' But Lausanne was the 'turning point,' 'the definitive step,' 'a watershed,' 'a catalyst' in which such views ceased, in all but the most right-wing circles, to smack of 'social gospel liberalism,' and became part of mainstream evangelical understanding of 'mission.'[26]

The Lausanne Covenant does not, of course, use the language of 'world-view.' It tackles the same issues, however, using the language of the relationship between evangelism and socio-political activity.[27] It remains, in my opinion, debatable as to whether or not these two categories are the best way to approach this issue,[28] but we should not underestimate the significant recovery of a vision for all of life that the Lausanne Congress signified for evangelicalism. Indeed, the extent of the shift became apparent at a follow-up meeting to Lausanne in which John Stott had to stand

---

26. Dudley-Smith 2001: 218.
27. Stott 1996: chs. 1 and 7, for the Lausanne Covenant and the 1982 Grand Rapids Report on the relationship between evangelism and social engagement.
28. My own view is that tackling this issue through the two categories of social concern and evangelism is in danger of building in a dichotomy into the discussion from the start.

his ground for this wider vision against Billy Graham and others who wanted to refocus on a narrower vision for 'evangelism'.[29] Fortunately the broader view triumphed. It is exemplified in Stott's superb *Christian Mission in the Modern World*, and Stott models the issues we need to tackle if we are to take this wider understanding seriously in *Issues Facing Christians Today* and in his establishment of the London Institute for Contemporary Christianity.[30]

How are we doing at the start of the twenty-first century?

Blamires wrote in 1963 – it is now some 40 years later – so how is evangelicalism doing? This is not an easy question to answer. Alister McGrath writes very positively about the future of evangelicalism.[31] David Wells and Mark Noll appear to be less optimistic. In his *No Place for Truth* Wells argues that evangelicals have allowed their confessional centre to dissipate and have abandoned doctrine in favour of 'life'.[32] Noll's *Scandal of the Evangelical Mind* is that there is little evidence of such a mind![33] The differences among these three authors may not, however, be as large as they appear at first sight.

In my opinion, there can be no doubt that in all sorts of ways tremendous progress has been made by evangelicals in terms of a Christian world-view. There is hardly an area of study or cultural life in which one can't find some serious evangelical writing, whether it be the arts, politics, literature, economics, family life, counselling or psychology.[34] Evangelicalism, not least in terms of world-view and cultural involvement, has experienced a major resurgence in the latter half of the twentieth century. Oliver Barclay relates this resurgence to four areas in particular:

---

29. See the fascinating description in Dudley-Smith 2001: 220–224.
30. Stott 1975; 1990; see also Dudley-Smith 2001: ch. 9.
31. See McGrath 1996 for example.
32. Wells 1993: 128, 131. For a response to Wells by McGrath see McGrath 2000.
33. Noll 1994.
34. A few examples are Jeffrey 1996; Harris 1993; Starkey 1995.

- A love of biblical doctrine reflected in the commitment to expository preaching.
- A commitment to finding the whole biblical outlook – a 'vision of the great biblical scheme from creation to eternity captured the evangelical community in a new way, and gave depth to both preaching and evangelism'[35] – that emerges from a study of the Bible.
- A new awareness of the need to love God with all our minds and to develop a Christian mind in relation to all areas of life: 'The old defensiveness was lost. They believed that there are Christian approaches to be worked out in every sphere, from academic theology to art, science, education and medicine, and in society. Evangelism and apologetics were greatly improved. Many were, by God's special blessing, converted and then well taught.'[36]
- The recovery of biblical themes like creation and providence gave Christians perspectives for dealing with the contemporary world of culture and society. 'A belief that "everything God created is good" (1 Tim. 4:4) enabled them to value the material world and to have an approach to the environment and to society. They recovered a responsibility to alter society for the better, which had been such a marked feature of the evangelicals of the early nineteenth century. In brief they arrived nearer to a biblically balanced position.'[37]

However, at the end of the twentieth century Barclay feels that all is not well in evangelical circles. Evangelicalism has become more respectable and has certainly made major strides in terms of cultural awareness and involvement, but Barclay fears that some evangelicalism is going soft on the Bible and fundamental doctrine. Barclay calls for evangelicals to be clear on and committed to the core Christian doctrines and to make these the basis of a Christian mind. Barclay's concerns at this point echo those of Wells.

---

35. Barclay 1997: 136.
36. Ibid.: 136.
37. Ibid.: 136, 137.

The difference between Blamires' context and ours can perhaps be summed up in one word: *postmodernism* – the word used to articulate the ethos of our culture at the start of the twenty-first century. If you ask anyone what time it is in our culture this is the response you are most likely to hear. Such analysis is a breathtaking case of painting on a large scale, but it does at least alert us to the fact that we operate in a different context with some different challenges to that of Schaeffer, for example.[38]

David Harvey's characterization of postmodernism is a useful way into a complex debate. He points out that whereas modernity rejected tradition and the security it provided, while hoping that reason would lead us to new truths and certainties, postmodernity no longer hopes that reason will lead us to Truth. Postmodernism is thus characterized by an undermining of old certainties, and an embrace of radical pluralism and flux. The spirit of 'cheerful nihilism' that pervades much postmodernism is captured in Neil Smith's statement that, 'The Enlightenment is dead, Marxism is dead, the working class movement is dead, . . . and the author does not feel very well either'![39] The result is that the following sorts of views are common currency:

- Objective truth, what Schaeffer called 'true truth', is unattainable.
- Cheerful nihilism – the view that we ought to live cheerfully and playfully without hoping to find true truth – is the right attitude to take.
- If an approach to life works for you that's great, but don't claim that it is true in any ultimate sense and don't impose it on me.
- Everyone comes at things from their own perspective – everyone has their own world-view, but we can't say that one world-view is better than another.

A factor that helps to explain the unease that Oliver Barclay feels about current evangelicalism is the diversity of evangelical

---

38. On postmodernity see Bartholomew 1997.
39. Smith 1984. Quoted in Harvey 1989.

responses to postmodernism. These range from the Reformed critique of Carson and Wells, to post-evangelicalism, to the sort of approach in Walsh and Middleton's *Truth is Stranger than it Used to Be* among many others.[40] It is clear that evangelicals are divided and fragmented in their response to postmodernism, and I agree with Barclay and Wells that there are some worrying signs of evangelicals capitulating to postmodernism and consumerism in surprising ways at the cost of the authority of Scripture and doctrinal truth.[41] It could be argued that, failure to be sufficiently critical of modernity[42] has made evangelicalism vulnerable to the powerful winds of postmodernism, with evangelicals either polarizing towards rational propositionalism or towards irrationalistic subjectivism. At the end of the twentieth century evangelicalism, for all its recovery of an interest in culture, has, in my opinion, shown a worrying tendency to be shaped by culture rather than shaping culture.[43]

This is not to say that all that is postmodern is bad. On the contrary, I believe that postmodernism provides evangelicalism with a great opportunity to forge ahead in shaping and incarnating a Christian mind. If evangelicalism is to retain and increase its concern with culture but do so with integrity, what ought its priorities to be?

The priority of a Christian world-view

Despite their different assessments of contemporary evangelicalism, McGrath, Noll and Wells all agree that development of a Christian mind or world-view should be a priority for evangelicals today. For all its strengths, McGrath agrees with Noll that evangelicalism needs to develop an evangelical mind and that in

---

40. Walsh & Middleton 1988; see also Lyon 1994; Grenz 1996; Erickson 2001, etc.

41. On consumerism see Bartholomew & Moritz 2000.

42. Wells 1993 focuses in particular upon evangelicalism and modernity.

43. Wells 1993; 1994 and 1998 are useful in exposing the dangerous tendency in evangelicalism to capitulate to some of the worst trends in contemporary culture.

order to do this we need an adequate theological vision.[44] Wells insists that 'Evangelicalism without a worldview is simply marketing with no purpose other than a desire for success and no criteria by which to judge the results other than mounting numbers of warm bodies.'[45] The church needs to recover its identity so that the cognitive dissident 'can return to a center and receive a fresh confirmation of his or her biblical worldview, a fresh understanding of the world and human life, fresh nourishment in believing, and a renewed connectedness with the people of God'.[46]

Missiology is one of the most exciting areas of theological study nowadays, and missiologists such as Lesslie Newbigin and David Bosch have done much to help Christians understand what it means to live as the people of God today. According to Bosch, the challenge of our time

> is not to talk about God in a culture that has become irreligious, but how to express, ethically, the coming of God's reign, how to help people respond to the real questions of their context, how to break with the paradigm according to which religion has to do only with the private sphere . . . This is not to suggest that we will build God's kingdom on earth. It is not ours to inaugurate, but we can help make it more visible, more tangible; we can initiate approximations of God's coming reign.[47]

Bosch rightly picks up on the kingdom of God as the central theme of Jesus' ministry (cf. Mark 1:14, 15). If, as Bosch says, the church's role in mission is to point to and to embody the reign/kingdom of God, what are the particular challenges of this for us at our time and place? 'What is it,' asks David Bosch, 'that we have to communicate to the Western "post-Christian" public? It seems to me that we must demonstrate the role that plausibility structures, or rather, worldviews, play in people's lives.'[48]

---

44. McGrath 1996: 9.
45. Wells 1994: 221.
46. Ibid.: 226.
47. Bosch 1995: 35.
48. Ibid.: 48.

There is thus widespread agreement that the urgent need of our time is a vibrant Christian community which is articulate in its understanding of the Christian mind and is prayerfully working together at embodying such a perspective in our world in all areas of life. How might this be taken further?

Different Christian world-views?

As one thinks through these issues it is important to realize that there is not one Christian world-view that all Christians agree upon. Historically, a variety of Christian perspectives upon the world have developed. If by 'culture' we mean the way human societies order their life, then another way of getting at the nature of a world-view is to ask how Christ relates to culture. This is H. Richard Niebuhr's approach in his classic *Christ and Culture*.[49] Niebuhr argues that there are five basic ways in which Christians have understood the relationship between Christ and culture:

- Christ *against* culture – this approach is intensely aware of how fallen cultures are and argues that Christians need to withdraw from secular cultures and witness to the world as an alternative group. Much anti-cultural evangelicalism has been of this sort.
- Christ *of* culture – in contrast to the above model, this approach is so impressed with the cultures of our day that it thinks the gospel can easily fit in with and develop all that is good in our cultures. This approach has little sense of the conflict between the gospel and human culture and easily accommodates Christ to our culture.
- *Churches of the Centre* – Niebuhr recognizes that few Christians nowadays would argue for either of these two extreme views. Most Christians try and understand the Christ–culture relationship in a more integrated way. Niebuhr calls these Christians 'Churches of the Centre'. Among them he discerns the following three approaches to the Christ–culture relationship:

---

49. Niebuhr 1951.

- Christ *above* culture – this approach thinks of nature as supplemented and fulfilled by grace. Aquinas and traditional Catholics represent this view.
- Christ and culture *in paradox* – according to this view, Christ and culture are a duality in which both have authority but are in tension with each other. Luther is an example of this approach.
- Christ *the transformer of culture* – this view argues that as a result of sin God's good creation has been corrupted by being misdirected, and that redemption leads to the healing / proper directing of culture.

If evangelicals are to develop a Christian worldview then they will have to work hard on the shape of a Christian world-view – how, for example, should we understand the Christ–culture relationship? Are Niebuhr's categories adequate? And so on and so forth. At present many evangelicals are finding the sort of Anabaptist world-view defended by Yoder, Hauerwas, Hays and Clapp very attractive with its strong sense of antithesis between Christianity and contemporary Western culture. We do not have time to explore that debate further here, but suffice it to say that, in my opinion, Niebuhr's transformational paradigm is the most biblical. I am, of course, assuming here that one expects the Bible to present or norm a coherent world-view, an assumption that many biblical scholars would question.[50]

---

50. Historical critics have long held that the Bible is full of conflicting traditions. Clements (1992: 142) says, for example, of Old Testament wisdom that it does not lead us 'to conclude that there existed, either in Israel, or in the spheres of Mesopotamia or Egyptian life any single agreed worldview that was embraced by wisdom'. The assumption here is that the Bible does express a consistent perspective upon reality or what we might call a world-view, and that Wolters (1991: 237) is correct in maintaining that '[b]iblical faith in fact involves a worldview, at least implicitly and in principle. The central notion of creation (a *given* order of reality), fall (human mutiny at the root of all perversion of the given order) and redemption (unearned restoration of the order in Christ) are cosmic and

The major reason for seeing the transformational Christian world-view as the most biblical is the justice it does to the comprehensive nature of Christianity. For unique to this world-view is its comprehensive understanding of creation, fall, redemption and consummation. As Wolters says:

> One way of seeing this difference is to use the basic definition of the Christian faith given by Herman Bavinck: 'God the Father has reconciled His created but fallen world through the death of His Son, and renews it into a Kingdom of God by His Spirit.' The reformational worldview takes all the key terms in this ecumenical, trinitarian confession in a universal, all-encompassing sense. The terms 'reconciled,' 'created,' 'fallen,' 'world,' 'renews,' and 'Kingdom of God' are held to be cosmic in scope. In principle, nothing apart from God himself falls outside the range of these foundational realities of biblical religion. All other Christian worldviews, by contrast, restrict the scope of each of these terms in one way or another.[51]

The authority of Scripture

I agree with Barclay and Wells that we need to recover a strong sense of the primary authority of Scripture and the secondary authority of the confessions today. However, far too often we seems to be in a situation where some evangelicals are strong on Scripture and the confessions but have little to contribute outside of a narrow focus on church and theology, and others are very *avant garde* but seem to have drifted from their scriptural moorings. It is surely true that confessing the authority of Scripture without relating it to all of our lives is not very helpful, just as being immersed in contemporary culture without living under the authority of God's Word is downright dangerous.

---

transformational in their implications. Together with other basic elements ... these central ideas ... give believers the fundamental outline of a completely anti-pagan *Weltanschauung*, a worldview which provides the interpretive framework for history, society, culture, politics, and everything else that enters human experience.'

51. Wolters 1985: 10.

At a local church level there is still a long way to go in helping preachers and church members recover a Christian mind. So much preaching fails to strike a comprehensive, kingdom note that extends across the whole of God's creation and embraces every aspect of the lives of its members.[52] This is not for a moment to suggest that the preacher should be an expert in every area of life, but it is to insist that the Word, rightly preached, calls for Christians to bring all of their lives under the Lordship of Christ. Worship, in the biblical sense of the only appropriate response to what God has done in Christ (cf. Rom. 12:1, 2), begins or at least continues when we leave the church door, and we ought to know that far more than we do. The church urgently needs to recover the Bible as a story, telling of the way from creation to re-creation, from a garden to a city, and that story needs to shape our reading of the individual texts so that when they are preached our congregations are hearing the call of the kingdom.[53]

We urgently need a Christian world-view that will take us wide and deep into contemporary culture at a practical and theoretical level, but which is thoroughly biblical and confessionally orthodox. This means that evangelicals need to make the following questions a matter of intense focus:

- How do we read the Bible as a whole, and how do we read it for the whole of life?

We need to rediscover what Scripture does *and* does not do. It seems to me that evangelicals often expect too much or too little from the Bible. Either we expect it to provide answers to questions it does not address, such as how do we counsel victims of rape. Or we expect too little when we think it has nothing to contribute to questions like the one just mentioned. Effective counselling needs to know far more than the Bible provides – one would need all the

---

52. Every pastor should read and reread Peterson (1998: 75–77) for a marvellous and timely articulation of the full-time service of all believers.

53. In a forthcoming book, *At Home in the Scriptures* (Baker), M. Goheen and C. Bartholomew seek to articulate the shape of the biblical story for first year undergraduates.

data available about rape and its effects and the experience of other counsellors in this area. But, of course, this needs to be interpreted through a Christian, biblical understanding of the world, sin and the human person.

- How does Scripture provide us with or authorize a world-view?

I am thinking here of the move from Scripture as a sprawling, capacious narrative to the more abstract contours of a world-view. Do elements such as theology and philosophy come in to play as we make this move, and from where do we get them?

- How do we move from Scripture through a world-view to issues like art, education and politics?

If we take a Christian world-view seriously, then work will need to be done in all the disciplines at the highest level, and a Christian perspective will need to be incarnated in practice with rigour. In practice and in theory, the journey to and from Scripture will have to made in an ongoing fashion, whether we serve in psychology, business, education, politics, homemaking or any other area, and this relationship to Scripture will have to made with integrity. Indeed, if we are going to relate Scripture to cultural and intellectual life in a serious way, we will need a conceptual apparatus to facilitate such a connection.[54] Evangelicals need to work far harder on the development of an appropriate conceptual apparatus for such work.

An adequate spirituality for the journey

Eugene Peterson, Dallas Willard, Joyce Huggett and many others have helped evangelicals recover a robust spirituality. It is vital, in this respect, to remember that spirituality is utterly central to a Christian world-view. No one articulates the dangers of a scholastic

---

54. O'Donovan (1996) rightly insists that to relate the Bible to politics we need more than an understanding of the Bible as story, we also need concepts arising from the story that will do the theoretical work in political theology. Wright (1992) is an excellent example of the positive role world-view can play in renewing a discipline, in this case New Testament studies.

world-view severed from roots in a living faith more strongly than Thomas Merton:

> It is not enough for meditation to investigate the cosmic order and situate me in this order. Meditation is something more than gaining command of a *Weltanschauung* (a philosophical view of the cosmos and of life) . . . such a meditation may be out of contact with the deepest truths of Christianity. It consists in learning a few rational formulas, explanations, . . . we should let ourselves be brought naked and defenceless into the center of that dread where we stand alone before God in our nothingness, without explanation, without theories, completely dependent upon his providential care, in dire need of the gift of his grace, his mercy and the light of faith.[55]

Merton rightly warns of the danger of a world-view becoming lifeless and scholastic. As evangelicals wake up to the comprehensive range of Christian faith, it is important that they do not forget that a world-view without a living faith at its heart is dysfunctional. Eugene Peterson has written most helpfully about a spirituality for pastors – this kind of work needs to be developed for all vocations. As Peterson himself notes, 'It is no more difficult to pursue the pastoral vocation than any other. Vocations in homemaking, science, agriculture, education, and business when embraced with biblically informed commitments are likewise demanding and require an equivalent spirituality. *But each requires its own specific attention.*'[56] Very little has yet been written helping Christians in different professions to develop spiritualities adequate for their particular journeys in life. Much work remains to be done in this respect.

Conclusion

As Barclay rightly notes:

> Having a Christian mind is not an optional extra for the learned; it is to have our outlook transformed by the biblical revelation, and much of

---

55. Merton 1969: 85.
56. Peterson 1992: 4. Italics mine.

that is doctrine . . . Anti-intellectualism and an anti-doctrinal stance are emphatically not what the Bible requires of us, and their dangers are evident today, as they have been in past history when people rely on what they feel is right.[57]

Evangelicalism has come a long way since the start of the twentieth century, but its future is not assured. A priority should be the further development and practice of a Christian world-view. A rich legacy in this respect has been bequeathed to us by Orr, Kuyper, Schaeffer, Henry, Stott and others. We should receive this with gratitude and build upon it.

Bibliography

Barclay, O. R. (1997), *Evangelicalism in Britain 1935–1995: A Personal Sketch*, Leicester, IVP.

Bartholomew, C. G. (1997), 'Post/Late? Modernity as the Context for Christian Scholarship Today', *Themelios* 22.2: 25–38. (Also published in abbreviated form in *Catalyst* 24.3 (1998): 4–6.)

Bartholomew, C. G. and T. Moritz (2000), *Christ and Consumerism*, Carlisle: Paternoster Press.

Blamires, H. (1963), *The Christian Mind*, London: SPCK.

Bosch, D. (1995), *Believing in the Future: Towards a Missiology of Western Culture*, Philadelphia: Trinity Press International; London: Gracewing.

Clements, R. E. (1992), *Wisdom in Theology*, Grand Rapids: Eerdmans; Carlisle: Paternoster Press.

Coetzee, J. M. (2000), *Disgrace*, Maryland: Penguin.

Cranfield, C. E. B. (1979), *A Critical and Exegetical Commentary on the Epistle to the Romans, Volume II*, Edinburgh: T. & T. Clark.

Dudley-Smith, T. (2001), *John Stott: A Global Ministry*, Leicester: IVP.

Erickson, M. J. (2000), *Truth or Consequences: The Promise and Perils of Postmodernity*, Downers Grove: IVP.

Grenz, S. (1996), *A Primer on Postmodernism*, Grand Rapids: Eerdmans.

---

57. Barclay 1997: 126.

Hamilton, M. S. (1997), 'The Dissatisfaction of Francis Schaeffer', *Christianity Today* 3: 22–30.

Harris, P. (1993), *Under the Bright Wings*, Vancouver: Regent College Publishing.

Harvey, D. (1989), *The Condition of Postmodernity*, Oxford: Blackwell.

Hauerwas, S. and W. H. Willimon (1999), *The Truth about God: The Ten Commandments in Christian Life*, Nashville: Abingdon.

Henry, C. F. (1947), *The Uneasy Conscience of Modern Fundamentalism*, Grand Rapids: Eerdmans.

Heslam, P. S. (1998), *Creating a Christian Worldview: Abraham Kuyper's Lectures on Calvinism*, Grand Rapids: Eerdmans; Carlisle: Paternoster Press.

Jeffrey, D L. (1996), *People of the Book: Christian Identity and Literary Culture*, Grand Rapids: Eerdmans.

Lyon, D. (1994), *Postmodernity*, Concepts in the Social Sciences, Buckingham: Open University Press.

McGrath, A. (1996), *A Passion for the Truth: The Intellectual Coherence of Evangelicalism*, Leicester: Apollos.

—— (2000), 'Evangelical Theological Method: The State of the Art', in J. G. Stackhouse (ed.), *Evangelical Futures: A Conversation on Theological Method*, 15–37, Grand Rapids: Baker; Leicester: Apollos.

Merton, T. (1969), *Contemplative Prayer*, London: Darton, Longman & Todd.

Naugle, D. K. (2002), *Worldview: The History of a Concept*, Grand Rapids: Eerdmans.

Niebuhr, H. Richard (1951), *Christ and Culture*, New York: Harper & Row.

Noll, M. A. (1994), *The Scandal of the Evangelical Mind*, Grand Rapids: Eerdmans.

O'Donovan, O. (1996), *The Desire of the Nations: Rediscovering the Roots of Political Theology*, Cambridge: Cambridge University Press.

Paton, A. (1948), *Cry the Beloved Country*, London: Cape.

Peterson, E. (1992), *Under the Unpredictable Plant: An Exploration in Vocational Holiness*, Grand Rapids: Eerdmans.

—— (1998), *The Wisdom of Each Other: A Conversation Between Spiritual Friends*, Grand Rapids: Zondervan.

Pollard, N. (1997), *Evangelism Made Slightly Less Difficult: How to Interest People Who Aren't Interested*, Leicester: IVP.

Sire, J. (1997), *The Universe Next Door: A Basic Worldview Catalog*, 3rd ed., Downers Grove and Leicester: IVP.

Smith, D. W. (1998), *Transforming the World: The Social Impact of British Evangelicalism*, Carlisle: Paternoster Press.

Smith, N. (1984), *Uneven Development: Nature, Capital and the Production of Space*, New York: Blackwell.

Stott, J. R. W. (1975), *Christian Mission in the Modern World*, repr. Eastbourne: Kingsway, 1986.

—— (1990), *Issues Facing Christians Today*, 2nd ed., London: Marshalls.

Stott, J. R. W. (ed.) (1996), *Making Christ Known: Historic Mission Documents from the Lausanne Movement 1974–1989*, Carlisle: Paternoster Press.

Thiselton, A. C. (2000), *The First Epistle to the Corinthians: A Commentary on the Greek Text*, Grand Rapids: Eerdmans; Carlisle: Paternoster Press.

Walsh, B. J. and J. R. Middleton (1988), *The Transforming Vision: Shaping a Christian Worldview*, Downers Grove: IVP.

Wells, D. F. (1993), *No Place for Truth, or, Whatever Happened to Evangelical Theology?* Grand Rapids: Eerdmans; Leicester: IVP.

—— (1994), *God in the Wasteland: The Reality of Truth in a World of Fading Dreams*, Grand Rapids: Eerdmans; Leicester: IVP.

—— (1998), *Losing Our Virtue: Why the Church Must Recover its Moral Vision*, Grand Rapids: Eerdmans; Leicester: IVP.

Witherington III, B. (1995), *Conflict and Community in Corinth: A Socio-Rhetorical Commentary on 1 and 2 Corinthians*, Grand Rapids: Eerdmans; Carlisle: Paternoster Press.

Wolters, A. (1984), 'Nature and Grace in the Interpretation of Proverbs 31:10–31', *Calvin Theological Journal* 19: 153–166, reprinted in Wolters, 2001.

—— (2001), *The Song of the Valiant Woman: Studies in the Interpretation of Proverbs 31:10–31*, Carlisle: Paternoster Press.

—— (1985), *Creation Regained: Biblical Basics for a Reformational Worldview*, Grand Rapids: Eerdmans; Leicester: IVP.

—— (1991), 'Gustavo Gutierrez', in S. Klapwijk et al. (eds.), *Bringing Into Captivity Every Thought*, 229–240, Lanham, MD: University Press of America.

Wright, N. T. (1992), *The New Testament and the People of God*, Minneapolis: Fortress.

—— (2002), 'Paul and Caesar: A New Reading of Romans', in C. Bartholomew, J. Chaplin, R. Song and A. Wolters (eds.), *A Royal Priesthood? The Use of the Bible Ethically and Politically: A Dialogue with Oliver O'Donovan*, Grand Rapids: Zondervan; Carlisle: Paternoster Press.

Recommended reading (+ = best introductory works)

+ Colson, C. and N. Pearcey, *How Now Shall we Live?*, Wheaton: Tyndale, 1999.

+ Harris, P., *Under the Bright Wings*, Vancouver: Regent College Publishing, 1993.

Heslam, P. S., *Creating a Christian Worldview: Abraham Kuyper's Lectures on Calvinism*, Grand Rapids: Eerdmans; Carlisle: Paternoster Press, 1998.

Holmes, A., *Contours of a World View*, Grand Rapids: Eerdmans, 1983.

Naugle, D. K., *Worldview: The History of a Concept*, Grand Rapids: Eerdmans, 2002.

Noll, M. A., *The Scandal of the Evangelical Mind*, Grand Rapids: Eerdmans, 1994.

+ Schaeffer, E., *The Tapestry: The Life and Times of Francis and Edith Schaeffer*, Texas: Word, 1981.

+ Sire, J., *The Universe Next Door: A Basic Worldview Catalog*, 3rd ed., Downers Grove and Leicester: IVP, 1997.

Walsh, B. J. and J. R. Middleton, *The Transforming Vision: Shaping a Christian Worldview*, Downers Grove: IVP, 1988.

+ Wolters, A., *Creation Regained: Biblical Basics for a Reformational Worldview*, Grand Rapids: Eerdmans; Leicester: IVP, 1985.

8. EVANGELICAL SPIRITUALITY

Eugene H. Peterson

'Spirituality' is a net, that thrown into the sea of contemporary culture, pulls in a vast quantity of spiritual fish, rivalling the resurrection catch of 153 'large fish' that St John reports (John 21:11)[1]. In our times 'spirituality' has become a major business for entrepreneurs, a recreational sport for the bored, and for others, whether many or few, it's hard to tell, a serious and disciplined commitment to live deeply and fully in relation to God.

Once used exclusively in traditional religious contexts, the word is now used indiscriminately by all sorts of people in all sorts of circumstances and with all sorts of meanings. The attempt to reclaim the word for exclusively Christian, or other religious usage, usually begins with a definition. But attempts to define 'spirituality', and they are many, are futile. The term has escaped the disciplines of the dictionary.

Evangelical spirituality in this setting is not a particular brand of spirituality, but rather an impulse or concern to harness and direct

---

1. Biblical quotations in this chapter are from the NRSV.

the already seething energies of spirituality that are everywhere in evidence, harness them in biblical leather and direct them in following Jesus. The adjective 'evangelical' doesn't define a distinctive form of spirituality that sets it apart from all others; it seeks to provide biblical clarity and gospel focus. When spirituality develops élitist postures, or quits reading its basic spirituality text, the holy Scriptures, or lets the culture set its agenda, or becomes theologically amnesiac, the evangelical impulse, energetic in most denominations and movements, calls us home and articulates an insistence that the Christian life must be lived on God's terms as revealed in the Word and created by the Spirit.

I will employ two stories, three texts, two terms, and a dance to show how the evangelical impulse serves contemporary Christian spirituality in the four critical areas: two stories to return our feet to common ground so that we live humbly (countering élitism); three texts that define a scriptural foundation (countering self-helpism) so that we live obediently; two terms that provide gospel foci for living accurately (countering cultural fuzziness); and a dance to bring theology prominently into the action so that we live largely (countering a secular horizon).

The two stories

Spirituality, the way it is often understood and practiced in our culture, often develops airs of élitism – a way of life practised by advanced Christians. Nothing could be further from the truth. We are all beginners in this business and never cease being beginners.

Story is the most natural way of enlarging and deepening our sense of reality and then enlisting us as participants in it. Stories open doors to areas or aspects of life that we didn't know were there, or had quit noticing out of over-familiarity, or supposed were out-of-bounds to us. They then welcome us in. Stories are verbal acts of hospitality. St John tells two stories early in his Gospel that definitively welcome all into the Christian life.

The first is the story of Nicodemus, a Jewish rabbi (John 3). Nervous about his reputation, he came to talk with Jesus under cover of darkness. He would have lost credibility with his rabbi colleagues if it became known that he was consulting this disreputable itinerant teacher, this loose prophetic cannon out of the no-place Nazareth in Galilee, out of nowhere. So he came to Jesus by night. He came, it seems, simply to get acquainted, opening the conversation by complimenting Jesus, 'Rabbi, we know that you are a teacher who has come from God; for no one can do these signs that you do apart from the presence of God' (John 3:2).

But Jesus discerned an agenda, a yet unspoken question; Nicodemus was after something. And so Jesus dismissed the introductory small talk and got down to business; he read Nicodemus's heart and addressed himself to that: 'Very truly I tell you, no one can see the kingdom of God without being born from above' (John 3:3). So that is why Nicodemus was there, to inquire about getting into the kingdom of God, living under the rule of God, participating in the reality of God. That's odd.

Odd, because this is the kind of thing in which Nicodemus was supposed to be an expert. So why is he sneaking around, having a clandestine conversation with Jesus? Was it out of humility? That is plausible. Leaders who are looked up to constantly, who give out answers competently, whom everyone assumes are living what they are saying, often have acute experiences of dissonance: 'Who I am and what people think I am aren't anywhere close to being the same thing. The better I get as a rabbi and the more my reputation grows, the more I feel like a fraud. I know so much more than I live. The longer I live, the more knowledge I acquire, the wider the gap between what I know and what I live. I'm getting worse by the day . . .'

So perhaps it was this deep sense of unease, grounded in a true humility, that brought Nicodemus that night to Jesus. He wasn't looking for theological information but for a way in, not for anything more about the kingdom of God but for a personal guide/friend to show him the door and lead him in: 'How do I enter . . . ?'

Or was he there simply out of curiosity? This is also plausible. Leaders, if they are to maintain their influence, have to stay ahead of the competition, have to keep up with the trends, know what sells best in the current market. Jesus was attracting an enormous amount of attention these days – so what's his angle? what's his secret? how does he do it? Nicodemus was good at his work, but he knew he couldn't simply rest on his laurels. The world was changing fast. Israel was in a vortex of cultures – Greek learning and Roman government and Jewish moral traditions mixed in with gnostic sects, mystery cults, terrorist bands, and assorted messianic adventurers and fanatics. The mix changed weekly. Nicodemus had to be alert to every shift in the wind if he was going to keep his leadership out in front and on course. Jesus was the latest attraction and so Nicodemus was there that night to dig out some useful piece of strategy or lore. This is also plausible.

But our interest in teasing out the motive that brought Nicodemus to Jesus is not shared by the story-teller, St John. There is no authorial interest in motive here; this is a story about Jesus, not Nicodemus. Jesus does not question Nicodemus's motives and St John does not explore them. After the brief opening gambit, Jesus seizes the initiative by introducing a startling, attention-demanding metaphor, 'born again' or 'born from above': '. . . I tell you, no one can see the kingdom of God without being born from above' (John 3:3); and then, before Nicodemus can so much as catch his breath, Jesus adds another metaphor, even odder than the first, '. . . I tell you, no one can enter the kingdom of God without being born of water and Spirit' (John 3:5). Wind, Breath and Spirit are the same word in the Aramaic that Jesus presumably spoke and also the Greek that St John wrote. The necessity in those languages of using the same term for the movement of air caused by a contraction of the lungs, the movement of air caused by a shift in barometric pressure, and the life-giving movement of the living God in us, required an exercise of the imagination every time the word was used: What's being talked about here, breathing or weather or God?

No sooner have we asked the question than St John clarifies matters by putting the literal and the metaphorical side by side: 'The wind [*pneuma*] blows where it chooses, and you hear the sound of it, but you do not know where it comes from or where it goes. So it is with everyone who is born of the Spirit' [*pneuma*] (John 3:8). But then he complicates it even further by throwing in another metaphor, 'born', creating one of Jesus' most memorable sentences.

Nicodemus shakes his head. He doesn't get it.

Another story follows, this one of the Samaritan woman. This story takes place not at night as with Nicodemus, but in broad daylight by Jacob's Well in Samaria. Jesus is sitting alone when the woman comes to get water. Jesus opens the conversation by asking for a drink. The woman is surprised even to be spoken to by this man, this Jew, for there were centuries of religious bad blood between the two ethnic groups.

She is surprised, but is she also wary? Do we detect an edge to her voice in her reply, 'How is it that you, a Jew, ask a drink from me, a woman of Samaria?' (John 4:9). Does she mistrust this man sitting at the well? It would seem she had good reason to. She is a woman hard-used by life. Later in the narrative we will find that she has been married five times and is now living with a sixth man without benefit of marriage. It is not difficult to conjure up a scenario of serial rejections, multiple failures, a year after year accumulation of wounds and scars in mind and body. For her, to be a woman is to be a victim. To be near a man is to be near danger. What is this stranger going to do next, say next? Her guard is up.

Or is it just the opposite? Maybe that was not mistrust we detected in her question, but a teasing flirtatiousness. Maybe she is on the hunt. Maybe she used up those five husbands, one after another, and is now working her seductive ways on this sixth. Maybe she sees men as opportunities for gratification or access to power or advancement, and when they no longer serve her pride or ambition or lust she dumps them. It is entirely possible that from the moment she saw Jesus she began calculating strategies of seduction: 'Well, this is a nice surprise! Let's see what I can get out of this one.'

We love playing these little games, don't we? Filling in the blanks, guessing at the reality behind the appearances, getting the inside scoop on people's lives. But again, just as in the Nicodemus story, Jesus shows no interest in playing the game and John shows no interest in exploring motives. He takes her just as he finds her, no questions asked. We realize that, as before with Nicodemus, this is a story not about the woman but about Jesus.

After the opening conversational exchange at the well, Jesus starts talking in riddles: 'If you knew the gift of God, and who it is that is saying to you, "Give me a drink," you would have asked him, and he would have given you living water' (John 4:10). Soon it becomes clear to us that Jesus is using the word 'water' as a metaphor with the Samaritan, just as he used 'wind' as a metaphor with Nicodemus. The word 'water' that started out by referring to well water pulled up by a bucket is now being used to refer to something quite different, something interior, 'a spring of water gushing up [in them] to eternal life' (John 4:14). And then the earlier Nicodemus metaphor is added: 'God is spirit, and those who worship him must worship in spirit and truth' (John 4:24). 'Spirit' again, the word that connects our sensory experience of breath and wind with the nature and activity of God.

Then, just as the conversation is on the brink of degenerating into a squabble over where to worship, Jesus' words suddenly create a new reality in which God takes the centre ground. And the woman gets it. She makes the connection between things she knows about messiah and what Jesus says to her, what he is to her. She is converted on the spot.

The striking things about these two stories, set in parallel as they are by St John, is that God's Spirit is at the heart of the action: the aliveness of God, the creating presence of God, the breath breathed into our lives just as it was breathed into Adam, the breath that makes us alive in ways that biology can neither command nor account for.

There is a corresponding feature: the stories taken together insist on common ground accessibility. The unfortunate connotation that often accompanies the contemporary use of the word 'spiritual' – a tinge of élitism, the insinuation that only a select or in-the-know few can get in on it, is abolished. These two stories dismiss even a hint of it. The God-breathed life is common, totally accessible across the whole spectrum of the human condition. We are welcomed into life, period. There are no preconditions.

This realization of generous welcome is achieved first of all by the choice of vocabulary. The introductory metaphors in each story are completely accessible, everyone knows the words without using a dictionary; they come out of ordinary life. With Nicodemus it is 'birth'; with the Samaritan it is 'water'. We all have sufficient experience of those two words to know what is going on without further instruction. The metaphor common to both stories, wind/breath, is also plain. We all know what birth is: our being here is proof that we were born. We all know what water is: we drink or wash with it several times a day. We all know what wind/breath is: blow on your hand, take a deep breath, look at the leaves blowing in the breeze.

And then there are these features:

The first story is about a man, the second about a woman. There is no preferred gender in the Christian life.

The first story takes place in the city, the centre of sophistication and learning and fashion; the second in the country of small towns. Geography has no bearing on perception or aptitude.

Nicodemus is a respectable member of a strictly orthodox sect of the Pharisees; the Samaritan woman is a disreputable member of the despised heretical sect of the Samaritans. Racial background, religious identity and moral performance are neither here nor there in matters of spirituality.

The man is named, the woman is unnamed. Reputation and standing in the community don't seem to count for anything.

There is also this: Nicodemus opens the conversation with Jesus with a religious statement, 'Rabbi, we know that you are a teacher who has come from God' (John 3:2). Jesus opens the conversation with the woman with a question that doesn't sound the least bit religious, asking for a drink of water. It doesn't seem to make any difference in the Christian life who gets things started, Jesus or us, or what the subject-matter is, heavenly or earthly.

And in both stories a reputation is put at risk: Nicodemus risks his reputation by being seen with Jesus; Jesus risks his reputation by being seen with the Samaritan woman. There is an element of daring here on both sides, a crossing of the lines of caution, a willingness on both sides to be misunderstood. When we get close to the heart of things, we aren't dealing with assured results or conventional behaviour.

So: a man and a woman, city and country, an outsider and an insider, a professional and a layperson, a respectable man and a disreputable woman, an orthodox and a heretic, one who takes initiative and one who lets it be taken, one named and the other anonymous, human reputation at risk and divine reputation at risk.

There is also this: In both conversations 'spirit' is the pivotal word. 'Spirit' links the differences and contrasts in the two stories and makes them aspects of one story. In both conversations 'spirit' refers primarily to God and only derivatively to the man and the woman: In the first conversation the Spirit gives birth ('So it is with everyone who is born of the Spirit', John 3:8); Spirit is an agent, a source, a cause of the birth that makes a person able to 'see' and to 'enter' (both verbs are used in the conversation); in the second conversation, God is spirit; the consequence is that we worship him in spirit and truth, that is, according to who he is not as we want him to be. It is only because God is spirit that there is anything to say about what we do or don't do.

Finally, there is this: Jesus is the primary figure in both stories. Although Nicodemus and the Samaritan provide the occasion, it is Jesus who provides the content. In everything that has to do with living, the large context in which everything that we do and say takes place, Jesus is working at the centre. Jesus is far more active than any one of us; it is Jesus who makes it happen.

We are not used to this. For us, 'spiritual', the adjective formed off the activity of God's Holy Spirit, is commonly used to describe our moods or traits or desires or accomplishments. The unhappy result is that the word has become hopelessly garbled. These two stories rescue us from our confusion. We will no longer consult our own experiences or feelings or performance or those of our friends as we study the ways of God among us in Jesus Christ and the ways we are welcomed into those ways. We will start with these stories and make a clearing in which to stand. To begin with we have removed some of the clutter by observing that:

- Spirituality is not a body of secret lore.
- Spirituality has nothing to do with aptitude or temperament.
- Spirituality is not primarily about you or me; it is not about personal power or enrichment. It is about God.

The biblically instructed Christian church has always maintained an open door, a welcoming stance to 'the lost', to those disenfranchised by establishment religion and cultural acceptability or deficient in education or piety or social respectability. But not infrequently, especially when it has been adopted by the culture and is numerically successful, the church has strayed in this commitment and society's outsiders have also been left out of the church. At such times the evangelical has often been the one to recover the original welcome and re-include the left out.

Today, with 'spirituality' in the air, this old élitist voice reasserts itself on a new front. In matters of spirituality one often picks up the subtle insinuation that while the basic gospel is for everyone, in 'advanced' matters in the kingdom some are more suited than others, and these 'some' always seem to be socially and culturally from the middle or upper social strata. The poor and the minimally educated never seem to receive much attention in these matters. But 'evangelical' brings the same energy and acceptance to the outsiders as to the insiders. The storefront mission and the prairie outpost often have deeply developed Christian spiritualities, even though their vocabularies might not fit in easily with what is heard in mountain retreat centres and multiple-staffed suburban churches.

The three texts

The two stories set the word 'Spirit' front and centre for us, inviting one and all into a life of growing intimacy with our Lord. The text that reveals this word in all its complexity and comprehensiveness is holy Scripture. We cannot understand spirituality apart from the revelation conveyed in this text. The evangelical impulse keeps returning all considerations of spirituality to this definitive text.

The word 'Spirit', designating God's Spirit, or Holy Spirit, occupies a prominent place throughout our scriptures and traditions, designating God's living presence at work among us. Three representative texts mark the range of the formative work of Spirit in the world we find ourselves in: Genesis 1:1–3, Mark 1:9–11 and Acts 2:1–4. Each of these texts marks a beginning, and in each text it is the Spirit that initiates the beginning.

G. K. Chesterton once said that there are two kinds of people in the world: When trees are waving wildly in the wind, one group of people thinks that it is the wind that moves the trees; the other group thinks that the motion of the trees creates the wind. Most of humankind through most of its centuries has believed the former, that the wind moves the trees. But in recent times a new breed of people has emerged; they blandly hold that it is the movement of trees that creates the wind. The consensus has always held that the invisible is behind and gives energy to the visible; Chesterton in his work as a journalist, closely observing and commenting on people and events, reported with alarm that the broad consensus had fallen apart and that the modern majority now naively assumes that what they see and hear and touch is basic reality and it is that which generates whatever people come up with that cannot be verified with the senses, that is, they believe that the visible accounts for the invisible.

Having lost the metaphorical origin of 'spirit', we operate in our daily conversations, in the English language at least, with a serious vocabulary deficit. Imagine how our perceptions would change of we eliminated the word 'spirit' from our language and used only 'wind' and 'breath'? Spirit was not 'spiritual' for our ancestors; it was sensual. It was the invisible that had visible effects. It was invisible, but it was not immaterial. Air has as much materiality to it as a granite mountain: it can be felt, heard and measured; it provides the molecules for the quiet breathing that is part of all life, human and animal, waking and sleeping – the puffs of air used to make words, the gentle breezes that caress the skin, the brisk winds that fill the sails of ships, the wild hurricanes that tear roofs off barns and uproot trees.

It would clarify things enormously if we could withdraw 'spirit' and 'spiritual' from our language stock for a while.

But these three texts can serve as signposts in the muck of imprecision in which we find ourselves. The three texts mark the three beginnings, the beginning of creation, the beginning of salvation, and the beginning of the church: holy creation, holy salvation, holy community.

Genesis 1:1–3

In the beginning when God created the heavens and the earth, the earth was a formless void, and darkness covered the face of the deep, while the Spirit of God swept over the face of the waters. Then God said, 'Let there be light' . . .

God begins. He begins by creating. This act of creation accounts for everything there is, visible and invisible, 'heavens and earth'. Creation takes non-creation, or anti-creation, that which is 'without form and void'. that which is without light ('darkness on the face of the deep'), and makes something of it, gives it form and content, and floods it with light. Non-creation or pre-creation is pictured as ocean waters deep and dark. Formless, anarchic, wild, unpredictable, death-dealing.

God breathes or blows over these waters. The breath is life and life-making. We see the wind moving over these anarchic waters, these dark and lethal waters, God breathing life into this unlife, this nonlife.

And then this breath of God, no longer just an inarticulate blowing, is used to make words. The same breath/spirit that produces wind now makes language. We first see the effects of God's breath on the water, then we hear the articulation of God's breath in words: 'God said . . .'. Eight times in the narrative God speaks. The eight sentences account for everything that is; the scope is comprehensive. 'Create' accounts for everything that is in heaven and earth.

But there is more to this. The Spirit of God that moved over the face of the waters 'in the beginning' continues to move, continues to create. The Genesis creation text is not confined to telling us how the world came into being, it is also a witness to the creation work of the Spirit of God now. The verb 'create' in our Bibles is used exclusively with God as its subject. Men and women and angels don't create. Only God creates. And the most frequent use of the verb is not in the story of the beginning of heaven and earth, but in a prophetic/pastoral ministry that took place among the exiled people of God in Babylon in the sixth century BC. The Hebrew people had lost virtually everything – their political identity, their place of worship, their homes and farms. They had been force-marched across 600 miles of desert to eke out a bare exilic existence in a strange land. They had nothing. They were stripped not only of their possessions but of their very identity as a people of God. They were uprooted and plunked down in a foreign and idolatrous society. And it was there and in those conditions that they began hearing the Genesis verb 'create' in a fresh, unexpected way. The word 'create' (and

Creator) occurs more times in the preaching of Isaiah of the Exile than any other place in the Bible – seventeen times as compared to the six occurrences in the great creation narrative in Genesis. The Spirit of God created life out of nothing in the Babylon of the sixth century BC just as he had done in the formless void when the 'darkness was upon the face of the deep'. Through the text of Isaiah, the Creator Spirit is seen as creating both a structure to live in and lives adequate for living in it now. 'Create' is not confined to what the Spirit did; it is what the Spirit does. Creation is not an impersonal environment, it is a personal home – this is where we live. The superb accomplishment of Isaiah of the Exile was to bring every detail of the Genesis beginnings into this present in which we feel so uncreated, so unformed, and unfitted for the world in which we find ourselves. The work of the Spirit in creation no longer is confined to asking the questions, 'When did this take place? How did this happen?' We are now asking, 'How can I get in on this? Where is my place in this?' And praying, 'Create in me . . .' (Ps. 51:10).

Mark 1:9–11

In those days Jesus came from Nazareth of Galilee and was baptized by John in the Jordan. And just as he was coming up out of the water, he saw the heavens torn apart and the Spirit descending like a dove on him. And a voice came from heaven, 'You are my Son, the Beloved; with you I am well pleased.'

God begins again. A second beginning: Jesus is baptized and identified as God's 'beloved Son'.

Genesis is cosmological, presenting us with a watery chaos breathed on by God into form and fullness and light; life both inorganic and organic emerges out of no-life. Mark presents us with a local and named river in which Jesus is baptized, first drowned in the river and then raised from the river. Baptism is a replay of Genesis. As Jesus is lifted out of the water, God breathes life into him. The breathing is given visibility this time by means of what looks like a dove descending out of heaven.

And, as in Genesis, the breathing of God that is first given visibility then becomes audible in speech, 'This is my Son, my Beloved . . .'.

The descending dove on Jesus provides a visual link with Genesis 1. The verb used for the 'Spirit of God moving (*měraḥepet*) over the face of the waters' can also be translated 'hovering'. It is used in Deuteronomy (32:11) of an eagle nurturingly or protectively hovering over the young in its nest.

The birds, the hovering Genesis eagle and the descending Markan dove, provide our imaginations with an image of the Spirit of God.[2]

And, as in Genesis, the breathing of God that is first given visibility, immediately becomes audible in speech ('Let there be . . .'), so in Mark: 'You are my Son, my Beloved; with thee I am well · pleased' (Mark 1:11).

A lot has happened between Genesis and Jesus. The creation that was brought into being by the life-breath of God has been battered around a good bit. Death has become a major factor – death, anti-creation. Death, the denial of life, the elimination of life, the enemy of life. There is no energy in death, no movement in death, no words out of death. But death never prevailed. Always life, God-breathed, God-articulated life survived, at times even flourished. As death worked its way into the creation, an extensive vocabulary of death words was developed to identify its various forms, words like 'sin' and 'rebellion' and 'iniquity' and 'lawlessness'. Biblically, we are given an extensively narrated story of life assaulted by death but all the time surviving death, with God constantly, in new ways and old, breathing life into this death-plagued creation, these death-battered lives. A complex plot emerges as we read this story: God creating a way of life out of this chaos and misery, God countering death, God breathing life into creation and creatures and the life-breath becoming audible in language over and over again. The vocabulary of life words counters and surpasses the death words: words like 'love' and 'hope' and 'obedience' and 'faith' and 'salvation' and 'grace' and 'praise'. Hallelujah and Amen words.

The same Spirit of God, so lavishly articulated in words that create everything that is, 'heavens and earth', fish and birds, stars

---

2. Not all agree that there is a suggestion of bird-like hovering here. Some scholars prefer to translate the phrase 'a terrible storm' or 'God's storm' (von Rad 1961:47).

and trees, plants and animals, man and woman, now descends on Jesus who will now speak salvation into reality in our death-ravished and sin-decimated world.

The God-breathed-into-life of Jesus, the God-blessed person of Jesus at this moment begins to work out the consummation of salvation over death.

Acts 2:1–4

When the day of Pentecost had come, they were all together in one place. And suddenly from heaven there came a sound like the rush of a violent wind, and it filled the entire house where they were sitting. Divided tongues, as of fire, appeared among them, and a tongue rested on each of them. All of them were filled with the Holy Spirit and began to speak in other languages, as the Spirit gave them ability.

God begins again. A third beginning, as God breathes on a company of 120 followers of Jesus and creates the holy community, the church.

On the day of his ascension into heaven Jesus had told his apostles that God would breathe God's life into them just as God had breathed heaven and earth into creation, just as God had breathed blessing into Jesus at his baptism, confirming and authorizing the completion of salvation in him. Once having been breathed into life by God, 'baptized with the Holy Spirit' was the way he put it (Acts 1:5), they would have the strength and energy to continue the God-breathed creation of heaven and earth and the God-breathed salvation of Jesus. 'My witnesses' was the term he used to designate their new identity.

They believed the promise. They told other Jesus-followers. Soon there were 120 of them waiting for it to happen. They were waiting for the God-breathed creation of heaven and earth and the God-breathed baptism of Jesus to be God-breathed into them. They waited ten days.

When it happened, as it most surely did, there were surprises. The continuity with God's life-giving breath in the Genesis creation and the Jesus baptism was evident, but also augmented – the holy breathing became a holy wind, 'the rush of a violent wind' (Acts 2:2) and filled the room. Soon the wind that filled the room

(Acts 2:2) filled them (Acts 2:4). As if that were not enough, another sign was added, the sign of fire. Those gathered in the room that day were part of a tradition in which fire, commonly altar fire, was associated with the presence of God. But there was more to it here, this fire was distributed – each person individually was signed with a tongue of fire, each person became a sign of the presence of God. As the breathing of the Genesis creation and the Jesus baptism swelled into a wind, the old altar fires were multiplied into personalized fires burning above each waiting man and woman, each of them now a sign of God alive, God present.

And then, repeating the pattern of Genesis and Jesus, the breath/wind, that is, the living presence of God that filled each of them, was formed into spoken words by each of them. The tongues of fire became articulate in tongues of speech. The God-breathing that was formed into speech came out of the mouths of men and women speaking in all the languages (sixteen are named) represented in Jerusalem that day, and all the languages saying essentially the same thing, 'God's deeds of power' (Acts 2:11).

Everyone, of course, was properly astonished. The miracle of language is what first caught their attention, the God-originated and God-witnessing speech spoken in sixteen (at least) different languages by ordinary men and woman ('Galileans' – that is, provincials who presumably would know only one or two languages). The confusion of languages at Babel (Gen. 11) was reversed. The continuing miracle that continues to astonish is that the same breath (life) of God that created heavens and earth, that validated and blessed Jesus, is now being breathed into ordinary men and women and formed into words that continue to give witness to God's Genesis-creation and Jesus-salvation.

The three texts function like a tripod, grounding every aspect of life – creation, salvation, community – in the living (breathing) God. God alive who makes alive. God the Spirit who imparts spirit. God's Spirit is not marginal to the main action, it is the main action. Spirit is comprehensive. The three texts also make it clear that language is always involved in the making and saving and carrying on of life.

In the Christian tradition Spirit and Word are organically connected – they are not simply related or complementary – they are aspects of the same thing. There are attempts from time to time to launch wordless spiritualities, in which silence is set as the goal. And it is true that there is too much talk in most religion/spirituality. But the texts stand as authoritative: sooner or later something is said, reality is spoken into being.

The two words

Two words, rightly understood, provide a defence against the cultural erosion that obscures the core distinctiveness of Christian spirituality. The devil does some of his best work by ruining words – turning them into clichés or isolating them from the story in which they accumulate their meaning and then seducing us into using them in mere gossip and chatter. And so language is a primary evangelical concern: We guard our storehouse of words against reduction or distortion by a secularizing culture that uses words with no sense that 'in the beginning God said', or that 'the Word became flesh'. When the grammar of God no longer provides the syntax for our words, spirituality degenerates into a grab-bag of inspirational silly-putty. If words are no longer holy, more often than not they will be used to tell lies. Two words essential for maintaining accurate discourse in spirituality are 'Jesus' and 'soul'.

Jesus
The evangelical response to the amorphous limpness so often associated with contemporary spirituality is Jesus. Spirituality is given skeleton, sinews, definition, shape and energy by the term 'Jesus'. Jesus is a personal name of a person who lived at a datable time in an actual land that has mountains we can still climb, wildflowers that can be photographed, cities in which we can still buy dates and pomegranates, and water which we can still drink and in which we can be baptized. As such the name counters the vagueness and abstraction that accompanies 'spirituality'.

Jesus is the central figure in the spiritual life. His life is, precisely, revelation. He brings out into the open what we could never have figured out for ourselves, never guessed in a million years. He is God among us: God speaking, acting, healing, helping. Salvation is the big word into which all these words fit. The name Jesus means 'God saves' – God present and in action in our language and in our history.

The four Gospel writers, backed up by the comprehensive context provided by Israel's prophets and poets, tell us everything we need to know about Jesus. As we read, ponder, study, believe, and pray these Gospels we find both the entire Scriptures and the entirety of the spiritual life accessible and in focus before us in the inviting presence of Jesus of Nazareth, the Word made flesh.

But while the Gospel writers present Jesus in a down-to-earth setting not much different from the town and countryside in which we live, and in a vocabulary and syntax similar to the language we use around the dinner table and out shopping, they don't indulge our curiosity. There is so much that they do not tell us. There is so much more that we would like to know. Our imaginations itch to fill in the details. What did Jesus look like? How did he grow up? How did his childhood friends treat him? What did he do all those years of his growing up in the carpentry shop?

It didn't take long, as it turns out, for writers to appear on the scene who were quite ready to satisfy our curiosities, to tell us what Jesus was really like. And they keep showing up. But 'lives' of Jesus – imaginative constructs of Jesus' life with all the childhood influences, emotional tones, neighbourhood gossip, and social/cultural/political dynamics worked in – are notoriously unsatisfactory. What we always seem to get is not the Jesus who reveals God to us, but a Jesus who develops some ideal or justifies some cause of the writer. When we finish the book, we realize that we have less of Jesus, not more.

This itch to know more about Jesus than the canonical Gospel writers chose to tell us started early on in the second century. The first people who filled in the blanks in the story had wonderful imaginations but were somewhat deficient in veracity; they omitted to tell us that the supplementary entertaining details were the product of their imaginations. Some wrote under apostolic pseudonyms to provide authority for their inventions. Others claimed actual Holy Spirit inspiration for their fictions. It wasn't long before the church got more or less fed up with this imaginative tinkering and creative expansion with Jesus and said it had to stop. The church leaders rendered their decision: Matthew, Mark, Luke and John are the last word on Jesus. There is nothing more to be said on the subject.

It is essential that we honour this reticence on the part of the Gospel writers. Spirituality is not improved by fantasies. Spirituality is not a field in which to indulge pious dreams.

Jesus pulls every idea, every activity, every aspiration into a personal relationship, first with himself and his Father, and then with everyone around us, our 'neighbours'. Jesus takes a no-nonsense view of life, is wary of good intentions, is indifferent to 'making it' in the culture of the age, seems to delight in the company of disreputable men and women. It doesn't take long to realize that he doesn't fit the cultural stereotypes of what these days we are calling spirituality. The spirituality that Jesus offers for the asking is difficult, obedient and self-sacrificing – adjectives that are not calculated to win votes in the electoral process that goes on week by week in the decisions people make in how they are going to live their lives.

The often-documented reality that we must face is that spirituality is a, maybe the, primary breeding ground for sin. But Jesus does not for that reason keep his distance. This is where he does his work: Jesus saves.

Soul

If the name 'Jesus' keeps an awareness of the uniquely personal God in our spirituality, God historical, present, and in action, 'soul' maintains an equivalent awareness of ourselves. We are provided a biblical revelation of ourselves and the men and women we work with as persons-in-relationship. Each of us is a one-of-a-kind creature, a person-in-relationship, made in the 'image-of-God'. 'Soul' is our word for this. It is the most personal term we have for who we are. The term 'soul' is an assertion of wholeness, the totality of what it means to be a human being. 'Soul' is a barrier against reduction, human life reduced to biology and genitals, culture and utility, race and ethnicity. It connotes an interiority that permeates all exteriority, an invisibility that everywhere inhabits visibility. 'Soul' carries with it resonances of God-created, God-sustained, and God-blessed. 'Soul' is our most comprehensive term for designating the core being of men and women. 'Soul' in the Hebrew language is a metaphor, *nefesh*, the word for neck. The neck is the narrow part of the anatomy that connects the head, the site of intelligence, with everything else. Physically, the head is higher than the body, at least when we are standing up, and so we sometimes speak of the higher functions of thinking, seeing, hearing and tasting in contrast to the lower functions of digestion and excretion, of perspiring and copulating. But if there are higher and lower aspects to human life (which I very much doubt), it is not as if they can exist independently from one another. And what connects them is the neck. The neck contains the narrow passage through which air passes from mouth to lungs and back again in speech – breath, spirit, God-breathed life. It is the conduit for the entire nervous system stemming and branching from the brain. And it is where the mighty jugular vein, an extremely vulnerable 3–4 inches of blood supply comes dangerously close to the surface of the skin. Soul, *nefesh*, is what keeps it all together. Without soul we would be a jumble of disconnected parts, inert lumps of protoplasm. Our modern passion for analysis and dissection, trying to find out what makes us tick, is not a biblical passion. The Hebrews had a genius for metaphors and this is one of their finest. Synonyms proliferate – heart, kidneys, loins – accumulating metaphors that give a sense of inwardness and depth. But soul holds the centre.

The term 'soul' works like a magnet, pulling all the pieces of our lives into a unity, a totality. The human person is a vast totality; 'soul' names it as such. The biblical story that gives us this metaphor in Genesis 2, makes it clear that the breath that flows through the neck/soul is God's breath. And if God's breath is gone, the human being is gone. Apart from God there is nothing to us.

But in our current culture, 'soul' has given way to 'self' as the term of choice to designate who and what we are. 'Self' is the soul minus God. 'Self' is what is left of 'soul' with all the transcendence and intimacy squeezed out, the self with little or no reference to God (transcendence) or others (intimacy).

'Self' is a threadbare word, a scarecrow word.

'Soul' is a word reverberating with relationships: God-relationships, human-relationships, earth-relationships.

'Self' in both common speech and scientific discourse is mostly an isolating term, the individual.

'Soul' gets beneath the fragmentary surface appearances and experiences and affirms an at-homeness, an affinity with whoever and whatever is at hand.

When 'soul' and 'self' are turned into adjectives in our common speech, the contrast becomes even clearer: 'soulish' gives a sense of something inherent and relational, entering the depths, plumbing the underlying sources of motive and meaning (we even speak of soul food, soul music, the soulful eyes of a spaniel); 'selfish' refers to the self-absorbed, uncaring, and unrelational – a life all surface and image.

Setting the two words side by side triggers a realization that a fundamental aspect of our identity is under assault. We live in a culture that tries its best to replace 'soul' with 'self'. This reduction turns people into either problems or consumers. In so far as we acquiesce in that replacement, we gradually but surely regress in our identity, for we end up thinking of ourselves and dealing with others in marketplace terms: everyone we meet is either a potential recruit to join our enterprise or a potential consumer for what we are selling; or we ourselves are the potential recruits and consumers. We and our friends have no dignity just as we are, only in terms of how we or they can be used.

In our present culture all of us find that we are studied, named, and treated as functions and things. 'Consumer' is the catch-all term for what we become. From an early age we are looked upon as individuals who can buy or perform or use. Advertisers begin targeting us in those terms from the moment we are able to choose a breakfast cereal.

At present, unfortunately, there is a widespread and growing tendency among Christian leaders to define lay Christians as consumers. Spiritual consumerism, treating people in terms of what they will buy in matters of God and faith, and using people in terms of how they can support the religious enterprise, is parasitical, sucking the life-blood out of Christian spirituality. The evangelical response articulates a vehement 'No' to all such marketplace spirituality.

To be reduced from a soul to a consumer is to leave out most of what I am, of what makes me me. To be treated as a consumer is to be reduced to being used by another or reduced to a product for someone else's use. It makes little difference whether the using is in a generous or selfish cause, it is reduction. Widespread consumerism results in extensive depersonalization. And every time depersonalization takes over life leaks out.

Now here's the thing: The one place in our culture that by tradition and sanctions is most protected from this depersonalizing consumerism is the Christian congregation. 'Grace is everywhere', there is nothing to sell, no one to use. The one way of life that by its very nature is most exempt from the need to aggressively depersonalize in order to carry out its task is the Christian who is defined by his Lord as a servant: he or she can be used but cannot 'use'.

The evangelical occupies a key position in our culture for standing against the consumerist torrent that sweeps all and sundry before it as things to use or be used. A primary element in congregational identity involves treating everyone present with dignity, with reverence, with respect – as souls. Leaders are responsible for articulating and insisting on that identity.

Most of these people who show up in our churches have little to show for their lives; they are not distinguished in any way. They are for the most part men and women of modest gifts who have settled for a secure, consumer life. They are not distinguished by being looked up to as celebrities nor set apart by being looked down upon as victims. Our culture treats these people almost totally as consumers, to be used or put to use, to be preyed upon.

But the Christian church has the space and precedence and sanction to treat them seriously just as they are and not for what can be got out of them or even for what God can get out of them. We are in a position to treat these people with the dignity they have simply by being the image of God and baptized in the name of the Trinity. Who else treats them that way? But we can.

And a dance

The dance is *perichoresis*, a dance metaphor used by our Greek ancestors to refer to the Trinity. Imagine a folk-dance, a round dance, with three partners in each set. The music plays and the partners start moving in a circle holding hands. On signal from the caller, they release hands, changing partners, weaving in and out, swinging first one and then another. The tempo increases, the partners move more swiftly with and between and among one another, swinging and twirling, embracing and releasing, holding and letting go. There is no confusion, every movement is cleanly co-ordinated in precise rhythms, but each person maintains his or her own identity. To the onlooker, the movements are so swift it is impossible at times to distinguish one person from another, and the steps so intricate that it is difficult to anticipate the actual configurations as they appear. *Perichoresis* (*peri* = around; *choresis* = dance). The essence of Trinity, arguably the centrepiece of Christian theology, and sometimes considered the most subtle and abstruse of all doctrines, is captured here in a picture anyone can observe in an American neighbourhood barn dance or an Irish ceilidh.

Trinity is the most comprehensive and integrative framework we have for understanding and participating in the Christian life. Early on in our history, our teachers and pastors formulated the doctrine to express what is distinctive in the revelation of God in Christ. This theology provides an immense horizon against which we understand spirituality largely and comprehensively. Without an adequate theology, spirituality gets reduced to the cramped world reported by journalists, or the flat world studied by scientists, or the sorry world cooked up by our feelings. Trinity reveals the immense world of God creating, saving, and blessing in the names of Father, Son and Holy Spirit with immediate and lived implications for the way we live, for our spirituality. Trinity is the church's attempt to understand God's revelation of himself in all its parts and relationships. And a most useful work it has been. At a most practical level it provides a way of understanding and responding to God that enters into all the day-to-day issues that we face as persons and churches and communities from the time we get out of bed in the morning until we fall asleep at night. It prevents us from getting involved in highly religious but soul-destroying ways of going about living the Christian life.

Trinity understands God as three-personed: Father, Son and Holy Spirit, God in community, each 'person' in active communion with the others. We are given an understanding of God that is most emphatically personal and interpersonal. God is nothing if not personal. If God is revealed as personal, the only way God can be known is in personal response. We need to know this. It is the easiest thing in the world to use words as a kind of abstract truth or principle, to deal with the gospel as information. Trinity prevents us from doing this. We can never get away with depersonalizing the gospel or truth to make it easier, simpler, more convenient. That rules out knowing God through impersonal abstractions, knowing God through programmatic projects, knowing God in solitary isolation. Trinity insists that God is not an idea or a force or a private experience but personal and only known in personal response and engagement.

Trinity also prevents us from reducing God to what we can understand or need at any one time. There is a lot going on in us and in the world, far exceeding what we are capable of taking in. In dealing with God we are dealing in mystery, in what we do not know, what we cannot control or deal with on our terms. We need to know this for we live in a world that inordinately respects the practical. We want God to be 'relevant' to our lifestyle. We want what we can, as we say, 'get a handle on'. There is immense peer pressure to reduce God to fit immediate needs and expectations. But God is never a commodity to use. In a functionalized world, in which everyone is trained to understand themselves in terms of what they can do, we are faced with the reality that we are not in control. And so we learn to cultivate reverence. We are in the presence of one who is both before and beyond us. We listen and we wait. Presumption – God-on-demand on our terms – is exposed as simply silly. Defining God down to the level of our emotions and thinking, and then demanding that God work by our agenda, are set aside in favour a life of worship and prayer and obedience – a way of life open and responsive to what God is doing rather than plotting strategies to get God involved in what we are doing. Trinity keeps pulling us into a far larger world than we can imagine on our own.

And Trinity is a steady call and invitation to participate in the energetically active life of God – the image of the dance again. We are not spectators to God, there is always a hand reaching out to pull us into the trinitarian actions of holy creation, holy salvation and holy community. God is never a non-participant in what he does, nor are we. We need to know this. It is a lot easier to guide, motivate, plan and direct from a distance, whether in our homes or our work. We learn to keep a little distance, find ways to delegate. But the reality of the Trinity does not permit it. If we are going to know God we have to participate in the relationship that is God. We discover ourselves as unique participants – each of us one-of-kind – in the life of God. The Christian life is not preprogrammed; it is a release into freedom. Trinity keeps us alert and responsive to the freedom that derives from participation in the life of God. And every act of participation is unique.

Every expression of spirituality, left to itself, tends towards being more about me and less about God. The evangelical responsibility is to give witness to the living God in as large and comprehensive terms and images as possible. Trinity provides the theological language that enables us to maintain our Christian identity in the largest, most comprehensive, most involving understanding of the being and action of God.

Ten books to nurture the evangelical impulse and responsibility

1. John Bunyan, *Pilgrim's Progress* (1678), many eds., inc. introduced Monica Furlong, London: Vega, 2002.
2. C. S. Lewis, *Till We Have Faces: A Myth Retold* (1956), repr. London, Fount 1998.
3. Augustine, *The Confessions* (400), many eds., inc. trans. R. S. Pine-Coffin, Harmondsworth: Penguin 1961.
4. George Herbert, *The Temple* (1633), repr. in John N. Will (ed.), *George Herbert: The Country Parson, The Temple*, Classics of Western Spirituality, London: SPCK, 1981.
5. Hans Urs von Balthasar, *Prayer*, San Francisco: Ignatius Press, 1986.
6. Karl Barth, *The Christian Life*, Church Dogmatics IV/4, Lecture Fragments, Grand Rapids: Eerdmans; Edinburgh: T. & T. Clark, 1981.

7. James Houston, *Prayer: The Transforming Friendship*, Oxford: Lion, 1989.
8. James M. Gordon, *Evangelical Spirituality*, London: SPCK, 1991.
9. P. T. Forsyth, *The Work of Christ* (1910), repr. London: Collins, 1965.
10. Simon Chan, *Spiritual Theology*, Downers Grove: IVP, 1998.

Bibliography

von Rad, Gerhard (1961), *Genesis*, London: SCM Press.

9. EVANGELICALISM AND PHILOSOPHY

Gregory J. Laughery

Introduction

I remember the day, some years ago, when I arrived on the door-step of a rather large chalet, following many others to the small Alpine village of Huémoz, Switzerland. This tiny farming village is where L'Abri Fellowship has its home. When I got off the postal bus, after the long and arduous climb up the winding road, I met with a staff member and was welcomed into one of the L'Abri chalets for a period of study. Little did I know it then in 1980, but this day was to change the course of my life.

In the next days and weeks I discovered L'Abri was made up of a community of people from all over the world. Each student took part in gardening, preparing meals, studying, attending prayer meetings, lectures and discussions. All these activities, combined with the intense interaction of a community life, had the aim of being something of a demonstration of the existence of God. In addition to the centrality of Christ, a Christian world-view, spirituality and so on, one of the pivotal things that was emphasized at L'Abri, contrary to much of the evangelical focus at the time, was the relevance of philosophical ideas for understanding God, ourselves, others, the world and the cultures in which we live. Francis Schaeffer, who with his wife Edith started L'Abri, comments: 'Christians have tended to despise the concept of philosophy. This has been one of the weaknesses of evangelical, orthodox Christianity – we have been proud in despising philosophy, and we have been exceedingly proud in despising the intellect.'[1]

This detachment from philosophy and the intellect did not only have harmful effects on the credibility of the evangelical community and the wider church,[2] but it left evangelicals in a dilemma as to how to interact with people, especially the younger generation, in late modernism. According to Schaeffer, the significant philosophical questions of a pluralistic culture and the world-views it comprised were largely ignored. Unfortunately, this perspective was prevalent in many evangelical seminaries, which equally tended to marginalize philosophy. Schaeffer writes:

> Our theological seminaries hardly ever relate their theology to philosophy, and specifically to current philosophy. Thus, students go out from the theological seminaries not knowing how to relate Christianity to the surrounding worldview. It is not that they do not know the answers. My observation is that most students graduating from our theological seminaries do not know the questions.[3]

Schaeffer was convinced that evangelicals and evangelical seminaries were short-sighted here and he made every effort to broaden the vision. Christianity, Schaeffer argued, dealt with the whole of life, including the arts, music, literature and philosophy.[4] He consistently

---

1. Schaeffer 1982: I: 297.
2. Noll 1994. In this insightful work, Noll critiques Christians for similar reasons.
3. Schaeffer 1982: I: 297 and see also 152.
4. Schaeffer published books on philosophy, art, ecology, spirituality, ecclesiology, apologetics and ethics. See Erickson (1998: 63–80) for a discussion on Schaeffer and postmodernism. See also Naugle (2002: 29–31) for a positive assessment of Schaeffer's contribution.

reinforced with urgency the importance of having a grasp of the philosophical ideas that were influencing our generation, and philosophy played a key role in his thought. Ronald Nash comments:

> Philosophy plays a central role in the work of Francis Schaeffer. Schaeffer recognized that important developments in philosophy had helped push modern man into his present predicament . . . It was Schaeffer's method then to look at the broad flow of philosophy and culture in the West, and to focus upon key thinkers at critical points where these problems were most apparent.[5]

While Schaeffer was not a professional philosopher, he contributed to preparing the way for many who were to take up such a vocation. He discussed the works of Nietzsche, Foucault, Wittgenstein, Hegel, Kierkegaard, Sartre and other influential thinkers, seeing the necessity for Christians to interact with such philosophers and the issues they raised.[6] Philosophical poverty, too often an evangelical trademark, diminished the credibility of the truth of Christianity. Schaeffer, among others,[7] sowed the seeds for a renewed Christian interest in philosophy,[8] which has now grown and developed in a dramatic fashion.

At present, I am a third-generation staff member at L'Abri with a published doctoral thesis on the French philosopher Paul Ricoeur. I believe, more strongly than ever, that evangelicals need a clear understanding of historical and contemporary philosophical thought if they are to meaningfully evaluate their tradition and challenge their culture for the sake of Christ.

The aim of this chapter is threefold: First, to provide an overview of a striking resurgence of Christian involvement in philosophy in North America. Second, to trace out three core issues that are pivotal for the present and future of the evangelical faith and philosophy:

---

5. Nash 1986: 53.

6. Schaeffer 1982: I–V.

7. See Clark 1952; Holmes 1977.

8. Walls 1994: 107.

- the matter of the appropriate role of reason and evidence in belief in God
- the debate concerning realism and anti-realism, focusing on the discussion between the two philosophers Alvin Plantinga and Merold Westphal
- the problem of the relation between theology and philosophy, centring on Paul Ricoeur and Alvin Plantinga. This will be developed through a dialogue with two philosophically minded theologians, Kevin Vanhoozer and Craig Bartholomew, who have creatively attempted to clarify this issue.

Third, to outline a number of trajectories for future philosophical investigation.

The resurgence of Christian philosophy

An extraordinary resurgence of a Christian interest in philosophy is taking place and evangelicals are participating in this flourishing. Alvin Plantinga points out that Christians have addressed several weighty issues and contributed significantly to philosophical discussions.[9] He argues that the shining light in Christian philosophy is philosophical theology. Plantinga writes: 'At present, this enterprise is faring rather well, perhaps even flourishing; the last few years have seen a remarkable flurry of activity in philosophical theology as pursued by Christian philosophers.'[10]

Christian insights in philosophy and philosophical theology are having massive implications in their own right for studies on the divine attributes, God's eternity and action in the world, the argument from evil and so on, but they equally open fresh opportunities for other disciplines such as history, literature and biblical interpretation. Evidence of this, from both the analytic

---

9. Plantinga 1995: 29–53; also in Sennett 1998: 328–352. See also Noll 1994: 233–239.
10. Plantinga 1998b: 340.

and continental traditions, is found notably in the fecund work of A. C. Thiselton and Kevin Vanhoozer.[11] While Plantinga recognizes there is further work to be done in philosophical theology, positive and negative apologetics, and Christian philosophical criticism,[12] the current renaissance of a Christian concern for philosophy is extremely positive.

A powerful stimulus for this major change has been the founding by William Alston, Robert and Marilyn Adams, Alvin Plantinga, Arthur Holmes and George Mavrodes of the Society of Christian Philosophers. Remarkably, this Society is the largest single-interest group in the American Philosophical Association.[13] In addition to the Society of Christian Philosophers, one should also take note of the Evangelical Philosophical Society and its scholarly journal *Philosophia Christi*, renewed academic rigour, articulate published works, university postings of Christians in philosophy and so on. These are vital signs that philosophy being done by Christians from a Christian point of view is experiencing renewed vigour in North America.[14] Nicholas Wolterstorff, Alvin Plantinga, Merold Westphal, William Alston and many others have led the way to what has now become, in a relatively short period of time, a widespread phenomena: Christians are gaining respect for their philosophical positions and the cogency of their work calls for consideration in many philosophical debates.

This astonishing resurgence has been brought about by a diversity of factors, but analytic philosopher Alvin Plantinga has been recognized as one of its key figures.[15] In his 1983 inaugural address at the University of Notre Dame, Plantinga challenged Christians in philosophy to take the offensive and to display more integrity.

---

11. Thiselton 1992 and Vanhoozer 1998, whose influences include Gadamer and Ricoeur.

12. Plantinga 1998b.

13. Clark 1990: 9.

14. At present, regrettably, there are no similar movements in Britain or continental Europe.

15. Sennett 1998: xiv.

Among other things, this meant embracing a greater freedom from the agendas of secular philosophy and the forging of an independence that proclaimed the right to pursue philosophical questions from within a Christian framework.[16]

Plantinga has done a tremendous amount to stem the tide of atheistic philosophy in establishing that belief in God can be rational and defensible.[17] He has also contributed significantly to the growing collapse of the argument from evil, which attempted to deny the existence of a wholly good God on the basis of the existence of evil. Christianity, Plantinga declares, is on the move, not only in philosophy, but also in a variety of areas of intellectual endeavour. Evangelicals must take notice of such a progression, and in reliance on God, make every effort to shore up the resilience and attraction that evangelicalism desperately needs if it is to hope to have a significant impact on humanity.

Three core issues

I shall now focus on three core philosophical issues for evangelicals. These issues are at the heart of the debate between modernism and postmodernism, and furthermore they are connected to the broader question of the relationship between faith and understanding.[18]

The role of reason and evidence in belief in God

Questions concerning God's existence continue to be a 'consuming passion'[19] for philosophers, and especially for philosophers of religion in the twentieth and twenty-first centuries. The role of reason and evidence in responding to these queries is a highly significant epistemological issue for evangelicals. In the wake of the

---

16. Plantinga 1984: 253–271; also in Sennett 1998: 296–315.

17. Plantinga 1993; 2000.

18. Helm 1997; Evans, 1998; Davis 1997; have, in various ways, dealt with this larger question.

19. Davis 1997: x.

audacious proclamation of Friedrich Nietzsche with regard to the death of God, can belief in God be rational?

There have been several objections raised against belief in God: the statement that 'God exists' is nonsense; a lack of internal consistency in the logic that God is a personal being; the argument from evil; and that there is not enough evidence for such belief to be rational.[20] In this section, my main concern is with the latter argument: rationality and evidence.

The evidentialist objection to belief in God is that it would always be wrong to believe anything without sufficient reasons or evidence. Some evangelicals agree and contend that belief in God requires arguments, reasons and evidential proofs to be rational.[21] But others respond differently. Reformed epistemologists would disagree that arguments, reason and evidential proofs are required for belief in God to be rational.[22] As Kelly Clark points out, evangelical evidentialists have attempted to respond to the evidentialist objection by meeting its demands, while Reformed epistemology has chosen to question the credibility of such demands.[23]

In response to the evidentialist objection that belief in God requires proof to be rational, R. C. Sproul, John Gerstner and Arthur Lindsley have argued that the theistic 'proofs' must not just be respectable, but if they are to be worthy of belief they must prove that God exists. 'But if proofs do not prove, it is unreasonable to believe them as arguments. To do so is to say with the mind, that they do not prove and with the will, that they do prove. This is usually what we call fideism rather than rationality.'[24]

These writers contend that if belief in the existence of God does not measure up to the requisite standards of proof it would

---

20. Plantinga 1998a.

21. Sproul, Gerstner & Lindsley 1984; Geisler 1976. In contrast, Mercer (1995) calls for evangelicalism to shed its rationalistic-modernist framing and become 'post-evangelical'. See also Hilborn (1997: 56–73) for a discussion of this topic.

22. Plantinga & Wolterstorff 1983.

23. Clark 1990: 46–54.

24. Sproul, Gerstner & Lindsley 1984: 122–123.

be irrational to believe it. They attempt to offer proof against the evidentialist objector on the foundation of evidential certainty and therefore argue that belief in God is capable of being as rational and provable as those who claim it is not.[25] In this case, the objector maintains, 'Not enough evidence to believe God exists, therefore if you believe you are not rational.' This is challenged with the response, 'Of course there is plenty of evidence, even proof, to believe that God exists, therefore if I believe I am rational.'

It is important to recognize that these views are representative of a form of foundationalism. In the Western world, since at least the Middle Ages, foundationalism has been the central theory concerning how beliefs are to be ordered in a system of belief. A foundationalist asserts that we hold a series of basic beliefs and a series of non-basic beliefs. Non-basic beliefs require evidence if they are to be rationally accepted, while basic beliefs function as the foundation of the house of knowledge in that such beliefs are not dependent on other beliefs. But how can one be sure which beliefs are basic? In that there are various forms of foundationalism (and disagreements within them), it becomes crucial to have greater certainty that the house of knowledge is based on a solid foundation. This position is often referred to as strong foundationalism.[26] Jay Wood states:

> Strong foundationalists severely restrict what can count as basic belief, what kind of support it lends to other beliefs we hold, and the manner in which this support is communicated to non-basic beliefs. They claim that the foundations of human knowledge must be unshakably certain and that the only way this certainty is transferred to non-basic beliefs is by the ordinary logical relations of deduction and induction.[27]

---

25. Sproul, Gerstner & Lindsley 1984: 100.
26. See Wood (1998: 77–104) for a description of strong foundationalism. See also Wolterstorff (1984) for an illuminating discussion on the problems with foundationalism.
27. Wood 1998: 85.

A strong foundationalist demands that the foundation for belief in God be certain. Basic beliefs are those that are thought to be self-evident, self-evident to the senses and unmistakable, such as, 'I am alive' or 'I am in pain', but not 'I believe that God exists.' As belief in God here is not self-evident to the senses and unmistakable, such a belief cannot be considered properly basic, and therefore it requires rational evidential proofs in order to justify it becoming part of the house of knowledge. If belief in God is lacking such proofs it is assumed to be irrational.

An Enlightenment notion of evidentialism or rationality has been embraced by some evangelicals who attempt to meet the criteria for belief in God that evidentialist objectors such as W. K. Clifford, Bertrand Russell and Antony Flew have demanded.[28] Enormous weight is placed on reason and the natural world in the attempt to prove that God exists. Peter Hicks states: 'Throughout the history of evangelicalism, there has always been a tendency among thinking evangelicals to capitulate to the demands of the Enlightenment and to seek to justify their beliefs by the use of reason.'[29] Many complex arguments or theistic proofs for God's existence have proliferated: the ontological, teleological, cosmological and moral arguments as well as the argument from religious experience. Such a plethora of theistic proofs, however, brings with it even a fuller degree of complexity as each of these proofs or arguments is, in turn, a family of related but different arguments.[30]

With this proviso in mind, let us briefly consider the Kalaam version of the cosmological argument.[31] William Lane Craig states:

> The argument is basically this: both philosophical reasoning and scientific evidence show that the universe began to exist. Anything that begins to exist must have a cause that brings it into being. So the

---

28. Clifford 1879; Russell 1957; Flew 1976.
29. Hicks 1998: 102.
30. For a fuller discussion of the perplexity, see Davis (1997) and Geisler (1974).
31. A more detailed presentation of the cosmological argument can be found in Davis (1997: 60–77); Clark (1990: 17–26) and Evans (1982: 50–59).

universe must have a cause. Philosophical analysis reveals that such a cause must have several of the principal theistic attributes.[32]

One of these central theological characteristics is formulated in the following manner. If anything begins to exist it has a cause. The universe has a cause in that God created it. It is more credible to believe this than to believe that the universe came into being uncaused, out of nothing. This is a simplified version, but it legitimately represents one form of the cosmological argument.[33] In the minds of some evangelicals, if this or another type of theistic argument does not prove God's existence, it would be unreasonable to accept that God exists.[34]

A second response to Enlightenment evidentialism is Reformed epistemology. Plantinga, Wolterstorff[35] and others challenge the necessity of evidential proofs for belief in God's existence to be rational. They propose a different perspective of rationality. Nicholas Wolterstorff, for example, argues:

> A person is rationally justified in believing a certain proposition which he does believe unless he has adequate reason to cease from believing it. Our beliefs are rational unless we have reason from refraining; they are not nonrational unless we have reason *for* believing. They are innocent until proved guilty, not guilty until proved innocent.[36]

A return to reason, in Reformed epistemology, means a refusal to let Enlightenment criteria decide what is required for belief in God to be rational.[37] This view does not attempt to meet the standards of evidentialism, but, in contrast, questions the legitimacy of

---

32. See Craig 1994: 77–125, esp. 92, for more detail.

33. Geisler (1974: 190–226 and 1976: 238–239), who presents this argument in bullet form.

34. Sproul, Gerstner & Lindsley 1984; see also Geisler 1976.

35. Plantinga (2000: 247–251; 1998b) and Wolterstorff (2001) trace their roots back through Kuyper and Dooyeweerd to Reid and Calvin.

36. Wolterstorff & Plantinga 1983: 163 (emphasis his).

37. See Clark 1990: 123ff., Wolterstorff 1984.

its demands. Belief in God, it is argued, does not need evidential proof to be rational. Wolterstorff comments:

> Deeply embedded in the Reformed tradition is the conviction that a person's belief that God exists may be a justified belief even though that person has not inferred that belief from others of his beliefs which provide good evidence for it . . . We have to start somewhere! And the Reformed tradition has insisted that the belief that God exists, that God is the Creator, etc., may justifiably be found there in the foundation of our system of beliefs . . . We are entitled to reason *from* our belief in God without having first reasoned *to* it.[38]

In addition to a different perspective of rationality, Reformed epistemology sets out to examine what beliefs may be considered properly basic beliefs in one's foundation. In accord with foundationalism, Reformed epistemology accepts that one is rational to include basic beliefs that are self-evident, self-evident to the senses, and unmistakable in a belief structure, yet it disputes that it should only be restricted to these. Plantinga, for example, includes memory beliefs, testimony beliefs and belief in God. These sorts of beliefs, he contends, are basic beliefs in that they are not dependent on reason, evidence or other beliefs.[39]

Plantinga and Wolterstorff, along with C. Stephen Evans, Kelly James Clark and Stephen Davis have produced insightful and detailed work on the problematics raised in this section.[40] Reformed epistemology with its different definition of rationality and its refiguring of the notion of properly basic beliefs is funding much of the epistemological discussion today. In this view, it is not wrong to attempt to give reasons or evidence for belief in the existence of God, but these are not necessary for one's belief in God to be considered rational. There is no interest in attempting to prove God's existence on the basis of reason or evidence, yet

---

38. Wolterstorff 1992: 149 (emphasis his).
39. Plantinga 1998a.
40. Plantinga 2000; Wolterstorff 1984; Evans 1982 and 1998; Clark 1990; Davis 1997.

those who hold this epistemology forcefully maintain that God exists and that belief in God is rational.

The question of belief in God and the role of reason and evidence in such belief remain acute matters for philosophical investigation in our times. Have evangelicals too often drunk from the intoxicating well of the Enlightenment? If Enlightenment criteria and assumptions are now fading or have failed, it may indeed be the moment for evangelicals to reassess their epistemology. In contrast to a succession of barricades, which too often characterize our evangelical heritage, the aim of reassessment should be serious dialogue with the hope of coming to fecund conclusions for the Christian faith.

Realism versus anti-realism

As Plantinga has noted, this is an important issue for Christians in philosophy.[41] Realism and anti-realism are philosophical positions directly connected to the understanding and shaping of one's world-view. When we make a statement about the world are we speaking of the real world outside of us or merely using language to construct a world, which is dependent on human interaction?[42] This controversy is clearly linked to other domains of inquiry, such as metaphysics, epistemology and language, but my aim is to present this philosophical issue in the context of the question of our relation to the world.

Immanuel Kant, a prolific philosopher of the modern period, may still be one of the most influential and thought-provoking participants in this discussion.[43] The philosophy of Kant is extremely complex, yet I believe it is possible to draw some basic conclusions that pertain to this issue. Kant is seen by some as attempting to have the best, or the worst as the case may be, of two worlds. That is, by the time of Kant, the empiricism of David Hume had brought a significant challenge to a rationalist approach and

---

41. Plantinga 1998b.

42. Kirk & Vanhoozer (1999: 18–34) have an excellent discussion of the realism/anti-realism debate.

43. Kant 1929.

through Hume's trajectory Kant was awakened to what he envisioned as new possibilities for philosophy.[44] This jolt is referred to by Kant as a Copernican Revolution. What was it? Basically, Kant found himself in agreement with the rationalist notion that knowledge related to concepts formed by the mind, while at the same time he held that knowledge came from the senses.

What does this have to do with the question of the world and our access to it? Kant, as some propose, divided the world in two: the noumenal, which is the realm of things in themselves and the phenomenal, which is the world as we experience it in terms of categories we impose on it. The latter world is the world we are restricted to having knowledge about. J. Andrew Kirk puts it this way:

> The dilemma began when the culture in general accepted (following the arguments of Hume and Kant) that intellectual probity necessitated the assumption that the uniformity of natural causes required a closed-order universe. The dilemma is acute. No longer is there a sufficient reason for believing with certainty that anything exists, or that there is an adequate correlation between the observer (subject) and the thing observed (object) . . .[45]

The radical post-Kantian question, highlighted by many a postmodernist is the following: can one access the world as it is? As Kirk has pointed out above, there is a dilemma with regard to the object/subject interface. Christian philosophers continue to wrestle with these Kantian or reality types of questions. I shall briefly examine two responses to Kant. Alvin Plantinga, the analytic philosopher, claims that Kant's idea of creative anti-realism in the first *Critique* is 'incompatible with Christianity.'[46] A realist perspective assumes that our access to the world must conform to objects and not vice versa. Plantinga points out: 'But the fundamental *thrust* of Kant's self-styled Copernican Revolution is that things in the world owe their basic structure and perhaps their very existence to the noetic activity

---

44. See Scruton (1982) for a helpful introduction to Kant.
45. Kirk 1999: 170.
46. Plantinga 1998b: 331.

of our minds.'[47] Plantinga is highly suspect of anything profitable coming from the Kantian notion of creative anti-realism. He seems to argue that we either perceive the world as it is, or that we create it as it appears, and if the latter is the case, there is no connection between the noumenal and the phenomenal. On this second scenario of creating the world, the result would be that the things in the world owe their existence to the subject. Plantinga's interface of object and subject suggests there is only one world, that is, the world that the subject sees, is the world as it is.

On the other hand, Merold Westphal, who is a more continental type of philosopher, argues that creative anti-realism is to be defended and that Christian philosophers should be favourably inclined to Kantian idealism.[48] Westphal suggests that Plantinga may have under-read Kant, arguing that there are 'four types of Kantianism'[49] only one of which contains a negative humanist orientation which would be pejorative for a Christian point of view.

In his discussion of Kant, Westphal uses the example of the difference between watching a black-and-white TV and seeing the real colour of something in the TV studio. He wishes to make the point that Kant sees the mind as a 'receiving apparatus' whose 'spontaneity' allows things to appear in a particular way, whether they are this way or not. This, in Westphal's view, should not be understood as two worlds, but rather as two modes of a subject seeing the same object. If this is the case, the object remains what it is even though the receiving apparatus may modify it and Kant's position, Westphal argues, is more closely represented by this type of realism.[50]

How are we to understand these two Christian responses to Kant? What type of people are human beings and what sort of world is it that we live in? These questions are at the heart of the Christian faith. Plantinga seems to make the relation between the world and our access to it exactly the same, while Westphal aims to

---

47. Plantinga 2001: 129 (emphasis his).
48. Westphal 1993b: 162.
49. Ibid.: 163, for the detailed argument.
50. Ibid.: 166.

defend the distinction. That is, he is more concerned with our 'receiving apparatus' which may in fact, he contends, not receive things exactly the same way they actually are in the world.

Both these views concerning this arduous question, from a Christian perspective, seem to have valid points. Thus, I suggest the appropriateness of a configuration which respects *both* the relation and the distinction of the object/subject interface. There is indeed a complexity in tension that cannot be resolved by opting for *either* relation *or* distinction alone. Furthermore, it may be an opportune time for evangelicals in philosophy to acknowledge, to a greater degree, a place for human subjectivity with respect to the object/subject relation and distinction, without however, capitulating to modes of subjectivity that seek to remove or deny any objectivity whatsoever.

In my view, evangelicals who work in philosophy cannot ignore Kant and are obliged to interact further with his work, especially the *Critique of Pure Reason*. This is not to say that one must be overly preoccupied with Kant, but only to argue that this crucial debate needs further illumination if we are to come to increasingly fecund and clear conclusions. A greater precision in the understanding of whether we are talking about reality or knowledge, and what we mean when we use the terms 'realism' and 'creative anti-realism' will prove, I believe, profoundly useful for a Christian understanding of God, self and world.

Philosophy versus theology

The relationship between philosophy and theology has long been a debated issue. How are we to configure this relation? This is a massive and complex question, impossible to do full justice to here, yet it is important to bring some elements of a response into light. I shall first explore the views of two contemporary philosophers: Paul Ricoeur[51] and Alvin Plantinga.[52] Ricoeur and Plantinga

---

51. See Laughery (2002) for a full and detailed account of Ricoeur's work on biblical hermeneutics in the context of modernism and postmodernism.
52. Noll (1994: 235) points out the radical resurgence of an evangelical interest in philosophy in North America is largely due to the fecund

are postmodern: both are aware, in their own ways, of the pitfalls of classical strong foundationalism. These philosophers, Plantinga the evangelical, and Ricoeur not, both merit a close reading.[53] Evangelicals in philosophy, or theology for that matter, have much to learn from them as they each offer, in the twilight of modernism,[54] something of a way forward to a truly postmodern philosophy.

Plantinga and Ricoeur are opposed to any notion of a Cartesian self-authenticating self and steer clear of modernist forms of post-modernism. Ricoeur has been extremely sensitive about meshing together his philosophical work and his theological beliefs and understandings, although he readily admits some effects of the latter on the former.[55] Plantinga is much less cautious in this area and deliberately acknowledges Christian presuppositions as clas-sifying and influencing his philosophical work. Plantinga, the philosopher of religion, attempts to relate theology to philosophy, and dares to articulate a *Christian* philosophy; whereas Ricoeur, the philosopher, strives to keep the two distinct and would be reluctant to embrace any notion of *Christian* philosophy, as for him, this would amount to something like a round square.[56]

Plantinga lacks no zeal, and rightly so, in reminding Christian philosophers that they need not be favourably disposed to non-believing philosophies and that theologians and biblical scholars should not see themselves as indebted to the ideas and projects of unbelievers. Plantinga's work has clearly had a tremendous influ-ence on philosophers and the philosophy of religion, especially in North America. The resurgence of philosophical inquiry in the evangelical and wider Christian community is to be applauded, and

---

influence of those connected to the Dutch Reformed heritage. Two of the leading contributors to this renewal are A. Plantinga and N. Wolterstorff.

53. Recent works by Plantinga include 1993; 2000; by Ricoeur, 1984–7; 1991; 1992a; Ricoeur & LaCoque 1998.

54. Green 2000: 25.

55. Ricoeur 1992a: 24.

56. Ricoeur 1992b: 39–40.

Plantinga is to be given due credit for his outstanding contribution in making this venture philosophically credible and convincing.[57]

Ricoeur is heralded as one of the most important and versatile philosophers of the twentieth century. He attempts to avoid the accusation of crypto-theologizing[58] his philosophical work, yet his hermeneutically centred philosophy is theologically sensitive. Ricoeur's notion of philosophy is that it is basically an anthropology. In his perspective there is a difference between solving a question posed or responding to a call.[59] One may speak of law, conscience, guilt and so on in philosophy, although in Ricoeur's view, neither love nor the confession of sin, for example, are philosophical ways of speaking as both go beyond the limits of philosophical inquiry.

How shall we evaluate the views of these two philosophers? Ricoeur seems to begin with philosophy, recognize its limits and then turns to theology. Does he leave the two too far apart? Plantinga, on the other hand, seems to begin with theology, and from this, work out his philosophy.[60] Does he too quickly integrate the two? The questions concerning Ricoeur's distance and Plantinga's integration are not intended to be rhetorical, but inquisitive.

With these questions in mind, I shall now examine the perspective of two theologians, Kevin Vanhoozer and Craig Bartholomew, who are both well attuned to the importance of philosophy. In his recent treatment of the subject Bartholomew is concerned with the question of whether recent formulations of theological hermeneutics have sufficiently taken philosophy into account.[61] While he *affirms* these new formulations of a theological orientation, the pressing *question* of the relationship between philosophy and theology remains. I concur with Bartholomew's endorsement and with his query.

---

57. See 'The resurgence of Christian philosophy' pp. 249–251 above.

58. Ricoeur 1992a: 24.

59. Ibid.: 23–25, 39.

60. Plantinga (Sennet 1998: 146–147) suggests following Reformed thinkers and starting with God.

61. Bartholomew (2000) presents this in a concise and fecund manner.

The complexity of this issue has also been explored by Kevin Vanhoozer.[62] In putting forward what he terms a Chalcedonian view of the relationship, Vanhoozer argues for the individual integrity, the relative autonomy and the mutual accountability of philosophy and theology. Bartholomew, in dialogue with Vanhoozer, grants that precision on this problematic is difficult, but he remains cautious about Vanhoozer's framing of Christ (theology) and concept (philosophy). The concern, for Bartholomew, is that there seems to be a residue of the modernist distinction between philosophy and theology that is 'somewhat restlessly present throughout' Vanhoozer's point of view, although Vanhoozer is careful to relate the two.[63]

Bartholomew proposes an intriguing and valuable modified typology for elucidating the relationship between philosophy and theology. His query with some formulations of theological hermeneutics seems to be the unwitting or deliberate emphasis on keeping the two apart. Bartholomew's useful typology, which he readily admits is tentative, aims to integrate the two through an appeal to Christ as the *clue* to philosophy and theology. A Christian hermeneutic, he argues, is to be viewed as faith seeking understanding in both spheres of research.[64]

This proposal points us in a helpful direction, yet my concern is whether it relates theology and philosophy[65] in such a manner that it leaves little room to continue *really* to view them as distinct. If

---

62. Vanhoozer 1991.

63. Bartholomew 2000, esp. 31. In my reading of Vanhoozer's proposal he is careful to attempt to address both the 'distinctness' and 'relatedness' of theology and philosophy.

64. We have no space here to enter into the fascinating and crucially important debate concerning faith seeking understanding. Where do we really begin? See 'Trajectories for the future' (pp. 265–267) below.

65. Bartholomew refers to Milbank 1999: 23–24. See also Milbank 1999: 32 and footnote, 49, which offers another argument along these lines. Bartholomew points out that philosophy cannot give an account of being human on its own. 'Theology *can* evaluate philosophy.' While this is true, I would wager the reverse may also, at least in some contexts, have a role: philosophy can evaluate theology.

Christ is the *clue* to philosophy, how does philosophy remain distinct from theology?[66] The suggestion that Vanhoozer has been modernist in leaving philosophy and theology too distinct is countered by Bartholomew in more expressly relating the two. Does this proposal equally result in a modernist configuration in that it moves awfully close to dissolving a tension through seeing philosophy and theology as too related? If this is the case, Bartholomew's point of view seeks to perhaps resolve a tension of relation and distinction that should be embraced and left intact.

The principal difference between Bartholomew and Vanhoozer can be summed up in the following way. Bartholomew's theological orientation of relating philosophy and theology seems to promote an interaction with philosophy for the purpose of assessing its negative impact on theology. He rightly wants theology to be better able to critique anti-Christian philosophies, but to do so theology has to be more aware of how it may be pejoratively influenced by such points of view. Vanhoozer's relation and distinction of philosophy and theology on the other hand, seems willing not only to assess a potential negative impact, but also to rightly affirm the possibility that philosophy might make a positive contribution to and offer a critique of theology.[67]

My main concerns are the following. If these two disciplines are too related, is there a real possibility for one to offer the other a contribution or critique? Does relating philosophy and theology together too rapidly, in an unrestricted union, suggest a modernist underplay of a dialogue in tension? Should our aim be to preserve a place for philosophy to assert a relative autonomy for the sake of offering an affirmation or critique to theology, while at the same time to hold equally on to theology's task of providing the same for philosophy?

---

66. Following Newbigin, Bartholomew (2000: 33–34) writes that Christ is the clue to all creation. In my view, theologically, the Triune God , Father, Son and Spirit, is its clue.

67. This may be closer to Bartholomew's (2000: 32) notion of 'double truth' where, I would say, *different* not always conflicting, views 'sit in uneasy tension'.

In conclusion, I would argue that as we move into the future, evangelicals should aim to avoid unnecessary polarizations (realism and anti-realism; philosophy and theology) where they are not called for. This is not, in general, to propose a form of synthesis, nor to discount that some key issues will rightly remain in opposition, but only to suggest that discovering a relation and distinction perspective on some issues, as Evans notes,[68] in acknowledging a tension-filled alliance, may bring us closer to Christian truth.

Trajectories for the future

Any attempt to sketch out lines for the future may prove problematic, yet it is necessary for Christian philosophers to be aware of a number of topics that require attention. Several other issues, in addition to those already addressed, may prove worthwhile to investigate.

Plantinga has given us an excellent overview of the current state and future concerns of Christian philosophy.[69] His assessment is that Christian philosophers have done fairly well in a variety of areas, but that there is more work to be done. Pluralism, in Plantinga's opinion, will be a major question that must be addressed. He also posits that there are a diversity of positive arguments for the Christian position that should be developed and that theistic arguments are in need of greater development. Other concerns would be a vibrant cultural criticism, and a deepening philosophical theology, where major Christian doctrines are examined and better understood for the Christian community.

Plantinga has also declared that perennial naturalism and creative anti-realism are the 'hydra heads' that have arisen in the wake of the demise of logical positivism. He argues that each is pervasive in its own way, and it is essential for Christian philosophers to pay close attention as to how they infiltrate Christian thought in negative ways.[70]

---

68. Evans 1982: 25.
69. Plantinga 1995b: 29–53; also in Sennett 1998: 328–352.
70. Sennett 1998: 328–335.

In addition to the issues mentioned by Plantinga, others may also be relevant and merit further reflection. The philosophy of language remains an important subject.[71] There has been some, but not enough work done here. Wolterstorff,[72] Thiselton[73] and others[74] have explored the potential of speech act theory and produced excellent contributions. As the residues of positivism fade and postmodern queries proliferate, Christians have a new opportunity to join in and contribute to a theory of language.[75]

In light of the collapsing foundations of modernism the role of communicating the gospel may become more acutely significant. What are Christian modes of communication in a postmodern world? How might philosophers help in moving us from the more abstract to insightful and practical ways of communicating the truth of the Christian world-view? A practical philosophy, not only related to thinking but to living, is essential.

A pertinent question, closely connected to our three core issues above, is the relationship between faith and understanding. Faith seeking understanding and understanding seeking faith? Philosopher Paul Helm has recently investigated this relationship and made a fine contribution to moving us further along.[76] Where, when and how do we begin? In my view, this pivotal issue deserves more reflection. The statement 'faith seeking understanding' seems to be frequently cited in Christian contexts, but not always with a great deal of focus and clarity.

Another problematic deserves further research. Since at least the era of Augustine, the issue concerning God and time has produced a diversity of questions. How are God and time to be thought of? Are we to think of God as outside time, in time, or both at the same time? What is time? Who is God in connection to

---

71. Laughery 2001: 171–194.

72. Wolterstorff 1995.

73. Thiselton 1992.

74. Bartholomew, Greene & Möller 2001 has several fecund contributions. See also Vanhoozer 1998.

75. Bartholomew, Greene & Möller 2001.

76. Helm 1997.

time? These types of questions have begun to draw more wide-spread consideration. Ricoeur has produced a fascinating and insightful study on temporality and narrative.[77] He has also argued that if we are going to understand something of time and of God, it is essential to examine the biblical text in its narrative and other forms.[78] Evangelicals can certainly benefit from Ricoeur's investigations. Other recent work has much to commend it,[79] but there is more that could be done to address these questions.

The philosophical issues mentioned here, along with others, merit hard and careful thought. If evangelicals in philosophy are to continue on the road towards credibility there is a crucial need to face the many challenges ahead. In order to participate in the hope of renewing a thirst for the living God and a living spirituality that touches the whole of life, Christian philosophers must not only track their culture, but also trace it. This means it is essential to be aware of the personal and cultural impact of philosophical ideas, and to leave, through an involvement with culture, a Christian imprint. My hope is that such efforts, dedicated to God and the Christian community, will challenge others to take notice that the God of Scripture is there and that Christianity is true.

Bibliography

Bartholomew, C. G. (2000), 'Uncharted Waters: Philosophy, Theology and the Crisis in Biblical Interpretation', 1–39, in C. G. Bartholomew, C. Greene and K. Möller (eds.), *Renewing Biblical Interpretation*, Grand Rapids: Zondervan; Carlisle: Paternoster Press.

Bartholomew, C. G., C. Greene and K. Möller (eds.) (2001), *After Pentecost: Language and Biblical Interpretation*, Grand Rapids: Zondervan; Carlisle: Paternoster Press.

---

77. Ricoeur 1984–7.

78. Ricoeur 1995a; also in Ricoeur 1995b: 167–180.

79. Ganssle 2001: Helm, Padgett, Craig, Wolterstorff. See the helpful bibliographical listings in this book, 24–27.

Clark, G. H. (1952), *A Christian View of Men and Things: An Introduction to Philosophy*, 1–39, Grand Rapids: Eerdmans.

Clark, K. J. (1990), *Return to Reason*, Grand Rapids: Eerdmans.

Clifford, W. K. (1879), *Lectures and Essays*, London: Macmillan.

Craig, W. L. (1994), *Reasonable Faith: Christian Truth and Apologetics*, Wheaton: Crossway.

Davis, S. T. (1997), *God, Reason, and Theistic Proofs*, Edinburgh: Edinburgh University Press.

Erickson, M. J. (1998), *Postmodernizing the Faith: Evangelical Responses to the Challenge of Postmodernism*, Grand Rapids: Baker.

Evans, C. S. (1982), *The Philosophy of Religion: Thinking about Faith*, Leicester: IVP.

—— (1998), *Faith Beyond Reason*, Edinburgh: Edinburgh University Press.

Flew, A. G. N. (1976), *The Presumption of Atheism*, London: Pemberton.

Ganssle, G. E. (ed.) (2001), *God and Time*, Downers Grove: IVP.

Geisler, N. L. (1974), *The Philosophy of Religion*, Grand Rapids: Zondervan.

—— (1976), *Christian Apologetics*, Grand Rapids: Baker.

Green, G. (2000), *Theology, Hermeneutics and Imagination: The Crisis of Interpretation at the End of Modernity*, Cambridge: Cambridge University Press.

Helm, P. (1997), *Faith and Understanding*, Edinburgh: Edinburgh University Press.

Hicks, P. (1998), *Evangelicals and Truth: A Creative Proposal for a Postmodern Age*, Leicester: IVP.

Hilborn, D. (1997), *Picking up the Pieces: Can Evangelicals Adapt to Contemporary Culture?*, London: Hodder & Stoughton.

Holmes, A. F. (1977), *All Truth is God's Truth*, Downers Grove: IVP.

Kant, I. (1929), *Critique of Pure Reason*, trans. N. K. Smith, New York: St Martin's Press.

Kirk, J. A. (1999), 'Christian Mission and the Epistemological Crisis of the West', in Kirk & Vanhoozer 1999: 157–171.

Kirk J. A. and K. J. Vanhoozer (eds.) (1999), *To Stake a Claim: Mission and the Western Crisis of Knowledge*, New York: Orbis.

Laughery, G. J. (2001), 'Language at the Frontiers of Language', in Bartholomew, Greene & Möller 2001: 171–194.

—— (2002), *Living Hermeneutics in Motion: An Analysis and Evaluation of Paul Ricoeur's Contribution to Biblical Hermeneutics*, Lanham, MD: University Press of America.

Mercer. N. (1995), 'Postmodernity and Rationality: the Final Credits or just a Commercial Break?', in A. Billington, T. Lane and M. Turner (eds.), *Mission and Meaning*, 319–338, Carlisle: Paternoster Press.

Milbank, J. (1999), 'Knowledge', in J. Milbank, C. Pickstock and Graham Ward (eds.), *Radical Orthodoxy: A New Theology*, 21–37, London: Routledge.

Nash, R. H. (1986), 'The Life of the Mind and the Way of Life', in L. T. Dennis (ed.), *Francis A. Schaeffer: Portraits of the Man and His Work*, Westchester: Crossway.

Naugle, D. K. (2002), *Worldview: The History of A Concept*, Grand Rapids: Eerdmans.

Noll, M. A. (1994), *The Scandal of the Evangelical Mind*, Leicester: IVP.

Plantinga, A. and N. Wolterstorff (eds.) (1983), *Faith and Rationality*, Notre Dame: University of Notre Dame Press.

Plantinga, A. (1984), 'Advice to Christian Philosophers', *Faith and Philosophy* 1: 253–271.

—— (1993), *Warrant: The Current Debate*, Oxford: Oxford University Press.

—— (1995), *Warrant and Proper Function*, Oxford: Oxford University Press.

—— (1998a), 'Reason and Belief in God', in Sennett 1998: 102–161.

—— (1998b), 'Christian Philosophy at the End of the 20th Century', in Sennett 1998: 328–352.

—— (2000), *Warranted Christian Belief*, Oxford: Oxford University Press, 2000.

—— (2001), 'The Twin Pillars of Christian Scholarship', in *Seeking Understanding: The Stob Lectures 1986–1998*, Grand Rapids: Eerdmans.

Ricoeur, P. (1984–7), *Time and Narrative*, 3 vols, trans. K. McLaughlin and D. Pellauer, (vols. 1 & 2), K. Blamey and D. Pellauer (vol. 3), Chicago: University of Chicago Press (French original *Temps et récit*, Paris: Seuil, 1983–5).

—— (1991), 'Philosophical Hermeneutics and Biblical Hermeneutics', in *From Text to Action, Essays in Hermeneutics II*, 89–101, trans. K. Blamey and J. B. Thompson, Evanston: Northwestern University Press.

—— (1992a), *Oneself as Another*, trans. K. Blamey, Chicago: University of Chicago Press (French original *Soi-même comme un autre*, Paris: Seuil, 1990).

—— (1992b), *Talking Liberties*, 36–40, London: Channel 4 Television.

—— (1995a), 'Biblical Time', trans. D. Pellauer in 1995b: 167–180 (French original 'Temps biblique', in *Archivio Filosofia* 53 (1985): 29–35).

—— (1995b), *Figuring the Sacred: Religion, Narrative, and Imagination*, ed. M. I. Wallace, Minneapolis: Fortress Press.

Ricoeur, P. and A. LaCocque (1998), *Thinking Biblically, Exegetical and*

Hermeneutical Studies, trans. D. Pellauer, Chicago: University of Chicago Press (French original *Penser la bible*, Paris: Seuil, 1998).

Russell, B. (1957), *Why I Am Not A Christian*, New York: Simon & Schuster.

Schaeffer, F. A. (1982), *The Complete Works*, vols. I–V, Westchester: Crossway.

Scruton, R. (1982), *Kant*, Oxford: Oxford University Press, 1982; 1996.

Sennett, J. F. (ed.) (1998), *The Analytic Theist: An Alvin Plantinga Reader*, Grand Rapids: Eerdmans.

Sproul, R. C., J. Gerstner and A. Lindsley (1984), *Classical Apologetics*, Grand Rapids: Academie Books.

Thiselton, A. C. (1992), *New Horizons in Hermeneutics: The Theory and Practice of Transforming Biblical Reading*, Grand Rapids: Zondervan.

Vanhoozer, K. J. (1991), 'Christ and Concept: Doing Theology and The "Ministry" of Philosophy', in T. E. McComiskey and J. D. Woodbridge (eds.), *Doing Theology in Today's World*, 99–145, Grand Rapids: Zondervan.

—— (1998), *Is There a Meaning in This Text? The Bible, The Reader, and the Morality of Literary Knowledge*, Grand Rapids: Zondervan.

Walls, J. L. (1994), 'On Keeping the Faith', in T. V. Morris (ed.), *God and the Philosophers: The Reconciliation of Faith and Reason*, 102–112, Oxford: Oxford University Press.

Westphal, M. (1993a), *Suspicion and Faith: The Religious Uses of Modern Atheism*, Grand Rapids: Eerdmans.

—— (1993b), 'Christian Philosophers and the Copernican Revolution', in C. S. Evans and M. Westphal (eds.), *Christian Perspectives on Religious Knowledge*, 161–179, Grand Rapids: Eerdmans.

Wolterstorff, N. (1984), *Reason within the Bounds of Religion*, 2nd ed., Grand Rapids: Eerdmans.

—— (1992), 'Is Reason Enough?' in R. D. Geivett and B. Sweetman (eds.), *Contemporary Perspectives on Religious Epistemology*, 142–149, Oxford: Oxford University Press.

—— (1995), *Divine Discourse: Philosophical Reflections on the Claim that God Speaks*, Cambridge: Cambridge University Press.

—— (2001), *Thomas Reid and the Story of Epistemology*, Cambridge: Cambridge University Press.

Wolterstorff, N. and A. Plantanga (eds.) (1983) *Faith and Rationality*, Notre Dame: University of Notre Dame Press.

Wood, W. J. (1998), *Epistemology: Becoming Intellectually Virtuous*, Leicester: IVP.

10A. EVANGELICALISM AND THE CHARISMATIC MOVEMENT (UK)

Nigel Scotland

England's two largest churches, Kingsway International Christian Centre and Kensington Temple are both charismatic churches. The Alpha Course in basic Christianity with its emphasis on the Holy Spirit has impacted every continent in the world. Its home is Holy Trinity, Brompton, England's largest charismatic Anglican church. Charismatic experience has been, and is, the most significant influence in English evangelicalism during the last forty years. Its impact has been particularly marked among Anglicans and Baptists and in the birth of several significant strands of what are now termed 'New Churches', whose adherents number several hundred thousand. From being small minority groups in the 1960s, charismatic evangelicals have expanded to a point where they have profoundly influenced the life and worship of every major denomination. Charismatic experience has deepened faith, prompted prayer, brought the Bible to life, motivated evangelism, inspired healing ministries, produced worship which is more participatory and informal, and provoked concern for the poor and disadvantaged.

Early beginnings

The word 'charismatic' derives from the Greek word *charismata*, which means gifts of the Holy Spirit. Peter Hocken has asserted that Harold Bredesden (b. 1918) and Jean Stone (b. 1924) have the distinction of coining the term 'charismatic' to denote the new movement of the Holy Spirit within the older mainstream denominational churches. At the end of an article entitled 'Return of the Charismata' they stated, 'we call this movement "the charismatic revival"'.[1] Charismatic Christianity is a world-wide phenomenon of the Holy Spirit, which is rooted in the experience of the day of Pentecost. It emphasizes such gifts as speaking in tongues, prophecy and healing, but also sees the importance of other gifts mentioned in the New Testament. Charismatic Christians must therefore be those who emphasize the importance of the indwelling *charisma* or gracious gift of the Spirit[2] and who seek to use the particular gifts (*charismata*) of the Holy Spirit, which God has graciously entrusted to them. Charismatic evangelicalism is most obviously visible by its free 'expressions' of worship. These may be in the form of spontaneous singing, extempore prayers or impromptu words of encouragement or consolation and general congregational participation. Such contributions can be in the context of both liturgical and non-liturgical forms of service.

Charismatic Christianity clearly has its roots in the New Testament churches and the undivided early Catholic Church. Among its many prominent early exponents were the Montanists whose movement began in Phrygia (modern Turkey) in AD 157. Led by Montanus and two prophetesses, Maximilla and Priscilla, they announced a fresh outpouring of the Holy Spirit. They practised speaking in tongues and prophecy and preached an imminent

---

1. Hocken 1997: 185. Jean Stone was married to an executive of an American airline. She was subsequently divorced and remarried. She is now Jean Stone Willans.
2. Professor Max Turner has suggested that *charisma* means no more than 'gift'. See Turner 1996: 252–255.

second coming. It needs to be recognized that many of the bishops in Asia Minor regarded the Montanists as heterodox on account of their having women in leadership, their extreme asceticism and their failed predictions concerning the Second Advent which they held would take place as Pepuza in AD 177.[3] However, their movement gained credibility and became more widespread when they were joined by Tertullian (160–220), one of the church's leading theologians. A little later, Irenaeus (130–202), who was Bishop of Lyons in central Gaul, wrote at the end of the second century of those who 'through the Spirit do speak all kinds of language and bring to light for the general benefit the hidden things of men and declare the mysteries of God'.[4] Justin Martyr (100–165), a contemporary of Tertullian, declared: 'It is possible now to see among us men and women who possess the Spirit of God'.[5] Much later, Augustine (354–430) first held to a cessationist view that the gifts of the Holy Spirit had been withdrawn with the closing of the apostolic era. He taught, for example, that the sign of tongues for the individual believer had been replaced by Christian love.[6] In his later years however, events caused him to change his mind and he began to record what he took to be healing miracles in his diocese. He wrote: 'It is only two years ago that the keeping of records was begun here in Hippo, and already, at this time of writing we have more than seventy attested miracles.'[7]

From Augustine's time onwards, particularly through the long Middle Ages (800–1500), the wider church seems to have largely lost touch with the gifts of the Holy Spirit. There were occasional shafts of light in the exploits of Patrick (385–461)[8] and

---

3. See, for example, Hippolytus, *Refutation of All Heresies* (c. AD 222), chs. 11 and 12.

4. Irenaeus, *Against Heresies*, ch. 8.

5. Justin, *Dialogue with Trypho*, ch. 88.

6. See Christie-Murray 1978: 47.

7. For an extended consideration of the gifts of prophecy, knowledge, exorcism and healing in the early Catholic period see Scotland 2001a: 161.

8. For Patrick see Hood 1979.

Cuthbert (*c.* 636–87)[9] and in the movement inspired by John Wycliffe (1328–84). The eighteenth century witnessed great revivals prompted by Jonathan Edwards (1705–58) and George Whitefield (1714–70) in the American Colonies and John Wesley (1703–91) in England. Although Edwards declared himself to be a 'cessationist'[10] and Whitefield seems to have shared his opinions, both men were open to 'manifestations of the Holy Spirit'. John Wesley, who did not believe that the gifts of the Holy Spirit had come to an end with the passing of the apostolic age, taught that it was the birthright of every Christian 'to know the witness of the Holy Spirit with his spirit that he is the child of God'. One of Wesley's prominent helpers, Thomas Walsh, spoke with tongues.[11] Edwards, Whitefield and Wesley thus all paved the way for the greater openness to the Holy Spirit which emerged in nineteenth-century England and America. Nineteenth-century England also experienced a number of outpourings of the Spirit, most notably in the ministry of Edward Irving (1792–1834) at Cross Street Presbyterian Chapel in London in 1822 and in the succession of American revivalists who came to Britain in the Victorian years. Prominent among them were Lorenzo Dow (1777–1834) who impacted the Primitive Methodists with his Camp Meetings,[12] James Caughey (*c.* 1810–91)[13] and Walter and Phoebe (1807–74) Palmer who proclaimed 'holiness revivalism'.[14]

Touching the English denominational churches

The twentieth century witnessed Pentecostal outpourings on both sides of the Atlantic. In the British Isles the Welsh Revival of 1904 and the extraordinary moves of the Spirit at All Saints, Sunderland

---

9. For Cuthbert see, for example, Bede 1990, Book 4, ch. 28.

10. Edwards 1741: 140.

11. T. Walsh, Diary, cited in Christie-Murray 1978: 51.

12. See Sellers 1928.

13. See Caughey 1855.

14. See Palmer 1845.

in 1907 under the rector, Alexander Boddy (1854–1930), helped to bring to birth both the Elim and Assemblies of God Missions which together form the backbone of the modern Pentecostal churches.

English charismatic Christianity began in the early 1960s. Among the first to be touched in the initial stirrings was Michael Harper (b. 1931) who was curate to John Stott at All Souls, Langham Place in London. He was, in his own words, 'baptised with the Holy Spirit' at a conference in Farnham and later recalled, 'I was filled with all the fullness of God and had to ask God to stop giving me more – I couldn't take it.'[15] Harper left All Souls in 1965 after six successful years and became secretary of the Fountain Trust in the same year. This organization, together with its magazine, *Renewal*, played a major part in promoting what was termed 'Baptism in the Holy Spirit' in local churches. Much of its work was also achieved through conferences for clergymen and Christian leaders and the dissemination of audiotapes. The Trust's impact was reinforced by visits from a number of individuals from America, among them Dennis Bennett, an American Episcopal priest and two of his parishioners, Mrs Jean Stone and her husband, Don, followed a little later by Graham Pulkingham from the Church of the Redeemer in Houston and Terry Fullam, Rector of St Paul's Episcopal Church in Darien.

Prominent early centres of Church of England charismatic evangelicalism were St Mark's, Gillingham under John Collins, Pip and Jay in Bristol under Malcolm Widdecombe and St Paul's, Beckenham under George Forester. Subsequently, the most prominent centres of Anglican charismatic evangelicalism were to be St Michael-le-Belfrey in York where David Watson was rector, St Andrew's, Chorleywood under Bishop David Pytches and Holy Trinity, Brompton under Sandy Millar. Thus from small beginnings in the mid 1960s when some Anglican theological college principals questioned the fitness of charismatic students for ordination, attitudes changed over a thirty-year period. By the 1990s there were bishops, archdeacons and theological college principals

---

15. Hocken 1997: 86.

who were card-carrying charismatics.[16] Among the Church of England episcopate, Simon Barrington-Ward, the former Bishop of Coventry, and Richard Hare, the former Bishop of Pontefract, were overtly charismatic. Something of the way in which the Church of England has come to terms with the Charismatic movement is illustrated by the publication of its official reports. It was not until sixteen years after the formation of the Fountain Trust that *The Charismatic Movement in the Church of England*[17] was published. This was followed in 1986 by Josephine Bax's General Synod report on the Charismatic and Cursillo Movement[18] and in 1991 by *We Believe in the Holy Spirit*[19] and Anne Richards' Board of Mission's Occasional Paper on the Toronto Experience[20]

Among charismatic Anglican evangelicals it has been possible to discern two major strands: Anglican Renewal charismatics and New Wine Network charismatics. The former are epitomized by Anglican Renewal Ministries (ARM) which closed down in July 2002.[21] The former ARM still represents those whose primary concern is to express their charismatic experience through the legally prescribed Anglican liturgy. In the words of their former organizer, the Revd John Leach, their Anglican attachment is more important than their charismatic convictions. Many of their number are more focused on the Eucharist, vestments and symbol and are concerned with the renewal of the liturgy and theology. Some also have leanings towards Celtic spirituality. New Wine Network charismatics on the other hand, are Vineyard in style and

---

16. Among the present bishops who are identified with the charismatic movement are John Perry (b. 1935); Graham Dow (b. 1942), Bishop of Carlisle; John Sentamu (b. 1947), Bishop of Birmingham; David Gillett (b. 1945), Bishop of Bolton; Cyril Ashton (b. 1942), Bishop of Doncaster; Peter Broadbent (b. 1952), Bishop of Willesden and Graham Cray (b.1947), Bishop of Maidstone.

17. Church Information Office 1981.

18. Bax 1986.

19. Church of England Doctrine Commision1991.

20. Richards 1997.

21. See Anon. 2002.

values, much less warmly attached to traditional Anglicanism and their attitude to the liturgy is often minimalist. ARM-style charismatics would like to renew the Church of England's structures while in contrast the New Winers believe that their New Wine needs new wine skins! However the reality of the situation is that neither group has achieved anything significant in so far as changing or creating new structures are concerned.

The Methodist were introduced to things charismatic at an early point by Charles Clarke (1903–84), a Staffordshire Circuit Superintendent Minister, who was baptized in the Spirit in 1963 and edited *Quest* to promote the experience among British Methodists. In 1970 Clarke and others founded the Dunamis Renewal Group with the aim of promoting charismatic renewal in Methodist circuits and a magazine, *Dunamis Renewal,* was first published in 1972. Five hundred Methodist ministers were on the mailing list in 1993. A leading inspiration in the movement was the Reverend Dr Bill Davis, Principal of Cliff College until 1994. His successor, the Reverend Howard Mellor, continued to encourage charismatic renewal. In April 1995 the Dunamis Renewal Group combined with Headway, another Methodist Renewal group with similar objectives. *Dunamis Renewal* ceased publication and the group shared the quarterly magazine *Headline* which in 1999 had a circulation of 2,500 of whom about 500 were Methodist ministers.

A very similar renewal group was established among the Baptists with the founding in 1980 of Mainstream. Mainstream organizes an annual conference for Baptist Union ministers and other leaders and in recent years has come to have a considerable influence within the denomination. Key leaders include Paul Beasley-Murray, who was Principal of Spurgeon's College until 1992, and David Coffey, the Baptist Union General Secretary. Both are committed to charismatic renewal. There is a widely held view that charismatic Christian influence has changed the whole ethos of Baptist Union life and worship during the last ten years or so. It has been estimated that the Sunday services in 50% of Baptist churches have been impacted by renewal in the Holy Spirit. Douglas McBain wrote in 1997 that 'the majority of Baptist ministers in Britain who began their Ministry in the middle to late 1970s onwards appear willing to identify themselves with whatever they perceive as the positive attributes of renewal'.[22] Douglas McBain, who was President of the Baptist Union, and his successor in 1999–2000, Michael Bochenski, were both charismatics. Dr Nigel Wright, the President for 2002–2003, is a prominent charismatic scholar and theologian and Principal of Spurgeon's College. Significantly in 2001 and 2002 Mainstream seems to have taken on a new lease of life as a vehicle of the Word and Spirit and its most recent conference at Swanwick was marked by an increased number of participants and a new level of enthusiasm.[23]

New Churches

A major focus in the emergence of charismatic evangelicalism from the movement's beginnings has been what were at first termed the 'house churches'. Initially groups of Christians who had been 'baptized in the Holy Spirit' became increasingly dissatisfied with the coldness and formalism of the established and denominational churches. They began meeting together in one another's homes and then, as numbers grew, they began to hire schools, community halls and even cinemas.

House churches which have since become known as 'New Churches', although they are no longer new!, emerged in a variety of different strands and factions. In the 1970s and 1980s a large sector operated under the banner of 'Restoration', a term which denoted their commitment to 'restore' to the contemporary churches, the pattern of ministry and structure of the New Testament churches with a particular emphasis on all the ministries of Ephesians 4:11. This included oversight and direction by 'restored' apostles and prominence given also to the ministry of the prophet. In his classic text, *Restoring the Kingdom*, Andrew Walker attempted to distinguish between what he termed Restoration 1 and Restoration 2 (R1 and R2).[24] Although both groups recognized that the kingdom of God

---

22. McBain 1997: 46.

23. See Finnis 2002.

24. See, for example, Walker 1998: 41 ff.

would not be fully restored until the return of Christ, they began to believe that through their work and worship people would experience a foretaste of the kingdom now.

R1 Restorationists were those who exercised a much more rigorous control over their followings and expected a much greater level of commitment from them. They were particularly noted in the earlier days for their 'heavy shepherding', which in some cases was 'abusive'.[25] Restoration 1 emerged around the swashbuckling ministry of Bryn Jones (b. 1939), who took on a pastorate of New Covenant Church in Bradford in 1965.[26] In 1977 they purchased the Anglican Diocesan Church House headquarters and transformed it into offices, a coffee shop, lounge and worship area for 500 people. In the mid 1980s Jones and his associates, who published a glossy periodical under the caption *Restoration*, made energetic forays into Birmingham, Leicester and Leeds reaching a high point of perhaps 12,000–15,000 members, although others put the figure considerably higher.[27] For a brief period, Terry Virgo, a former London Bible College student of Baptist origins, worked alongside Bryn. He later separated, but continued to exercise apostolic responsibility for a cluster of churches in the South East known as 'Coastlands'. This group was later to become a powerful strand of R2 under the name New Frontiers International (NFI).

A significant member of R2 operated under the name Pioneer and has been led by Gerald Coates, a former postman and member of the Christian Brethren. In 1991 Team Spirit with a smaller number of fellowships under the leadership of John and Christine Noble, entered into a working relationship with Pioneer. Their total membership was reckoned at 7,400 in the year 2000.[28] In South East London, Roger and Faith Forster, assisted by musician and songwriter Graham Kendrick, established the Ichthus Fellowship. By 1999 they had established some 27 congregations in schools, halls

---

25. For a discussion of heavy shepherding see Scotland 2000: 109–110.
26. See Walker 1998: 46.
27. See Hocken 1997: 115.
28. Brierley 1999: 9, 11.

and disused church buildings. In addition, there were 120 Icthus-linked churches in the UK and Europe.[29] Ichthus's total membership at the close of 1999 was probably of the order of 5,000.

Charismatic New Church groups include Salt and Light, a large cluster of churches which looked to Barney Coombs for 'apostolic oversight' and input. Initially they were firmly in the R1 camp but became much more relaxed over shepherding issues in the mid 1980s. By 1994 there were 105 affiliated Salt and Light congregations including one or two Church of England churches. At the beginning of 2002 their overall leader was Stephen Thomas and their UK membership was 5,000. The Vineyard movement founded by John Wimber (1934–97), a Californian-based evangelist, expanded rapidly in America during the 1980s and early 1990s. Although its influence in the United States has begun to wane with numbers of its former pastors joining the Communion of Evangelical Episcopal Churches and affiliating with other major associations, it has grown steadily in the UK. Led by John Mumford, a former curate of St Michael's, Chester Square, there were 59 Vineyards in the British Isles by the close of 1999 and 72 by the middle of 2001.[30] There are a number of smaller clusters of New Churches which are located in the Midlands and the South of England.[31]

---

29. Icthus Christian Fellowship congregations updated 4 May 1999, in Icthus Christian Fellowship 1999: 3.

30. *Equipped*, June 2000.

31. For further details see Scotland 2000: 20–27. These include Cornerstone led by Tony Morton of Southampton with a membership of 5,000; Ground Level with about 3,000; the Kings Churches under Derek Brown who is based at the King's Centre in Aldershot; Lifelink established by Alan Scotland with its headquarters at South Wigston in Leicestershire; Partners in Harvest, a group of about a dozen or so churches emanating from Telford and under the oversight of John Arnott of the Toronto Airport Christian Fellowship and the Jesus Army with a core membership of some 2,000.

Core values

Despite this very wide spectrum which extends from liturgical Anglican and Methodist congregations to very recent fundamentalist offshoots of the 1960s and 1970s New Churches, charismatics do nevertheless share a number of common core values. The majority stress the importance of a definite and conscious experience of the Holy Spirit which is usually subsequent to conversion and is sometimes spoken of as the 'second blessing'. For some, this has to be authenticated by speaking in tongues; others eschew the terminology of 'Baptism in the Spirit' and are quite relaxed when it comes to glossalalia.

All charismatic evangelicals emphasize the importance of renewed worship. For some, this means a renewal of the liturgy such that there is greater freedom for people to participate and a willingness to allow for spontaneous contributions. Frequently there is a move away from traditional hymns to simpler more contemporary songs which are folk in style. Here, too, there is a wide variety, ranging from raucous praise songs to gentle repetitive Taizé chants or Vineyard choruses. Charismatic worship is usually a dress-down occasion, often informal in atmosphere, with the greeting of peace and individuals contributing prayers, readings, words and sometimes dance.

The Holy Spirit prompts fellowship, and charismatic churches are frequently characterized by an atmosphere of warmth, friendliness and care. There is a strong sense of belonging and mutual care which is sustained by small groups which meet during the week. Closely intertwined with this is an emphasis on 'wholeness' and prayers for healing. Such prayer often happens within house gatherings or at the close of public worship. In other cases people are invited to kneel at the communion rail and are anointed with oil.

Charismatic ecclesiology is inevitably focused on the Pauline model of the church as a body with every member having a gift or function to perform. A charismatic church is not for passive spectators and members are urged to discover their roles as teachers, evangelists, carers, healers, administrators, discerners, prophets, exorcists and whatever other contributions are felt to be necessary.

Central to charismatic theology has always been the doctrine of

the kingdom of God and particularly so in the teaching and strategies of the New Churches in the early 1970s. They felt themselves
to be the Lord's agents who had been raised up to restore the
kingdom. A renewed church was therefore of vital importance but
the kingdom was of altogether greater concern. In the early period
much of the emphasis was on an end time revival and the coming
of a future heavenly kingdom. By the 1990s however, a realized
eschatology was emerging and most Restorationists, and charismatics in general, were beginning to see the importance of the
kingdom as a present reality and were focusing on issues of practical care and social justice. Groups such as Pioneer and the
Vineyard in particular have become more concerned with issues of
health, poverty and the family.

Charismatic Christians in general find that the experience of
'baptism in the Holy Spirit' has given them a heightened awareness
of unseen spiritual realities. In broad terms charismatic evangelicals have a strong sense of a conflict with the unseen forces of
darkness and most engage in some kind of 'spiritual battle',
whether it be in the form of fasting and intercession, at one end of
the spectrum, or half-night gatherings for intercession and warfare
prayer and battle songs at the other. Charismatic Christianity has
seen a renewed emphasis on the need for exorcism, but the way in
which this is approached varies a good deal. Some sections of
charismatic evangelicalism are judicious in their approach and recognize that believers also have to struggle against the world and
flesh as well as the devil. The extremist elements tend towards an
over-heated demonology and seem ever ready to blame the devil
for almost anything which goes wrong!

Of particular significance is the charismatic emphasis on evangelism. The Holy Spirit experience has clearly issued in a major
growth in numbers and membership. In the early days of
Restoration, accusations were made with a strong element of truth
that the New Churches were siphoning off the discontented from
the mainline denominational churches. By the later 1970s however,
it was clear that there were significant numbers of new converts.
Charismatic evangelicals across the spectrum have been at the
forefront of church planting and in the case of congregations,
such as Holy Trinity, Brompton, re-establishing churches which

had been closed down. Since the mid 1990s there has been an enormous expansion of the introduction to Christianity Alpha Courses such that more than seven thousand such courses were run in Britain in 2001.[32]

Charismatic evangelicalism 1965–95

It has been customary among religious historians and sociologists to view charismatic Christianity in four phases: Pentecostal beginnings or the First Wave; charismatic renewal; the Third Wave initiated by John Wimber and the Toronto Blessing.

The First Wave had its roots in the Welsh Revival of 1904 and the outpourings of the Spirit at All Saints, Monkwearmouth, Sunderland in 1907 where the Reverend Alexander Boddy[33] was vicar. In November of that year Mrs Boddy laid hands on Smith Wigglesworth (1859–1947), the Bradford plumber, who was to become one of the most dynamic leaders of early Pentecostalism. In the year following more than five hundred seekers were 'baptized in the Holy Spirit', among them George (1876–1943) and Stephen Jeffries (1889–1962). In 1915 George went to Ireland and established The Elim Evangelistic Band and planted the first Elim Church in Belfast the following year. In 1926 Stephen began to travel extensively with the Assemblies of God. During the same period his older brother, George, engaged in extensive evangelistic work and founded The Elim Foursquare Gospel Alliance of the British Isles in 1926 with the expectation that it would become an umbrella for all Pentecostals in Great Britain.[34] In the event, only Elim members joined and the name was subsequently changed to Elim Pentecostal Churches. From these beginnings in the 1920s and 1930s both the Elim churches and the Assemblies of God congregations have grown steadily such that by 1998 the former

---

32. See Combe 2001.

33. For Alexander Boddy see Lavin 1986; Blumhofer 1986.

34. For George and Stephen Jeffreys see Boulton 1928; Cartwright 1986 and Kay 2000.

had 62,000 members and the latter 58,500.[35] Of much greater significance, however, was the formation in the same year of The Pentecostal Churches of the United Kingdom (PCUK) with a combined membership of 350,000.[36]

The second phase extends from the beginnings of charismatic renewal in the early 1960s through to the arrival on the British scene of the American evangelist, John Wimber. In the Church of England, as has been noted, much of the initial impetus came from Michael Harper and his work organizing conferences and publishing articles in *Renewal* magazine. By the 1970s there were several charismatic evangelical members of staff at St John's College, Nottingham and chapel worship was markedly informal. In 1978 an Anglican Charismatic Conference was held to coincide with the Lambeth Conference of Bishops. Over two hundred Anglican leaders, including thirty bishops, gathered at Kent University. Archbishop Coggan attended a packed Cathedral for a festival of praise and spoke in glowing terms of renewal in England. By 1980 there were a number of prominent charismatic Anglican churches which included Holy Trinity, Brompton; St Mark's, Gillingham; St Aldate's, Oxford; St Michael-le-Belfrey in York; St John's, Harborne in Birmingham; St Thomas Crookes in Sheffield; St Nicholas, Nottingham and St Andrew's, Chorleywood. The faith-sharing ministry teams led by the Revd Barry Kissell who was on the staff of St Andrew's, played a very significant role in extending charismatic renewal across the whole of England over a twenty-year period. Among the Baptists and Methodists charismatic Christianity was less influential in this early phase.

In the 1970s the Restorationist New Churches were strongly impacted by visits from a number of American brothers, among them Derek Prince (b. 1915), Ern Baxter (1914–93) and Bob Mumford (b. 1930). Together with Charles Simpson and Don Basham they were known as the 'Fort Lauderdale Five'. Led by Baxter, they were influenced by the teachings of Carlos Ortiz of

---

35. *Elim Church Conference and Agenda Report* 1999: 60. Information received from David Gill, Assemblies of God Head Office, October 1999.

36. For further details see Scotland 2000: 253.

Argentina and set up networks of congregations who submitted to their apostolic oversight. Basham was reported to be 'dead keen on demons' and well known in the States for his deliverance ministry. Derek Prince, despite his early years as a Fellow of King's College, Cambridge, was noted for extreme biblical interpretations and passionate Zionism.[37] From these brothers the English leaders learned the significance of terms such as 'covering' and 'submission' which required individuals 'to obey' their elders, even if, on occasion, they were wrong or unwise. It was this American influence which contributed to groups such as Bryn Jones' New Covenant Ministries and Barney Coombs' Salt and Light establishing apostolic circuits and setting up systems of personal shepherding some of which were undoubtedly felt to be oppressive and were in some instances even abusive.

For the House churches, the 1970s were a decade of enthusiastic advance marked by church planting, triumphalist singing and jamboree Bible weeks in the Yorkshire Dales, Exeter and Builth Wells. However, by the early 1980s triumphalist warfare songs such as 'The Battle Belongs to the Lord' and 'It's God who makes my hands to War' were much less evident and in truth the early charisma and momentum of the movement was already beginning to peak.[38] Andrew Walker has suggested, and probably rightly, that Restorationists lost their earlier radical vision with its emphasis on community, co-operative Christian enterprises and committed relationships in a world that had become dominated by the hedonistic individualism of late modernity and the consumerism of the Thatcherite era.[39]

1981 saw the arrival in England of John Wimber and his particular brand of Christianity which brought about a major change to charismatic thinking and practice which is usually designated 'the Third Wave'.[40] Wimber, who came from a Quaker background, had taught a very effective course on church growth at Fuller

---

37. See Walker 1998: 93.
38. See Walker 1998: 202–223.
39. Walker 1998: 23.
40. See Wimber 1981.

Theological Seminary. His theology, which was simple and practical, asserted that the words of Jesus must be validated by the works of Jesus. This, as he perceived and taught it, was the function of the Holy Spirit. When invoked in a simple 'Come Holy Spirit' petition, he comes to confirm the spoken message by signs and wonders. In Wimber jargon this was 'power evangelism' and it included healing the sick and casting out demons. Two other things were of particular significance in Wimber's approach. The first was his laid-back easy-going style and the second was his insistence that this was a ministry not just for the apostle and the elder but for all the people of God.

Wimber was also a musician who at one time had helped to form a Las Vegas-based band, 'The Righteous Brothers', who gained international acclaim. He introduced his own church to music that was 'soft rock' and worship that was contemporary and informal in style. He soon spawned a small network of congregations called 'Vineyards' which expanded rapidly across the United States and subsequently took root in the United Kingdom. Despite the 'holy carnage'[41] of prostrate bodies on the floor at Wimber meetings, the Vineyard movement took strong root in central North America and among the middle and professional classes in the United Kingdom. The Vineyard movement, as has been pointed out, was, and is, essentially a middle-class phenomenon. Vineyard music, ethos and ministry came to have, and still has, a profound impact on the Church of England. Michael Mitton wrote:

> During the 1980s the renewal of the Church of England was profoundly helped and encouraged by the ministry of John Wimber and his teams from California. Thousands of Anglicans, clergy and lay, will testify to profound experiences of God at Wimber conferences which have changed their ministries.[42]

Despite his ill-judged and brief association with the Kansas City prophets and their misguided predictions of imminent revival,

---

41. See *Renewal* (January 1989) 1: 152.
42. *Renewal* 189 (February 1992): 27.

John Wimber's arrival in England brought a new dimension to charismatic Christianity which was at a point where it was starting to lose its way. Many Restorationist congregations who were beginning to reject the notion of authoritarian apostolic brothers and total commitment, enthusiastically embraced Wimber's easy-going style which barely entertained the notion of church membership lists or electoral roles.

Some charismatics, among them Mark Stibbe,[43] have seen 1994 as beginning a new stage in English charismatic Christianity and have designated it, 'the Fourth Wave'. This began with a series of meetings which were held at the Toronto Airport Vineyard Church. Many people attending were remarkably overcome with what they took to be an experience of the Holy Spirit and the nightly meetings were noted for the accompanying religious phenomena which included falling, jerking and animal noises. There was nothing new in these 'holy exercises', all of which had featured in earlier awakenings on the American continent, yet they served to attract the curious and the journalists in large numbers. Sociologists have pointed out that not only was the charismatic movement in need of a fresh injection of enthusiasm at this point in time but also that Toronto, as a cosmopolitan city in the centre of the North American continent, was an ideal location to stage it.

Great numbers of English church leaders went on pilgrimage to Toronto to receive 'the blessing' and many of those who returned to the British Isles were able to transfer their experience to others.[44] At one point it was reckoned that as many as 3,000 UK churches were experiencing the Toronto Blessing. The Toronto Blessing seems either to have had a very positive effect on the lives and ministries of those attending or to have left them seemingly untouched and confused in their minds as to whether what they had seen was psychologically induced or simply brought about by hypnotic music and the platform rhetoric of John Arnott. This divide has been well charted in the Evangelical Alliance Papers of

---

43. See Stibbe 1995.
44. See Percy 1996.

2001.[45] Vineyard leaders, John and Eleanor Mumford, the Holy Trinity, Brompton staff and Chorleywood leaders were among those who felt themselves to be transformed by the Toronto Experience. The Alpha Course which emanated from Brompton expanded out of all recognition in the years after Nicky Gumbel came under the influence of Toronto, although whether the two facts are interrelated is probably an open question.

The Toronto Blessing undoubtedly fits with what Iain Murray has termed 'revivalism', as opposed to 'revival', on account of its pronounced human element and its use of 'means'.[46] It has brought about a marked divide among English charismatic evangelicals. There were many whose lives had been deeply transformed by their experience of 'the baptism of the Holy Spirit' at a Fountain Trust meeting or a Lee Abbey conference but who felt quite unable to endorse what they perceived as the unnecessary hysteria of the Toronto meetings. Their suspicions were further fuelled by accompanying strong predictions of an imminent end-time revival which failed to materialize. Their stance was typified by Peter Fenwick, a prominent charismatic church leader in Sheffield. In his early years in the city he had started a meeting for charismatic leaders but with the onset of Toronto he had with others felt compelled to quit his own initiative.[47] On the other hand, some congregations such as Holy Trinity, Brompton; Holy Trinity, Cheltenham; St Paul's, Ealing and large numbers of the Pioneer and NFI network churches saw a significant growth in membership following their embracing of Toronto.

One major result of Toronto was that it led numbers of people to leave their places of worship altogether, and significant groups of churches to disown the term 'charismatic evangelical'. Peter Brierley's estimate that the number of charismatic Christians in the UK dipped steeply by 16% following 1995 probably reflects this. It is not necessarily the case that the clergy or their congregations have disowned their charismatic experience, it is

---

45. Hilborn 2001.

46. See Murray 1994: 163–190.

47. See Scotland 2000: 247; Walker 1998: 14.

simply that they feel more comfortable under the label of 'mainstream evangelical'.

Charismatic evangelicals now!

At the beginning of the third millennium it is clearly vital that charismatic Christians take stock of their situation. As I perceive it, the picture is by no means a uniform one. Some Anglican dioceses, for example, have only a handful of overtly charismatic churches. In a survey conducted in January and February 2002, Bradford diocese was reported as having approximately 120 benefices but could only claim 2 congregations with an obvious charismatic tradition. The diocese was described as 'not a charismatic hotspot' and 'full of dull Anglican evangelical churches that feel beleaguered but often with small charismatic elements on their fringes who feel neglected'.[48] The Lincoln diocese could only report 1 overtly charismatic church, that of St Laurence, Skellingthorpe, out of approximately 500 parish churches.[49] Chelmsford diocese claimed only 6 overtly charismatic parishes out of approximately 500.[50] Clearly here there is evidence of what the sociologist of religion, Max Weber, termed 'routinization of charisma'.[51] Weber's theory, which can be applied to any religious group, is that in the initial or early period, the leader's energies and qualities of personality (charisma) thrust the movement forward. However, with the passing of time, the initial leader and his co-workers begin to run out of steam and the impetus is slowed down and often put into a set routine or structure in order to make it more manageable. Eventually the incipient freedom of the Spirit and spontaneity become absorbed into bureaucratic structure. This has undoubtedly been the case in regard to the charismatic movement in certain parts of the UK.

On the other hand, there are areas of strong and resilient growth

---

48. Scotland 2002, report of the diocese of Bradford.
49. Scotland 2002, report of the diocese of Lincoln.
50. Scotland 2002, report of the diocese of Chelmsford.
51. Weber 1966: 2–5, 60–61.

among charismatic Anglicans. Churches such as St Barnabas, Woodside Park and St Paul's, Ealing have seen substantial growth, as has Holy Trinity, Cheltenham under the leadership of Mark Bailey where there are approximately eight hundred to a thousand worshippers a Sunday with two evening services. St Thomas Crookes in Sheffield, under Mike Breen, now has a cluster of associated churches which meet in other parishes across the city. Perhaps most obvious is the continuing influence of Holy Trinity, Brompton and its network of churches which is continuing to stretch out across south west London.[52]

Another significant indicator of charismatic growth was the fact that a total of 456 clergy attended the New Wine Conference on the Bath and Wells Showground at Shepton Mallet in the summer of 2001, the majority coming from the Church of England.[53] Of those clergy, 137 were identifiable as Anglican incumbents by virtue of their addresses being listed as either the 'vicarage' or the 'rectory'.[54] This means that of the order of 150 parishes quite probably reflect at least some New Wine or Vineyard values. Significantly, of these 137 New Wine clergy, 108 came from parishes which were south of a line drawn from Birmingham to the Wash in Norfolk. This would seem to suggest that charismatic

---

52. The Holy Trinity, Brompton network includes includes St Paul's, Onslow Square; St Mary's, Bryanston Square; St Paul's, Hammersmith under Simon Downham; St Stephen's, Westbourne Park; St Mark's, Battersea; St Barnabas, North Kensington and the Oaktree Anglican Fellowship, Acton. Holy Trinity, Brompton itself currently runs two evening services and is about to start a third morning service. Both St. Barnabas and St. Mark's, Battersea have planted churches of their own in Acton, Balham and Hammersmith. Oaktree have planted Riverside Community Church in Chiswick and Holy Trinity give input and support to World's End Community Church. Additionally, Holy Trinity sends out teams to help churches who want to establish something new on Sunday evenings.

53. Information received from Dr John Knight of New Wine Networks by e-mail, 7 February 2002.

54. This figure is likely to be larger than 130 since some clergy who are incumbents simply give their house number and road name.

evangelicalism tends to be more strongly rooted in the southern half of the country. This fact is further reinforced by statistics reported in *The Body Book*, a directory of charismatic churches published in 2000. It gives membership details of 1,023 charismatic churches including Anglicans, Baptist and the New networks. Of these churches, 67% are located in the southern half of the country. The statistics also show that eight of the top ten churches in 1998 had not increased in their attendance figures for 2000.

This picture is further endorsed by the remarkable and continued resilient growth in the main New Church networks. For instance, New Frontiers International (NFI) led by Terry Virgo had 74 affiliated congregations with 8 church plants in 1990 with a membership of 13,000. By the close of 2001 this figure had risen to 152 with 50 church plants and a membership of 26,500.[55] During the same period Pioneer, led by Gerald Coates, grew from approximately 50 affiliated congregations with 3,000 members in 1990 to 80 affiliated congregations with an estimated membership of 10,000 in 2001.[56] Other New Church strands, notably Salt and Light,[57] Cornerstone and Vineyard continue to show comparable growth. They all report an ongoing emphasis on spiritual gifts in their worship, Vineyard-style music and prayer ministry.

As will be apparent from these statistics, one of the great strengths of charismatic evangelicalism is its continued emphasis on evangelism and church planting. Nowhere is this more visible than in the spectacular expansion of the Alpha Courses emanating from Holy Trinity, Brompton. Since 1990 when Nicky Gumbel took over the course and revamped it, Alpha grew from 5 courses in 1992 to 7,287 in Britain by the close of 2001.[58] Significantly in 2001 there were also 12,600 courses abroad and Alpha ran in 3,500 churches in America.[59] Nicky Gumbel was reported to have more

---

55. Written information received from Steve Blaber of NFI Office, 24 Station Road, Sidcup, Kent DA15 7DU, dated 5 February 2002.

56. Written information received from Pioneer, 5 February 2002.

57. For Salt and Light see Scotland 2000: 24–25.

58. See Askwith 1998; Combe 2001.

59. Combe 2001.

staff than the Archbishop of Canterbury, with 64 working solely on Alpha in offices built in the grounds of Holy Trinity.[60] Alpha has also stimulated other mainstream evangelicals to engage in evangelistic enterprise. Some have taken up with Alpha, while others have produced similar courses with slightly different emphases.[61]

Related to this emphasis on evangelism among charismatic evangelicals has been their growing concern with the summer Bible Conferences in which seminars are given by a variety of scholars and Christian practitioners from across a wide spectrum on practical issues. These range from marriage and family to ethical and moral issues such as the environment and resolving conflict. Charismatic Christians have been actively involved in the organization and running of Spring Harvest since its inception. This is by far the largest annual Christian gathering in the British Isles. It drew an attendance of 80,000 mostly middle-class individuals to several centres at Easter 1991. This figure had reduced to 60,000 by 1999 largely, however, on account of using smaller sites. The attendance remained at the same level in 2001.[62] Among the largest annual summer events are New Wine hosted by John and Anne Coles which attracted 25,000 in 2001 and the New Frontiers International Bible week at Stoneleigh which drew in 28,000 in the same year. Associated with New Wine has been Soul Survivor organized by Mike Pilavachi with its headquarters in Watford. In addition to major summer events which drew in some 18,000 young people in 2001, Soul Survivor has sponsored a number of Youth Churches and youth congregations. These include The Path at Holy Trinity church, Cheltenham. Since the dramatic collapse and scandal surrounding Chris Brain's *Nine O'clock Service* (N.O.S.)[63] in Sheffield, the enthusiasm for youth churches has receded, though it is clearly not altogether off the charismatic agenda.

In 1999 George Otis Junior impacted many charismatic churches

---

60. Combe 2001.
61. For example All Souls, Langham Place have produced a course entitled 'Christianity Explored'.
62. Information received from Spring Harvest, 25 February 2002.
63. Howard 1996.

with his *Transformations* video. This had the effect of reinforcing the social concern which had been emerging among charismatic evangelicals during the previous decade. Since the early beginnings of the 1960s there had been a strong belief in the Spirit's power to bring wholeness and renewal to the individual. However, with the growing interest in Celtic spirituality in the 1980s, and an emergent theological stress on the operation of the Spirit embracing the cosmos,[64] charismatics increasingly, began to give serious attention to transformation within their local communities. Those who had focused on a future revival and the coming millennium in the 1970s and 1980s now came to concern themselves with a present renewal and the healing of the land. Mark Stibbe put the matter succinctly in the following lines:

> In the final analysis, any pneumatology or doctrine of the Holy Spirit which is purely concerned with the work of the Spirit in the church, or, worse still, in us as individual Christians, is hopelessly myopic. The Holy Spirit is concerned not only with our own liberation, but also with the liberation of societies, cultures, nature and indeed the whole cosmos.[65]

It is significant therefore to note that charismatics have been at the forefront in the leadership of both the Care Trust and the Evangelical Alliance. Pioneer, New Frontiers International and Vineyard all report a growing and active involvement in many social projects, both locally and nationally.[66]

The not so good!

The foregoing paragraphs should not be taken to imply that charismatic evangelicals are without their weak spots. There are several continuing dysfunctional aspects which need careful thought and

---

64. Moltmann 1992: 7.
65. See Stibbe 1992: 6.
66. Information received in response to structured questionnaires, February 2002.

action. In general, charismatics find it hard to listen and wait. If the next wave appears slow in arriving and nothing of significance seems to be happening, there is a tendency to invent something new or to re-package an aspect from the past. This means in practice that certain sections of the charismatic world are always running after the next new thing, be it words of knowledge, personal prophecy, warfare prayer, another anointing, Celtic worship, Christian Zionism, Toronto Blessings, gold teeth-fillings or spiritual mapping. Often the pace up front is so fast that there is barely time to assess or evaluate the present because another big name preacher is pushing the agenda on to the next new thing God is believed to be doing.

The following are the main areas over which people, both within and outside charismatic evangelicalism, are currently expressing concern. In the matter of prophetic utterance there is still considerable need for careful pastoral handling, particularly is this so where directive words are offered to churches or individuals or where messages which are charged with political content are given. It needs to be recognized that many of those who engage in predictive prophecy are people who are looking for affirmation or a way of imparting their agenda to a wider audience. An American Vineyard pastor recently suggested that 90% of what most people prophesy is purely for themselves. Where individuals attempt to speak prophetically about issues or circumstances of which they are a part, it inevitably becomes very difficult indeed to filter out their own opinions and personal preferences on the matter concerned.

Perhaps what is needed here is the establishment of Schools of Prophets after the pattern established by the Revd Barry Kissell in London.[67] Here an open debate can take place as to the worth and relevance of what are felt to be significant prophecies. Only then should they be endorsed and presented to others, but still with the proviso that they need to be judged by the hearers. It is widely acknowledged that there have been far too many rash and ill-judged prophecies about the coming of revival. Not only have most of those which have been given concerning the UK been

---

67. Kissell 2002: 133–139.

proved wrong, they have caused much heartache and discouragement. The giving of very personal words by one individual to another, particularly where the prophet so-called reveals information which is essentially personal or private, is fraught with danger. A number of Vineyard leaders in the United States confessed that they had fallen into 'divination' on this particular score.[68] This apart, the practice of inspirational prophecy where members of the congregation are invited to speak brief positive and encouraging words of strengthening, encouragement and comfort after the injunction in 1 Corinthians 14:3 needs to be fostered. It gives people the opportunity to participate and to encourage others in their local Christian community.

Closely allied to the prophetic is the matter of guidance, and there are still too many in the charismatic world who allow themselves to be led by instantaneous impressions rather than by growing convictions which are strengthened by reflection on the principles of Scripture. Generally speaking, the danger with 'hot line impulse guidance from God' is that there is no time to assess the issues involved and make a wise decision. There are still some, though few in number, who ask God to bring a Scripture to their mind and then promptly act on it without any further consideration. This is what the eighteenth-century philosophers judged to be 'enthusiasm' and it clearly has an inbuilt capacity for disaster.

Many are also of the opinion that there is still too much emphasis on the demonic amongst contemporary charismatic evangelicals.[69] The danger of an over-heated demonology is that individuals can quickly lose their grasp on reality and begin to see everything through a demonic grid. There is still also a tendency in some circles to blame the devil for everything which goes wrong[70] and, in consequence, to bind and rebuke every problem be it great or small. There needs to be a recognition that Christians have to grapple with three sources of evil, the world, the flesh and the devil and probably in that order. There is in some quarters a persistent unhealthy emphasis

---

68. Payne 1998.

69. For an example of an extreme demonology see Hammond 1992.

70. See Scotland 2001b.

on demonic entry points and territorial spirits, neither of which have solid biblical foundations. Entry point teaching asserts that evil spirits enter into people through particular points in the body such as the eyes, the mouth, the ear or even the genitals. Release, according to some exorcists, can only come as the entry point is prayed over, signed with the cross and anointed with oil. Rowland Howard in his book *Charismania* charted some of the disastrous consequences which have resulted from this type of ministry.[71]

On the second matter of territorial spirits, the current fashion for 'spiritual mapping' is putting far too much focus on the presence of evil and demonic blackspots. At the very least some balance could be brought into the situation if the individuals who engage in this activity plotted the endeavours of faithful churches and godly ministries alongside the dots they stick on Spiritualist churches and Masonic lodges.

Dénouement

One thing seems very clear and that is that charismatic Christianity has lastingly impacted evangelicalism as a whole. There has taken place what David Tomlinson termed 'charismaticisation'[72] and this is still very much an ongoing process. By this term Tomlinson referred to the way in which many mainstream evangelical churches have come to absorb and imbibe aspects of charismatic culture and indeed, in some cases, aspects of charismatic experience. Thus an evangelical church which may well eschew charismatic experience and charismatic theology may yet have assumed a dress-down culture, use informal and Vineyard songs and music and offer prayer counselling at the close of their Sunday worship. 'Charismaticisation' is in fact observable well beyond the boundaries of evangelicalism. I was informed for example, that when the diocese of Derby hold their annual conference at Swanwick there is informal worship, congregational participation

71. Howard 1997.
72. Tomlinson 1995: 15–17.

and prayer ministry.[73] The Revd Paul Smith, a circuit minister in Plymouth, made the same observation of Methodism in general and noted that charismaticisation was particularly marked in parts of East Anglia and the West Country.[74]

The emergence of growing 'charismaticisation' in the early 1990s marked the ending of the charismatic movement if indeed such a thing ever existed. Certainly by the beginning of the last decade of the twentieth century, charismatic Christianity had become a very diverse phenomenon and it was no longer easy to decide who was a charismatic and who was not.

There are still some significant sections within British evangelicalism that do not consider contemporary charismatic phenomena to be genuine manifestations of the Holy Spirit. This stance may in part be driven by exaggerated claims of healing on the part of charismatics.[75] Indeed, in some circles, the rhetoric about healing considerably exceeds the reality. It is the case that charismatics in general have been reluctant to acknowledge that the percentage of full and lasting physical, mental and emotional healings is relatively small and that organic healings are few in number. Nevertheless, even some of those churches which are avowedly cessationist in their theology are happy to offer worship which is led by robe-free clergy with lay participation and Vineyard and Kendrick songs. Additionally, many of them offer some form of prayer counselling at the close of their services.[76]

Martin Percy in his assessment predicted an increasingly fragmented future for charismatic evangelicalism in the third millennium. Significantly, despite the emergence of one or two smaller strands, charismatics have shown a remarkable capacity to hold together in a unified way. Indeed it is the Episcopal churches which are fragmenting, most notably in the United States where

---

73. Information from the Revd John Leach, Anglican Renewal Ministries, Derby, February 2002.

74. Information from the Revd Paul Smith, Methodist minister of Plymouth Circuit, February 2002.

75. See Glover 1997: 83–111; Sedden 1990.

76. See, for example, Masters & Whitcombe 1992; Glover 1997.

there are now thirty-five different Anglican Episcopal Communities, but also in England where there are several independent
Anglican churches which have broken away over matters such as
homosexuality, women priests and gay and lesbian issues.

The strong emphasis on evangelism on the part of many charismatics and their growing concern for political issues and societal
transformation must bode well for the future. Conscious efforts are
being made within the New Church strands to put new leaders in
the key positions and to give proper theological training. This is particularly visible, for example, in the case of the Ichthus network
churches in South London and at the Bristol Christian Fellowship. It
is clear that charismatic Christianity is at its most resilient within the
New Churches rather than within the denominational churches.
Charismatics within the established church face particular difficulties. This is true of both those whose sympathies lie with the former
Anglican Renewal Ministries and those who affiliate with New Wine
Networks. The former are becoming increasingly captivated by
Anglican structures, liturgy and elements of Catholic spirituality.
The latter have always declared that the new wine of the Holy Spirit
demands 'new wine skins', yet the New Wine leaders have, until very
recently, consistently turned away from their own agenda at this
point. However, a significant step forward was made in the summer
of 2002 by which the New Wine Network have agreed to offer vali-
dation and give pastoral input to those affiliated churches which
have no other denominational allegiance. This is a development
which will mean that New Wine will move closer towards becoming
an organization such as New Frontiers and Pioneer.

Worship has been another major focus among charismatics and
it is this aspect which has drawn, and continued to attract, people to
their ranks. Here perhaps there is something which Anglican charismatics and those from other strands can learn from each other.
Many charismatics have tended to regard liturgy as the law which
kills and the lack of it as the Spirit which gives life. In fact, a number
of charismatics are rediscovering the value of at least some sort of
liturgical and sacramental framework. There is in fact an observable
growing recognition among charismatics that there can be greater
freedom within liturgy rather than from it. A simple structure can
indeed provide a secure context in which congregational members

will feel free both to contribute and yet also to enjoy moments of silence, waiting, watching, listening and meditation.

If there is one matter of particular importance as charismatic evangelicals contemplate the years ahead at the beginning of the third millennium, it is the issue of rootedness which relates to questions of liturgy. Many charismatics have been aware of what they are reacting or fighting against, but what they have not always been clear about is what they are contending for. Perhaps, like many mainstream evangelicals, they are realizing the need for roots, a historical base and a biblically informed tradition which runs back through the centuries. It is this need for roots which has caused numbers of charismatics, including Michael Harper, to find a new base in the Greek Orthodox Church. By the same token, significant numbers of former Vineyard pastors and congregations have gone over to the Communion of Evangelical Episcopal Churches in the United States. Indeed more than fifty former Vineyard pastors are now ministering in an ordained capacity in one or other of the American Episcopal churches.

Far from a declining outlook, charismatic evangelicalism still offers a prospect of hope for the future. The postmodern world of the early third millennium is a pluralist culture which can only be effectively engaged and addressed by a variety of differing expressions of church. In this respect the wide diversity and breadth of charismatic evangelicalism should mean that it is well placed to play its part, together with other sections of evangelicalism, in carrying forward the contemporary church's mission.

Bibliography

Anon. (2002), 'C of E to be ARM less', *Christianity and Renewal* (June): 5.

Askwith, R. (1998), 'God's Own Spin Doctor', *The Independent*, 17 September.

Bax, J. (1986), *The Good Wine: Spiritual Renewal in the Church of England*, London: Church House Publishing.

Bede (1990), *History of the English Church and People*, Harmondsworth: Penguin.

Blumhofer, E. (1986), 'Alexander Boddy and the Rise of Pentecostalism in Britain', *Pneuma* 8 (Spring): 31–40.

Boulton, E. C. W. (1928), *George Jeffreys: A Ministry of the Miraculous*, London: Elim Publishing House.

Brierley, P. (1999), *UK Christian Handbook: Religious Trends 1998/1999*, Carlisle: Paternoster Press.

Cartwright, D. W. (1986), *The Great Evangelists*, London: Marshall Pickering.

Caughey, J. (1855), *Earnest Christianity*, Boston: J. P. Magee.

Christie-Murray, D. (1978), *Voices from the Gods: Speaking with Tongues*, London: Routledge & Kegan Paul.

Church of England Doctrine Commission (1991), *We Believe in the Holy Spirit*, London: Church House Publishing.

Church Information Office (1981), *The Charismatic Movement in the Church of England*, London: CIO.

Combe, V. (2001), 'Curate's Course Feeds Spiritual Hunger', *Daily Telegraph*, 26 December: 8.

Edwards, J. (1741), *The Distinguishing Marks of a Work of the True Spirit*, repr. Edinburgh: Banner of Truth Trust, 1991.

Finnis, M. (2002), 'Too Much Work in Our Churches', *Baptist Times*, 24 January.

Glover, P. (ed.) (1997), *The Signs and Wonders Movement Exposed*, Epsom: Day One Publications.

Hammond, F. and I. (1992), *Pigs in the Parlour*, Chichester: New Wine Press.

Hilborn, D. (ed.) (2001), *Toronto in Perspective: Papers on the New Charismatic Wave of the Mid-1990s*, Carlisle: Paternoster Press.

Hocken, P. (1997), *Streams of Renewal*, Carlisle: Paternoster Press, 1997.

Hood, A. B. E. (1979), *St Patrick: His Writings and Muirchu's Life*, Newton Abbot: Phillimore.

Howard, R. (1996), *The Rise and Fall of the Nine O'clock Service*, London: Mowbray.

Howard, R. (1997), *Charismania*, London: Mowbray.

Icthus Christian Fellowship (1999), *Welcome to Icthus Christian Fellowship*, London: Icthus.

Kay, W. K. (2000), *Pentecostals in Britain*, Carlisle: Paternoster Press.

Kissell, B. (2002), *The Prophet's Notebook*, Eastbourne: Kingsway.

Lavin, P. (1986), *Alexander Boddy: Pastor and Prophet*, Wearside Historic Churches Group.

Masters, P. and J. C. Whitcombe (1992), *The Charismatic Phenomenon*, London: The Wakeman Trust.

McBain, D. (1997), 'Mainstream Charismatics: Some Observations of

Baptist Renewal', in S. Hunt et al. (eds.), *Charismatic Christianity*, Basingstoke: Macmillan Press.

Moltmann, J. (1992), *The Spirit of Life*, London: SCM Press.

Murray, Iain (1994), *Revival and Revivalism: The Making and Marring of American Evangelicalism*, Edinburgh: Banner of Truth Trust.

Palmer, P. (1845), *The Way of Holiness*, New York.

Payne, L. (1998), '"Substitution" in Prayer, False Prophecy, and the Virtue of Hope', *Wheaton Pastoral Care Ministries School*, Tape 12.

Percy, M. (1996), *The Toronto Blessing*, Oxford: Latimer House.

Richards, A. (1997), *The Toronto Experience: An Exploration of the Issues*, London: Church House Publishing.

Scotland, N. A. D. (2000), *Charismatics and the New Millennium*, Guildford: Eagle.

—— (2001a), 'Signs and Wonders in the Early Catholic Church 90–451 AD and Their Implications for the Twenty First Century', *European Journal of Theology* 10.2: 161.

—— (2001b), 'Don't Blame the Devil for Everything which goes wrong!' *Skepsis/Anglicans for Renewal* 85 (Summer): 27–34.

—— (2002), Survey of Charismatic Churches in Church of England Dioceses, January–February. This survey consisted of structured questionnaires sent to the chairperson of all Diocesan Renewal Groups.

Sedden, P. (1990), 'Spiritual Warfare V Medical Reflections', in P. Jensen and T. Payne (eds.), *John Wimber Friend or Foe?*, 32–35, n.p.: St Matthias Press.

Sellers, C. C. (1928), *Lorenzo Dow: The Bearer of the Word*, New York: Minton, Balch.

Stibbe, M. (1992), 'The Renewal of Harvest – a Charismatic Theology of Creation', *Skepsis*.

—— (1995), *Times of Refreshing: A Practical Theology of Revival for Today*, London: Marshall Pickering.

Tomlinson, D. (1995), *Post-Evangelical*, London: Triangle.

Turner, M. (1996), *The Holy Spirit and Spiritual Gifts: Then and Now*, Carlisle: Paternoster Press.

Walker, A. (1998), *Restoring the Kingdom: The Radical Christianity of the House Church Movement*, Guildford: Eagle.

Weber, M. (1966), *The Sociology of Religion,* London: Methuen.

Wimber, J. (1981), *Riding the Third Wave*, London: Marshall Pickering.

10B. BACK TO THE FUTURE FOR PENTECOSTAL/CHARISMATIC EVANGELICALS IN NORTH AMERICA AND WORLD WIDE: RADICALIZING EVANGELICAL THEOLOGY AND PRACTICE

Jonathan Ruthven

What does the future look like for Pentecostal/charismatic evangelicals? It depends on where one starts. For me, it was summer, 1967. Since I had just graduated from a well-known evangelical seminary nearby, I dropped in on a friend who was a resident of the 'Faith Homes' in Zion, Illinois. The 'Faith Homes' provided solace for spiritual refugees in a utopian town built by a faith healer, John Alexander Dowie, who, though amazingly gifted, came to believe in his later life that he was the prophet Elijah and that he deserved more than his share of women.

During my visit, I learned that in one of these houses lay an elderly, housebound saint whose ministry it was to pray all night, every night for the salvation of the world. My friend, with an air of reverence, ushered me into the bedroom. We chatted briefly, then I was told that the Lord had promised this intercessor that before Jesus returned there would be a billion 'Spirit-filled believers' on the earth.

I was incredulous. It never occurred to me then (and probably neither to the elderly gentleman) that the term, 'Spirit-filled' could refer to anyone other than Pentecostals, or perhaps, to the new charismatics, whose presence was just beginning to be felt in North America. But a *billion*?! We were a tiny minority. Hadn't I just overheard a faculty member from my seminary heatedly insist that, along with Mormons and Jehovah's Witnesses, Pentecostals should not be allowed to matriculate there? Another professor demurred, who, in Christian charity, clung to the hope that Pentecostal students might be salvageable.

In the intervening years, my sins have swung from doubt to vainglory. 'Spirit-filled' Christians, secure in their experience that God performs miracles today,[1] number around 543 million[2] – on cruise control to that prophetic figure of one billion. The movement, originally dismissed by some as 'the last great vomit of Satan',[3] has now become the largest active group in Christianity.

Not all evangelicals, however, want to be in that number. This raises the issue of the 'evangelical' nature of Pentecostals and their offspring, the charismatics and the third wave movement.[4]

---

1. A *Newsweek* Poll conducted by Princeton Survey Research Associates, 13–14 April 2000, asked the question, 'Do you believe that God performs miracles?' Eighty-four per cent of the American general population said 'Yes'. Of these respondents, of course, few were Pentecostals, but the responses show the fertile ground in North America for a Pentecostal/charismatic world-view.
   http://www.pollingreport.com/religion2.htm

2. David M. Barrett, World Evangelization Research Center http://www.gem-werc.org/. Barrett projects that by 2020 the figure will reach 811 million. See also Barrett 2002.

3. This characterization of Pentecostals is widely attributed to G. Campbell Morgan, e.g. by Ewart 1975: 38–39; Synan 1971: 144.

4. Classical Pentecostals, a movement beginning around the 1900s, tended to be strict fundamentalists until the rise of the charismatic movement, springing up within, and frequently abandoning, mostly mainline churches during the 1960s. The 'Third Wave' of Pentecostalism, comprised of many independent and denominational churches, is more focused on the spiritual gifts as edification rather than as a distinguishing 'evidence'. The world-view and worship styles of Pentecostalism have penetrated broadly across not only evangelicalism, but within the

Evangelicals, of course, see themselves as faithful to the Protestant tradition, against the 'mainline' denominations who have drifted leftward.[5] Historically, Pentecostals conducted an unrequited love affair with the precursors of the evangelicals, that is, the fundamentalists, who were characterized by their shrill polemics and bitter splits from the traditional major denominations over their drift into modernism/liberalism – and the denial of historic tenets of the Christian faith such as the infallibility of Scripture, the virgin birth of Jesus, his miracles, atoning sacrifice for sin, resurrection, and literal return to earth.

So when it came to relating to the Pentecostals, the early fundamentalists (from about the 1920s to the 1950s) were in no mood for ecumenical trysts with anyone messing with Reformation doctrine. This was particularly true of their doctrine of cessationism, that is, the notion that miracles were limited to around the time of the apostles strictly to accredit the authority of the New Testament. Any claim to a miracle, such as speaking in tongues, was tantamount to adding new text to Scripture – the ultimate heresy to those often accused of bibliolatry.[6] To gain acceptance, Pentecostals desperately tried to behave and believe more fundamentalist than the fundamentalists, but mostly they received rejection for their efforts. Nevertheless, classical Pentecostals fervently shared the fundamentalist refrain: 'My hope is built on nothing less/ Than Scofield's notes and Moody Press!'

By the 1960s and 1970s, most rigid fundamentalism had mellowed into evangelicalism, becoming less brittle about most of its issues, including cessationism. The National Association of

---

increasingly marginalized 'mainline' denominations as well. Some remain unhappy with this development, e.g. Wood 1996; Noll 2002.

5. Barna (2001) has discovered, however, that more than four out of five American Senior Pastors (83%) describe themselves as 'evangelical'. 'Large majorities of clergy representing churches not generally thought of as evangelical embraced that label, such as seven out of ten who serve mainline churches.'

6. For a history and theological analysis of cessationism see Ruthven 1993.

Evangelicals included Pentecostals, who served in many joint ventures, such as Billy Graham crusades and world-wide missions conferences. Presently, the Pentecostal/charismatic constituency world-wide vastly outnumbers their evangelical counterparts; the tail now wags the dog. Interest among Pentecostals in being identified with evangelicals remains strong, but may be waning. Bellwether Pentecostal scholars are increasingly more drawn to the Society for Pentecostal Studies, the Society for Biblical Literature, and to ecumenical conferences, than to the Evangelical Theological Society. The second and third wave charismatics seem increasingly vague about their identity as evangelicals, though all Pentecostals and virtually all charismatics share essential doctrines with evangelicals.

The current scene

In North America, classical Pentecostalism,[7] which had grown rapidly during the decades of the 1970s and 1980s, have seen its growth flatten during the 1990s, the so-called 'Decade of Harvest'.[8] In North America, it is independent Pentecostal/charismatic or 'apostolic' churches and emerging denominations like the Association of Vineyard Churches that are experiencing the most growth. Perhaps the growing institutionalization of even this new movement made them uneasy with the extremely popular charismatic manifestations of the Toronto Airport Fellowship which saw some 300,000 visitors spreading its 'blessing' back to their

---

7. Represented by such denominations as the Assemblies of God, Pentecostal Assemblies of Canada, The Church of God (HQ Cleveland, TN), Church of the Foursquare Gospel, and the largest, The Church of God in Christ, an African-American body of some five million.

8. A term coined by the Assemblies of God leadership to apply to the 1990s, partly in response to a cooling of evangelistic fervour after two decades of almost effortless but sizeable windfall numerical increases, that is, the influx of many whose experiences with the Spirit tended to alienate them from their 'mainline' denominations. See the statistics in Lindner 2002.

home churches.[9] Similarly, the 'Pensacola revival' served to revitalize Pentecostalism.

Despite these expressions, North America is no longer the focus of church growth. Instead, in the non-Muslim Third World, in Asia and especially Latin America and Africa, the Pentecostal/charismatic movement is remarkable for its vitality. Reinhart Bonnke often draws crowds of a million in a single meeting, proclaiming an aggressive gospel of counterattack against the power of the devil in sickness, demonic oppression and sin. The Third World, nevertheless, has long ago moved beyond dependence on white missionaries. Missions statistician David Barrett offered that 'according to our estimates, the specifically new independent churches in Christianity number about 394 million, which is getting on for twenty percent of the Christian world'.[10]

Why this growth in the Third World? The answers vary. Many academics who study missions offer social, economic and political reasons galore for the success of Christian missions, but, as another expert pointed out, they failed at the most elementary level as historians: to take the primary sources seriously, that is, the testimonies of the original missionaries themselves, who routinely recorded that the penetration of new areas for the gospel was a result of the power of God in healings, exorcisms, revelatory spiritual gifts and miracles.[11]

Harvey Cox, by contrast, suggests that Pentecostalism, on a spiritual level, scratches where it itches: this charismatic gospel resonates across all cultures with the 'primal spirituality' common to humanity.[12]

---

9. Lester 2002.

10. Cited by Lester 2002.

11. McGee 2001.

12. Cox 1995: 81–84. Cox (1995: 83) sees Pentecostalism as representing the 'recovery of primal speech (ecstatic utterance), primal piety (mystical experience, trance, and healing), and primal hope (the unshakable expectation of a better future)'. This seems to be true in North American experience as well. 'We maintain that ecstatic religious experience is an important factor in evangelistic activities that undoubtedly promote church growth': Poloma & Pendleton 1989: 415.

Humans are hard-wired, it seems, to believe not only in the afterlife, but in revelatory experiences, demons and supernatural power. These experiences fit more closely with the world-view of Jesus and the New Testament than to that of the cessationism of the Reformers and the rationalism of the Enlightenment which colour much traditional evangelical theology. Certainly the future of Christianity, then, resonates with St Paul's hope: 'That your faith not rest on words of wisdom, but on God's power' (1 Cor. 2:5).

Perhaps the question of why Pentecostal/charismatic growth worldwide contrasts with that of North America and Europe is best answered by another question: what is this movement in the Third World doing differently?

1. Unlike the powerfully anaesthetizing effect of materialism of the West, which insulates its adherents from almost every form of suffering and want ('fat, rich and in need of nothing'), Third World people face starker choices and see more clearly their need for intensive prayer for the power and life of God. For a Westerner, God can be an expendable comfort; but for the poor, he is survival. The Western impulse to solve spiritual problems by more expertise, buildings and technology is seductive, but in the long run will likely be counterproductive.

2. Unlike the private individualism of North Americans, those in the Third World tend to think and act more communally. Families and villages are much more needed in cultures without welfare state government programmes and powerful economies that can supply every whim. With the rise of urbanization in the Third World and the breakdown of family and village ties, the church often steps in as a surrogate family, providing security, nurture and, above all, a larger sense of responsibility for others in the communal presence of God.

3. Unlike the professional, formally-educated ministers of North America, ministry in the Third World is the business of lay people. The Pentecostal principle of encouraging spiritual empowerment as broadly as possible undergirds the practice of ministry training by apprenticeship rather than by a detached, academic and often irrelevant formal education.

In keeping with the model of 1 Corinthians 12, each 'member' (spiritually-gifted person) in a Pentecostal church body is expected to express their charisms of the Holy Spirit. The oft-misinterpreted proverb, 'A man's gift makes a way for him' applies to a young person whose spiritual yearning to be useful in the kingdom of God finds encouragement to ministering to those around her or him, all the while learning, as an apprentice, while doing. By contrast, traditional theological education may well contribute to the stagnation of church growth in North America.[13] This system has that same potential overseas. Missionaries frequently complain that when they send their best and brightest young people to North America for Bible college or seminary training they rarely return, and if they do, they often return infected with materialism, status-seeking and a loss of their original zeal for ministry.

4. Unlike their Western counterparts,[14] Third World Christians may actually enjoy a more accurate and sophisticated grasp of 'theology'. If 'theology' is the understanding and articulation of the Christian faith, then they have penetrated beneath evangelical traditions to perceive more profoundly the emphases of New Testament theology. Salvation is viewed by Third World Christians more holistically, encompassing the physical and social dimensions of life as well as the spiritual focus on regeneration and sanctification. Prayer and faith for God's miracle power is scarcely mentioned positively in traditional evangelical theology, but they play a huge role both in the New Testament and in Third World Christianity.[15]

---

13. See Ruthven 2001.

14. Barna 2002. 'Shockingly few Americans understand the power and significance of the supernatural world . . . Most Americans deny the existence of Satan and the Holy Spirit and are blissfully ignorant of the spiritual battle that rages around and within them. Who will inform and motivate God's people about the realities of the battle?'

15. Jenkins 2002: 123–131.

The future of evangelical Pentecostal/charismatic theology and practice

This observation brings us to our principal speculation on the Pentecostal/charismatic 'evangelical future', namely, that either descriptively or prescriptively, evangelicalism is in line to redefine its key theological vocabulary to conform more to New Testament doctrine and Third World (or, primal human) experience. Whether or not theology precedes or follows religious experience is debatable – most likely they are mutually conditioned, but the church could profit from a theology that did not, at least, ignore or thwart the major factors for church growth.

Within traditional evangelical systematic theology, a number of key biblical doctrines, outlined below, evolved toward a common characteristic: the denial or evasion of their inherent charismatic significance. By contrast, the biblical studies showed the NT emphases within these doctrines to be a great deal more informed by the charismatic power of God. More disciplined study suggests this charismatic emphasis to be even greater. Nowadays, however, even the growing Pentecostal/charismatic branch of Christianity lacks a thoroughgoing theology that treats these themes from a radically biblical/charismatic perspective rather than from scholastic categories of traditional Protestantism. Pentecostal doctrine has been popularly attributed more to personal experience than to Scripture. In fact one could say, potentially at least, that in the area of the application of Scripture, Pentecostals may finally 'out fundamentalist the fundamentalists', or at least their evangelical counterparts in a radical (in the sense of returning to the root) biblical grounding for a truly evangelical theology.

However, traditional Protestant hermeneutics can be shown consciously to deny or minimize charismatic themes in the NT. For example, Luther's ranking of NT canonical books was based primarily, and inversely, on their emphasis on miracles.[16] Pentecostal interpreters simply adopted the traditional view of miracle to articulate their experience of the Spirit: 'miraculous' gifts existed only as

---

16. Luther, Works: 35: 361. See the discussion in Althaus 1966: 83.

apologetic devices to serve as 'signs' or 'evidence' of otherwise invisible divine actions. Further, Pentecostals followed the Protestant *ordo salutis* to place the 'Baptism of the Holy Spirit' as a subset of the stage of sanctification: hence and experience that served only as 'evidence' of the Spirit, occurring 'subsequent' to 'salvation'. The following paragraphs suggest that the New Testament itself would shift the experience of the Spirit from these old conceptual 'old wineskins' into newer, more useful and biblical paradigms.

Holy Spirit

Traditional theology has discussed the Holy Spirit as an adjunct to extraneous concerns: the Trinity, the procession of the Spirit, ethics and, in Protestantism, the *ordo salutis*. A number of key biblical studies laid out a more charismatic portrayal of the Spirit.[17] Statistical methods show that the OT and NT share essentially the same profile of emphases about the Spirit, one that is overwhelmingly active in charismatic expression. It is this charismatic Spirit of revelation, prophecy and miracle, who is normative for all Christians – not a Spirit mostly limited to the traditional functions of regeneration and sanctification.

Kingdom of God

The kingdom of God has received scant attention in traditional systematics, being identified with either the 'visible church' (RCC), the 'invisible church' (Protestant), or with the ideal theocracy at the end of the age. This latter concept devolved into the 'just society' of the Enlightenment, theological liberalism and the 'liberation' theologies. The biblical studies from Schweitzer onward showed how the kingdom was the central motif in Jesus' ministry (Luke 4:43). Where the few NT contexts actually describe the nature of the kingdom (e.g. Matt. 12:28//Luke 11:20; Rom. 14:17; 1 Cor. 4:20)

---

17. For example, Hermann Gunkel's *Die Wirkungen des heiligen Geistes* (1889), ET 1979. Gunkel's work was popularized in a *Theological Dictionary of the New Testament* article by G. Freidrich, which was translated into English in the late 1960s, radically reframing the doctrine of the Holy Spirit toward a much greater charismatic emphasis.

analysis shows its profoundly charismatic nature, almost a synonym for 'Spirit',[18] though the overwhelming emphasis in the NT is on the radical demand that one enter the kingdom.

The 'new covenant'

The 'new covenant', a major theme in traditional Protestant thinking, particularly in classical Reformed. The traditional 'covenant' focuses on the movement from law to grace in dealing with sin. However, the covenant promise of the Old Testament is centrally a promise of the Spirit of prophecy (e.g. Is. 59:21; Jer. 31:31; Ezek. 11:19; 36:26; Joel 2:28–30) to those normatively in the 'new covenant', that is, in the proleptically experienced 'age to come'.

The human condition

The Reformation saw man centrally as sinner in need of grace. In the redeemed order there was growth in sanctification (ethics) and in vocation (Calvinism), but there was little appreciation for the breadth and depth of human charismatic perception and experience outside of these categories. A biblical world-view appreciates the range of 'charismatic' experiences indigenous to all mankind (Jer. 32:20; Rom. 1:18–20), involving demonic, revelatory or physical phenomena. The 'bondage to decay' must include demonic oppression, disease, the religious traditions of men, as well as the effects of social, physical and environmental forces. This theological emphasis asks, 'Before we provide the theological solution, what is the problem – that is, the human condition?'

Salvation

Related to the human condition is salvation. Traditionally, 'salvation' involves forgiveness of sin, regeneration, ethical living and one's acceptance into heaven. Biblical studies expanded the notion to include rescue from oppressors (human and demonic) and physical healing. Analysis of the semantic field for salvation in the NT drives the term even more toward the physical, though including the ethical. For example, where the context is clear, virtually all

---

18. Dunn 1970.

of the references in the gospels to 'salvation' (*sotēria*) apply principally to physical healing. Salvation in the NT is a much broader
term than in traditional evangelicalism.

Miracle

Traditional concepts of 'miracle' rely on a highly rationalistic epistemology and anti-biblical concepts of nature. The function of
miracles was largely evidential (they were 'proof' for the gospel) or
metaphorical of traditional 'salvation' (the blind see the light of the
gospel; the deaf hear the Word, and so on). Biblical research
moved the concept of miracle much closer to a biblical world-view,
involving elements of revelatory disclosure and faith. On scriptural
grounds one may argue that God's 'mighty acts' did not 'point' to
the gospel, as the unfortunate English translation 'sign' implies, but
rather *express* the Gospel: they do not *prove* the gospel, they *are* the
gospel. This does not diminish Christ's atonement for sin, but it
does affirm his atonement for sickness as well (Matt. 8:16).

Christology

Traditional Christology has stressed the uniqueness and deity of
Christ to save from sin, as over against his humanity and role as an
example, a role emphasized in theological liberalism and hence,
largely rejected by evangelicals. Biblical theology restored a greater
balance. In this regard, the New Testament emphasizes Jesus as
the bearer and expresser of the Spirit, the 'anointed one', who
served as the *prototype for ministry* of the ideal Spirit-led Son for all
believers.

Discipleship

A biblical Christology leads inextricably to a crucial purpose: the
imitation of Christ as a pattern for discipleship for all believers –
a huge theme in the NT – a theme largely neglected in both traditional and biblical theology. The Third World is more in tune,[19] it

---

19. Blank 1996: 213. Blank uneasily notes (1996: 212) trends toward formal
    education in Latin America, however, cited in an excellent survey article,
    Matviuk 2002: 164.

seems, with the NT demand for a replication of *all* aspects of Christ's ministry, including that of the miraculous and charismatic. This insight is then applied more faithfully in their expressions of training for ministry than in traditional evangelical institutions, which tend to see the ministry of Jesus more as an object of academic study than of personal replication. This state of affairs echoes the criticism of traditional Protestantism that it is more a religion *about* Jesus than *from* Jesus.

Faith

Faith served in traditional Protestant theology as one of the three key *sola*s and was primarily defined over against 'works' – the referents of both terms competing as the means of 'salvation'. Reformation scholastics developed the dichotomy of 'saving faith' (for every Christian) and 'miraculous faith' (limited to the apostolic era as proof of doctrine). Where traditional systematic theology texts discuss 'faith', it is almost exclusively associated with Protestant 'salvation'. This is not the emphasis of the NT. As with the other major doctrines of the NT, above, the doctrine of 'faith' strongly connects to a broad and normative charismatic experience. Content analysis shows that a substantial proportion – about one-half – of Jesus' teaching to his disciples dealt with the areas of faith, most often in the context of miracle stories. An analysis of the *pistis* family of words ('faith/believe') in the NT, shows that, where the context is explicit as to the 'intended result' of faith, 93 of all 230, or over 40% of the passages, refer to healings and other acts of power.

Prayer

Though usually subsumed under ecclesiology, the doctrine of prayer has received scant attention, either in traditional evangelical systematics texts or in biblical studies. By contrast, prayer is a major NT theme. Jesus is recorded as praying some 26 times. Paul often frames the objectives for the spiritual growth of the church in terms of that for which he prays. Much of the NT participation in the eschatological dimension is expressed in prayer, praise and worship. Future evangelical theology and praxis needs to embrace prayer as a central emphasis.

Ecclesiology

The traditional doctrine of the church has failed to engage the NT contexts of ecclesiology in that the charismatic dimension is usually ignored. Rather, traditional ecclesiastical structures have evolved which have demanded theological attention and justification. Biblical theology has demonstrated more sensitivity to the processes of the gathered community, particularly recovering the notions of 'mutual edification' via the charismata. Systematic analyses of NT contexts discussing the church reveal a model quite close to the modern 'cell church' whose notion of church 'member' is not simply a consumer of spiritual information, but rather describes a charismatic function toward the 'building up of the body of Christ'.

Conclusion

Ideally, Pentecostal and charismatic evangelicals worldwide are on a trajectory back to the future. Their destiny lies not by denying their evangelical roots, but by affirming them – specifically its commitment to Scripture and *its own explicit emphases on God's power permeating all areas of our Christian faith and life*. If the principle of *sola scriptura* truly grounds the evangelical identity, we must be willing to re-examine the New Testament mandate to express the Spirit-anointed *euangelion* of its Author, the Lord Jesus Christ, and its role in a truly 'evangelical' future.

Bibliography

Althaus, P. (1966), *The Theology of Martin Luther*, trans. R. C. Schultz, Philadelphia: Fortress Press (German original 1963).

Barna, George (2001), 'A Profile of Protestant Pastors in Anticipation of "Pastor Appreciation Month"', September 25, 2001', http://www.barna. org/cgi-bin/PagePressRelease.asp? PressReleaseID=98&Reference=B

—— (2002), 'Barna's Beefs: His Nine Challenges for American Christianity', *Christianity Today* 46.17 (5 August): 35.

Barrett, David M. (2002), *The Encyclopedia of Christianity*, New York: Oxford University Press.

Blank, R. (1996) *Teología y Misión en América Latina* [Spanish: Theology and Mission in Latin America], St Louis: Concordia.

Cox, Harvey (1995), *Fire from Heaven: The Rise of Pentecostal Spirituality and the*

Reshaping of Religion in the Twenty-First Century, Reading, MA: Addison-Wesley.

Dunn, James D. G. (1970), 'Spirit and Kingdom', *Expository Times* 82.11 (November): 36–40.

Ewart, Frank J. (1975), *The Phenomenon of Pentecost*, rev. ed., Hazelwood, MO: Word Aflame Press.

Gunkel, Hermann (1979), *The Influence of the Holy Spirit: The Popular View of the Apostolic Age and the Teaching of the Apostle Paul: A Biblical-Theological Study*, trans. Roy Harrisville, Philadelphia: Fortress Press (German original *Die Wirkungen des heiligen Geistes*, 1889).

Jenkins, Philip (2002), *The Next Christendom: The Coming of Global Christianity*, New York: Oxford University Press.

Lester, Toby (2002), 'Oh Gods!' *Atlantic Monthly* (February) http://www.The-Atlantic.com/issues/2002/02/lester.htm

Linder, Eileen W. (ed.) (2002), *Yearbook of American and Canadian Churches 2002*, Nashville: Abingdon.

Luther, M. (Works) *The Works of Martin Luther* (1955–), St Louis: Concordia.

Matviuk, Sergio (2002), 'Pentecostal Leadership Development and Church Growth in Latin America', *Asian Journal of Pentecostal Studies* 5.1: 164.

McGee, Gary (2001), 'Miracles and Mission Revisited', *International Bulletin of Missionary Research* 25.4 (October): 146–156.

Noll, Mark A. (2002), *The Old Religion in a New World: The History of North American Christianity*, Grand Rapids: Eerdmans.

Poloma, Margaret and Brian F. Pendleton (1989), 'Religious Experiences, Evangelism and Institutional Growth within the Assemblies of God', *Journal for the Scientific Study of Religion* 28.4 (December).

Ruthven, Jon (1993), *On the Cessation of the Charismata: The Protestant Polemic on Post-Biblical Miracles*, Sheffield: Sheffield University Press.

—— (2001), 'Between Two Worlds: One Dead, the Other Powerless to Be Born' – Pentecostal Theological Education vs. Training for Ministry', *The Spirit and Church* 3:2 (November): 273–297.

Synan, Vinson (1971), *The Holiness-Pentecostal Movement*, Grand Rapids: Eerdmans.

Wood, Laurence W. (1996), 'The Third Wave of the Spirit and the Pentecostalization of American Christianity: A Wesleyan Critique', *Wesleyan Theological Journal* 31 (Spring): 110–140.

11. EVANGELICALISM AND POLITICS

Stephen Lazarus

Introduction

What does the adjective 'Christian' mean when placed before the word 'politics' today? To many, the very thought of 'Christian politics' might seem a bit odd or contradictory. The words just don't seem to go together. However, when this question was debated at a recent symposium of evangelical Christians in Washington, DC, it sparked a lively debate.[1] People proposed many different answers.

One professor argued that *Christian* politics should concern itself first and foremost with promoting individual freedom, including the freedom of citizens to live and worship as they choose, even if some people will choose lifestyles that are immoral or wrong. Other participants argued that Christian politics should work mainly to restrain sin and evil and preserve order in society. Others contended that Christians should encourage the state to pursue justice. Other voices

---

1. Collegium Conversations on Public Policy, 10–11 May 2002, sponsored by Gordon College (Wenham, MA), Center for Christian Studies.

called the Christian community primarily to promote the witness of non-violence and peacemaking in international conflicts. At the end of the day, it was clear that there was little or no consensus on what a comprehensive approach to Christian politics should look like.

Decades ago, Harry Blamires, the British cultural observer and student of C. S. Lewis, diagnosed the loss of distinctively Christian thinking in the church. He concluded that most Christians had surrendered in their thinking to the secularizing drift of the modern age. 'There is no longer a Christian mind', he lamented.[2]

Many troubling consequences of this continue today. The consequences are painfully evident both in the church and in the world. Chief among them is that the public impact of Christianity on culture and society in many countries has diminished and dwindled to an almost imperceptible level. Instead of providing direction for Christ's disciples in all of life, including in their political and cultural engagement in society, the message of Jesus and his invitation to abundant life in this world under the reign of God often becomes reduced to a private way of worship or to a ticket to an angelic afterlife in heaven. In either scenario, the Christian faith has little to do with 'this-worldly' matters such as politics or statecraft.

The argument of this chapter is that if evangelicals want to shape the future of politics, they need to develop not only a Christian mind, but also a Christian *political* mind. One part of developing a Christian mind is developing the ability to think and act *politically* in obedience to Christ.

However, in many countries today, most students of politics as well as most government leaders and most Christian believers would consider a debate about the connection between Christian faith and politics to be quaint and perhaps quite irrelevant. Some might even regard it dangerous. It is simply assumed that a Christian faith perspective or world-view offers very few if any distinctive insights into political affairs. Religion, after all, is a 'private' matter, as the saying goes.

---

2. See Blamires 1963: 3. Concerning the situation today, American historian of religion Mark Noll notes similarly that 'the scandal of the evangelical mind is that there is not much of an evangelical mind'. Noll 1994: 3.

To the contrary, the Christian faith – pointing as it does to God, the sovereign Creator, to his purposes for this world, and to the coming reign of God in Christ – is as inherently public and political as it is spiritual.[3] Both Christians and non-Christians often ignore this truth. Evangelicals are citizens of political orders in countries all around the world. Christian tradition even declares Christ to be the 'King of kings and Lord of lords', a very political title indeed![4] The question is not whether there is such a thing as a Christian or evangelical politics, but rather, what shape does it take – or should it take – when evangelicals seek to serve their Lord through political involvement.[5]

Evangelicals should do more than simply call for politicians to be honest, or advocate increases or decreases in funding for particular government programmes. Evangelicals in politics need to develop a Christian framework for making informed judgments about public policy concerns. To sharpen the question debated at the symposium, what are the proper duties of government as an institution ordained by God? What are proper limits to the state's use of power? How can Christians evaluate whether a government is properly carrying out the specific duties that belong to it? To answer those questions effectively, Christian citizens and policy-makers need a comprehensive vision for politics and human flourishing grounded in their deepest beliefs as followers of Christ. To be an *evangelical* framework, its controlling concepts should be informed and shaped by the witness of the Bible and the work of the Father, Son and Holy Spirit in this world. Evangelicals in politics should take seriously the whole biblical witness as it has been historically known.

---

3. Oliver O'Donovan notes that biblical terms such as 'king', 'kingdom', and 'reign', for example, cannot be fully understood apart from their overt political meanings. See O'Donovan 1996. For a comprehensive treatment of the recurring interplay between political thought and Christian theology in the Western political tradition, see O'Donovan & O'Donovan 1999.

4. Rev. 19:16, NRSV.

5. For example, see Paul Freston's path-breaking study of evangelical engagement in politics in Freston 2001.

The argument of this chapter develops as follows: The first section considers several different positions evangelicals have adopted towards political involvement in the twentieth century. Because many of these positions have impeded and not nurtured the growth of an integrally Christian political witness, believers have much work ahead of them in the next 100 years. Is current evangelical thinking about politics faithful to the basic storyline of the Bible and its message for our lives? This is an important question for all Christians to ask, whether as citizens of particular countries, or – for some – as political office holders with special responsibilities before God and others. By avoiding some pitfalls of the past, evangelicals can work to develop a new approach to governing and politics for the future that is grounded in faith and more consistent with a biblical world-view.[6]

Politics, however, is always more than merely an intellectual exercise. Evangelicals need more than just a new way to *think* about politics. Political obedience to the Lord requires renewed political *action* that flows from renewed political thought and renewed devotion to Christ. To truly shape the future of politics, evangelicals will need to incarnate in practice the difference Christ makes for politics.

This renewal is possible because Christ's redemption is real. It is far-reaching. The challenge for evangelical political leaders and citizens is to engage in politics and governing as a response to God's redemption and gracious rule in Christ. Obedience to Christ's love and reign must impact social structures and the work of governing, as well as the 'religious' or 'personal' lives of individuals and families. Thus, evangelicals working in politics have the opportunity – indeed the calling – to envision and enact new public policies designed to manifest Christ's purposes. How might society look different if evangelicals led the charge to promote justice for all citizens and serve the public good? The second section considers one such example of transformative political engagement by American and British evangelicals. Their work in the public policy arena as part of the 'faith-based movement' provides several instructive lessons.

---

6. For more on the idea of a biblical world-view, see Wolters 1985, and the chapter on world-view in this volume.

Should evangelicals decide to engage their culture with a Christian political witness, they will likely face many challenges in the modern (and increasingly postmodern) public square. The final section proposes some basic steps evangelicals can take to shape the future of politics from a distinctly Christian motivation. By advancing the standard of greater justice in public life for the faith commitments of all citizens, evangelicals can offer a compelling response to the growth of secularism and can witness to God's mercy in expectation of Christ's coming kingdom.

Evangelical approaches to politics

Evangelicals often do not agree on whether or how to engage the rough and tumble world of politics. Ask 100 evangelicals from churches in North America or the United Kingdom about the role of Christians in politics and one is likely to hear a wide range of often conflicting views.[7] There are at least four distinct positions one frequently encounters.

Withdrawal
The first of these is 'Withdrawal' or 'Separation'. This approach counsels Christians not to become involved in politics or the work of government. The advocate of the 'Withdrawal' position stresses that politics is often a very 'dirty business', fraught with temptations. Power corrupts. Christians in politics will be tempted to compromise their principles and trade in the gospel to gain influence and power. Thus, they should avoid politics to preserve their moral purity. Ed Dobson, an American evangelical minister, and Cal Thomas, a conservative Christian journalist, adopt a form of this position in their book *Blinded by Might*. They write:

> unless you play dirty, you can't win, and if you are a nice guy who plays
> by ethical rules, you will surely lose. Is this the kind of process in which

---

7. For a detailed survey of positions held by American evangelicals and other Christians over the past decade, see Skillen 1990 and Skillen, Herbert & Good 2001.

conservative Christians ought to immerse themselves? And if so – if
they must descend to this level of politics – can they really be said to be
serving a greater kingdom and greater King?[8]

According to advocates of withdrawal, if you want to change
society, you should work primarily to save individual souls from
sin. When individuals convert, it is presumed, they will adopt new
political and social positions. Believers are encouraged to work as
evangelists in mission agencies and churches – and not to place
much hope in government or politics, because they are sinful
beyond redemption.

It is true that politics and governing can present many moral
challenges and temptations – as can other callings such as business
or medicine, and even church work. However, there are serious
problems with the 'Withdrawal' position from an evangelical perspective. First, it presumes that God's presence and power are
somehow not active or effective for believers who serve in government or politics. Scripture teaches, however, that Christ is Lord
over *all* of creation, over every sphere of life, including government. He is the image of the invisible God.[9] Why should God's
sovereign hand be powerful to help his disciples only when they
save souls or conduct mission outreaches, and not also when they
seek to remedy injustice in society or protect the vulnerable
through lawmaking?

Second, when Christians choose separation and withdrawal,
they neglect God's call to be salt and light and agents of reform
and redemption in a fallen world.[10] Newspaper headlines reveal a
world in desperate need of wise political leadership and social
reform as well as spiritual renewal. Yet by isolating itself, the
church may risk becoming so 'heavenly minded' that it indeed
does no earthly good.

Third, there is a price for surrendering to others one's God-
given duty to help shape public life: politics, lawmaking and the

---

8. Thomas & Dobson 1999: 142.

9. Col. 1:15–20. See also Wolters 1985, ch. 4: 57–71.

10. Matt. 5:13–16.

enforcement of justice are permitted to operate free from the claims of Christ who declared, 'All authority in heaven *and on earth* has been given to me'.[11] The cost to human life and justice in the modern world is enormous and painful when the reign of Christ is regarded as irrelevant in the use political power. Politics goes on, whether or not Christians are involved. Political decision-makers follow some guide or another. Apart from Christ, we follow our own ideals and false 'saviours' to our own destruction: communism, the Holocaust, abortion, apartheid, economic exploitation, terrorism, and the list goes on. Often, today, it is secularism – and not the presence of religion in politics – that threatens justice and respect for human life.[12]

Behind political conflict lies a clash of spiritual visions.[13] When we withdraw from influencing politics and culture, we withdraw from the struggle for God's kingdom and glory that involves every area of life. The world suffers because of this loss of faith. Christian political thinker Bernard Zylstra writes:

> The 'principalities and powers, the world rulers of this present darkness, today's spiritual host of wickedness' – they are not exposed for what they are. And thus *these* forces condition our lives as they come to us by means of the educational system, the media, the political parties, and the myths of the industrial establishment. And it should not come as a surprise that those who make the decisions for our time and its sensitive youth do not turn to Christianity in searching for answers to the problems of a society falling apart at the seams. For the adherents of Christianity . . . those who proudly bear the name *evangel*-icals [good news], these do not evidence a faith in the radical renewing power of the Evangel as the source of Light for dark and dreary days.[14]

---

11. Matt. 28:18, NIV (italics added).

12. Marshall 2002: 1–17.

13. Dooyeweerd 1979: 105–110; Professor Robert George of Princeton also illustrates this with respect to issues such as abortion, pornography, homosexuality and bioethics in George 2001.

14. Zylstra 1970: 91 (second italics and bracketed note added).

Dominance

A second, quite opposite, position some evangelicals adopt is to strive for dominance in the public square. When faced with growing immorality, secularism and social problems in society, withdrawal is no option for these activists. 'If one world-view is to dominate, let it be ours!' is their cry. These evangelicals seek to use the power of government to secure a privileged place in public life for a Christian way of life over against other belief systems and cultures. They argue that the government should give special recognition and status to their faith, practices and traditions. Unless the government of a nation like the US or the UK returns to its Christian foundations and heritage, the moral decline in society will only worsen, they claim.[15]

For example, the Christian Coalition – an influential political lobby group in the United States – advocates as part of its platform that government-run, secular schools should restore the practice of Christian prayer in the classroom. In 1962, the United States Supreme Court declared school prayer unconstitutional on the grounds that government-sponsored prayer violated the requirement that the US government may not establish any religion as the nation's official faith.[16] The Court objected to prayer in schools in part because the practice required children of other faiths to participate in Christian religious activities against their will or the will of their parents. However, adopting the 'Dominance' strategy, defenders of school prayer contend that America is a 'Christian nation', founded by Christians, and made up of a Christian majority. On these grounds, they argue, school prayer should be permitted. If America is a Christian nation, then the government can give its official sanction to specifically Christian beliefs and practices. Minority groups do not possess the same rights.

---

15. For a detailed, historical profile of advocates of this position in the US see Brown 2002.

16. *Engel v. Vitale*, 320 U.S. 421 (1962). The idea of separation of church and state is often misused today to make government the engine of aggressive secularism. Properly understood, the idea need not have the effect of pushing religion to the margins of public life.

This 'majority rules' approach to Christian politics urges evangelicals to organize politically and mobilize large numbers of voters to elect Christian candidates at all levels of government. The aim is to win electoral majorities to enact public policies like school prayer to 're-Christianize' America, counter secularism, and restore Christianity to its special place in public life through legal and political means. Because American Christians represent the 'moral majority', the logic goes, they should be able to use democracy to regain control of American politics and society. 'The mission of the Christian Coalition is simple', says the Revd Pat Robertson. It is 'to mobilize Christians – one precinct at a time, one community at a time – until once again we are the head and not the tail, and at the top rather than the bottom of our political system'.[17]

Unlike the 'Withdrawal' position, this stance properly summons Christians not to abandon their political and civic responsibilities. The Christian Coalition and other organizations on the 'Religious Right' have mobilized and channelled the political activism of millions of American Christians in recent decades. However, the problem with the 'Dominance' strategy is that it is not *Christian* enough.

In using the power of government to favour Christians above others, advocates of this strategy fail to treat people of other faiths with the same respect they would want to be shown to them. Just as Christians desire the religious liberty to live out their faith in public and private, they should be willing to extend this same freedom to others as a matter of Christian conviction. A Christian may disagree strongly with the religious beliefs of a friend who practises another faith, yet think the friend should be equally free to practise his or her faith without interference by the government. This forbearance is not a sign of weakness, but of strength.

God is patient and gracious towards sinners. He desires repentance, but will not coerce it. As with Jesus' story about the wheat and the tares, God mercifully allows the saved and unsaved to enjoy the blessings of life side by side until the final judgment, while the

17. Quoted without citation on 'Quotes from the Religious Right' website at www.geocities.com/capitolhill/7027/quotes.html.

Good News is going forth into all lands.[18] By seeking complete dominance over their opponents in the public square, some evangelicals miss this grace of God. They also mistakenly assign to the government a responsibility that properly belongs to the church. It is the church's responsibility – and not the government's – to correct mistaken religious beliefs in society and encourage religious orthodoxy.

If a proposed law for school prayer permits only Christian students to practise their faith publicly, families of other faiths would be quite right to question what authority the state has to deny them the same opportunity. The 'majority rules' or 'Dominance' approach to governing does not recognize the government's unique responsibility to pursue justice for *all* its citizens, and not only for Christians. In today's religiously diverse societies, a political strategy that seeks to control public authority or monopolize public space for just one faith (or one secular belief system) – while disregarding or penalizing others – creates an injustice that should concern all Christians.

It is true and deeply regrettable that for many centuries Christians insisted that a good government was one that officially promoted Christianity. But Catholics and most Protestants reflecting on the Bible and history have come to see that that traditional teaching gives to the government duties properly belonging to the church or to God. As a result, statements of faith like the Westminster Confession have been amended. Some churches, like the Baptists, have distinguished themselves as standing against state-sponsored religion. The Roman Catholic Church decisively repudiated its previous position that a Christian government should favour the Catholic Church.

It is important to emphasize that affirming religious liberty in no way requires that the public square be 'naked' (to invoke Father Richard John Neuhaus's memorable phrase) and free of all religious influence as the zealous secularist would have it.[19] Evangelicals today do not have to choose either the dominance

---

18. Matt. 13:24–30.
19. Neuhaus 1986 and Willis 2001.

position or a relentless secularism – an either/or that modern politics has often served up in reductionist fashion. This will become clearer when we consider the fourth position below.

Grudging acceptance

The controversial British journalist Peter Hitchens conveys well the third position evangelicals often adopt. He writes:

> It would be absurd for any of us to imagine that politics in its current form is anything other than a threat and rival to religion. We should go into it and affect it, but only to reduce its influence and return to people the choice between good and evil that they alone can make.[20]

For many Christians today, government is a necessary evil. At best, it serves as a means to other ends such as freedom or economic prosperity. At worst, government poses a specific threat to freedom or a Christian way of life. This position regards the idea of Christian politics as a paradox. While Christians should participate, they should not deceive themselves into thinking that politics or governing can be a specifically Christian undertaking. Politics and sin are inextricably linked. This is a negative or defensive idea of Christian political involvement.

This view has a long history in the church and in Western political thought.[21] St Augustine, for example, believed that God ordained government on account of human sin. Had humans not rebelled against God and fallen into sin, we would have no need for government. While government is necessary in a sinful world to preserve peace and punish evil, it was not part of God's original plan for a good human society. Or as one American Founding Father wrote: 'If men were angels, no government would be necessary'.[22] Other thinkers, such as St Thomas Aquinas, later objected to Augustine's

---

20. Hitchens 1999.

21. Skillen 2000b explores this theme in depth; See also St Augustine, *City of God*, Book XIX.

22. Madison, *The Federalist Papers*, No. 51 in Hamilton, Madison & Jay 1961: 322.

view, arguing that the need for government grows naturally out of our social nature as humans.[23]

Christians who adopt the Augustinian position grudgingly recognize the need for government. They realize that governments provide important services such as a police force and a national military to protect and defend citizens from harm. Like other citizens, they look to government to provide order and stability in society. They may favour government efforts to combat poverty and other social problems. Unlike evangelicals advocating withdrawal, they participate in politics. However, their goals are more modest than those seeking to 're-Christianize' society by seeking political dominance. These evangelicals may join a political party of their choice, but they do so as a matter of practical necessity. They do not seek to advance a distinctively Christian agenda through politics, but merely to advance their own personal interests and concerns more or less as other citizens and interest groups do.

Vocation

The fourth position adopted by evangelicals holds that governing is not a necessary evil, but an opportunity for full-time Christian service in God's world. Serving as a political leader can be as much a vocation that pleases God as serving as a pastor. These evangelicals believe that engaging in politics and governing is much like raising a family or operating a business. Politics is one specific arena of responsibility that God built into the world for the good of his creation. Governing is part of human nature and ordained by God to advance justice and promote the common good. God endowed humans with the capacity to rule and to administer justice as stewards over his creation with specific duties. As Paul Marshall writes, 'Politics involves matters in the world that are vitally important, and for which there is no substitute. It is a fundamental part of creation in which we were made to live.'[24]

As with the work of parenting or managing a business, you can conduct your political responsibilities either in obedience or

---

23. Aquinas, Summa, I q. 96, art. 4.
24. Marshall 2002: 35.

disobedience to God's will. These evangelicals seek to engage in politics as a response to God's call for governments and citizens to pursue justice. They seek to participate in the political process from a distinctive standpoint by advocating a Christian understanding of justice for public policy and public life. They favour taking as their starting-point a different kind of political approach, one not directed predominantly by secular political ideologies such as conservatism or liberalism.[25] They seek to discern God-given norms and biblical principles to guide their political involvement in local, national and international affairs. In contrast to the 'Withdrawal' and 'Dominance' strategies, they advocate a form of political involvement that is active and engaged, but one that encourages the government to promote justice for people of all faiths in the public square. The purpose of engagement is not narrowly to advance Christian special interests, but to contribute a Christian perspective on justice and the common good for the restoration and proper ordering of society. 'The key to a revival of Christian social and political life today', writes James Skillen, an advocate of this approach, 'must be a revived understanding of God's ordinances – God's normative will for all of life, including politics.'[26]

Foundations for Christian politics

This fourth strategy, I believe, offers the most promise for evangelicals who seek to shape the future of politics today. It can provide a new direction beyond the escapism, triumphalism and resignation of past failed strategies. But it also presents a serious challenge to evangelicals. If Christian politics for evangelicals does not mean withdrawing for purity's sake, or driving for dominance, or accepting politics as usual, but, instead advancing a distinctively Christian vision of justice for all, what might this look like? Are there specific principles that can guide evangelicals?

First, any proper framework for Christian politics is shaped by a

---

25. See, for example, Lecture II 'Antithesis' in Runner 1974: 45–102.
26. Skillen 1981: 195.

biblical world-view. A biblical world-view takes as its guiding light the biblical story of creation, fall and redemption. These biblical themes provide the lens through which to view political life. We can't tell the story of the Bible (or of politics) by beginning with our fall into sin, or even by beginning with Jesus the Saviour. In the beginning God created the world and he created it good. He created the world with the potential for human society to develop with all its complexity, including a role for government and politics. Evangelicals can engage in political activity knowing that God created humans to flourish in perfect justice and righteousness. But human sin disrupted, and now distorts, everything – from family life to political life, from parenting to parliaments and everything in between.[27] For this reason, the work of government is often (but not only) about restraining sin, protecting the innocent and ensuring that people obey the law.

God is at work calling people to justice from the earliest chapters of Genesis throughout the Old Testament and into the New Testament. Consider, for example, the Bible's story of the first recorded murder. After Cain kills Abel, the Bible records that as part of Cain's punishment, God placed a mark on Cain to protect him from attack and limit the cycle of violence he had sinfully begun.[28] As Paul Marshall explains, this story shows how God's action served to create an early form of a legal order upon which later generations would build to restrain human sin and maintain justice. He writes:

> Penalties were established for Cain's murder of Abel, but, in turn, Cain himself was not left to suffer anarchy. This order incorporated both Cain and anyone who would seek private revenge on him. The mark of Cain was not merely particular to Cain as an individual: it was also a sign that God had appointed an order to maintain justice. This order embraced all human beings and demanded that they treat each other as God intended.[29]

But sin is not the end of the story in the Bible or in political life.

---

27. Spykman 1992: 301–322; Monsma 1984: 9–31.

28. Gen. 4:15.

29. Marshall 2002: 39.

Christ has promised he will return to establish his kingdom on earth, triumphing over the effects of sin's curse.[30] By offering the way to salvation through repentance, Christ has also 'delivered us from the dominion of darkness and transferred us to the kingdom of his beloved Son, in whom we have redemption, the forgiveness of sins'.[31]

Living under the creation-wide reign of God's righteousness is not only a future hope, but it is in part also a present reality. Christ is even now restoring his creation. His kingdom, touching every aspect of human life, grows every day like a small but thriving mustard seed through the work of Christ's faithful followers.[32] When Christians administer justice through governmental service or undertake other responsibilities in obedience to God, they share in the task of caring for and restoring God's creation.

According to St Paul, God has not abandoned his creation. Rather, the world 'stands on tiptoe' in anxious anticipation of its full liberation from sin's destructive consequences.[33] And even now, by God's grace, governments can promote justice instead of permitting or committing injustice. By seeking for God's will to be done 'on earth even as it is in heaven', Christians seek to bring the blessings and benefits of Christ's redemption to every corner of creation – even into issues of statecraft such as debates over welfare policy or international affairs.[34]

There is a pressing need for evangelicals to connect the witness of Scripture with real-world political situations. As a spiritual discipline, evangelicals should live with the Bible in one hand and the newspaper in the other in order to shape strong political convictions to bring into the public square for the sake of the common good, and ultimately for the glory of God. John Calvin captures the comprehensive claim of Christ on our lives (including our political lives) by reminding us that 'We are dedicated to God and

---

30. Wright 1999.

31. Col. 1:13–14, RSV.

32. Matt. 13:31–32.

33. cf. Rom. 8:18–25.

34. See, for example, Carlson-Thies & Skillen 1996; Marshall 2002, ch. 8.

therefore should not henceforth think, speak, design, or act, without a view to his glory.'[35]

For example, the Bible tells us in the book of Genesis that humans were created in the image of God.[36] For this reason, evangelicals believe that all people, regardless of their differences, possess God-given dignity by virtue of their existence as God's handiwork. Without exception, each person is 'fearfully and wonderfully made', knit together by God.[37] Thus, an evangelical view of citizenship quickly dismisses as illegitimate and unjust any laws that would declare some people as inferior or 'second-class citizens' based solely on their race or their religion. It is a Christian view of the human person that shapes this political judgment.

Second, a Christian framework for politics is justice-driven. Justice means rendering to each person or thing in society what is rightfully due them. Justice is not an abstract or speculative theory, but a personal obligation to keep covenant with the Creator and the creation.[38] Scripture repeatedly teaches that God loves justice and despises injustice.[39] A Christian approach holds the state accountable to render justice to all its citizens. As part of this duty to do justice, governments have particular responsibilities that no other institutions have. In modern democratic societies, governments guarantee citizens the right to vote and participate in the political process. They also have a duty to maintain a fair court system to settle legal disputes with impartiality. Governments develop policies to promote fair economic structures for citizens to have access to the resources necessary to fulfill their God-given callings in life. These tasks represent only a few examples of how a state pursues justice.

In carrying out these tasks, politics and governance are not simply matters of 'might makes right' or 'whoever has the gold or

---

35. For Calvin's challenging discussion of the virtue of Christian self-denial from which this quote comes, see Calvin, Inst: 3.7.

36. Gen. 1:26.

37. Ps. 139:14, NRSV.

38. Jackson 2003: 36; see also Skillen 2000a.

39. Ps. 11:7; Amos 5:7–17, 24; Mic. 6:8; Luke 18:1–8; Sherman 1999.

the guns makes the rules'. Government policies are subject to the norm of justice. God holds those who bear political responsibility accountable to use the powers of their office wisely and justly.[40]

Third, an evangelical framework for politics holds that justice is about maintaining right relationships among different institutions in society. In order for the state to promote justice in its specific arena of responsibility, it needs to relate properly to other institutions and organizations in society each of which has its own authority from God to exist and flourish. For example, a government's laws should encourage (and not hinder) the ability of schools to educate, congregations to worship, and parents to nurture their children. Justice requires the state with its lawmaking power to recognize the limits of its own authority so other institutions can carry out their distinct purposes.

While the state has the duty of administering justice, it is not responsible to administer everything in society. If instead of upholding a public legal order for citizens, a government begins acting like a family or a church, great harm will result. Imagine if a government presumed to require parents to raise their children according to one bureaucratically approved parenting model, penalizing anyone who relied on their own methods! . . . or a state that used its laws or police force to compel citizens to worship one particular way. Many former communist countries, for example, attempted to impose atheism on their citizens by outlawing the practice of Christianity and other faiths. The injustice was great and history records many martyrs. Because citizens are also family members, parents, worshippers, employees, and members of a wide variety of other associations and communities, justice or 'giving to each what is due' requires government to respect the many other non-governmental responsibilities citizens have in God's world as part of everyday life.

These examples illustrate two important principles of Christian politics. The first is known as 'structural pluralism'. This principle recognizes that God created society with the potential to unfold into an array of diverse institutions and relationships. It reminds

---

40. Ps. 82; Rom. 13:1–4; Col. 1:16–17.

policymakers that a state's laws should respect with care these necessary parts of a healthy civil society.

The second principle is known as 'confessional pluralism'. It recognizes that human beings are essentially and inescapably religious creatures. Everyone has a God-shaped hole in their hearts that seeks to be filled. Even those who claim to be 'non-religious' or atheist or agnostic act on their own deep beliefs about the ultimate meaning of life. Human life cannot simply be divided up into religious and non-religious compartments, because all of life (including the tasks of governing and citizenship) is at every moment a response to the Creator who made us.

However, because of sin and human rebellion, all people in society do not share the same faith. How then should the state deal fairly with citizens who belong to many different religious communities? The principle of confessional pluralism holds that until Christ returns, a just government will uphold the right of its citizens to be free to practise their diverse faiths in public and private life. This fundamental freedom (and restraint on government) is recognized for American citizens in the First Amendment of the Constitution of the United States, which requires the government to respect religious liberty and not to establish an official religion.

Evangelicals can use these two principles of structural and confessional pluralism to guide their thinking about politics and public policy. These principles hardly address every political question that arises. Few principles can. But they do help to establish the parameters of the proper role of government in relation to other institutions in society. By evaluating whether a state is acting within or outside its own sphere of authority and competence, evangelicals can better assess whether a state is preserving and promoting justice in society or not. Some evangelicals, as we shall see, have worked hard to translate these principles and their Christian world-view into action in the public square. They provide a living, breathing illustration of evangelicals working to advance justice on behalf of all citizens.

Evangelicals and the Faith-Based Initiative

Consider these facts: In the United States today some 15 million young people are at-risk for becoming involved in drugs, crime, and gang activity. About 1.5 million children are growing up without much parental guidance because they have a mother or father in prison. Statistics suggest that they too are likely to go to jail at some point in their life if they live to adulthood. And even though the United States is the richest country in the world – in the history of the world – more than 1 out of 6 American families with children live on a yearly income of $17,000 or less.[41]

In January 2001, in only his second week in office, US President George W. Bush launched the Faith-Based and Community Initiative in an attempt to address these and other social concerns. He stated:

> Government has a solemn responsibility to help meet the needs of poor Americans and distressed neighborhoods, but it does not have a monopoly on compassion. The indispensable and transforming work of faith-based and other charitable groups must be encouraged. Government cannot be replaced by charities, but it can and should welcome them as partners. We must heed the growing consensus across America that successful government social programs work in fruitful partnership with community-serving and faith-based organizations – whether run by Methodists, Muslims or Mormons, or good people of no faith at all.[42]

The aim of the Initiative is to build a new partnership between the government and faith-based and other grassroots organizations that house the homeless, help the addicted, train the unemployed and perform other compassionate works to meet a variety of social needs. At the heart of it all, President Bush has pledged to change and improve how government works with religious organizations. 'Starting now,' he has stated, 'the Federal Government is adopting a new attitude to honor and not restrict faith-based

---

41. Bush 2001a: 1.
42. Ibid.: Foreword.

and community initiatives, to accept rather than dismiss such programs, and to empower rather than to ignore them.'[43]

To advance these policy goals, the President established the White House Office of Faith-Based and Community Initiatives and other offices in key federal agencies that administer social programmes. In August 2001, the White House documented that many evangelical and other religious groups have often faced discrimination and unnecessary barriers when applying to the government for funding for community programmes.[44] Government agencies have often operated with the mistaken perception that if a community organization was religious, the government could not contract with that group to provide services the way it can with other groups because of religious restrictions in the law. For many years, community programme leaders in states across the country have been told that their programmes could only be funded if they could first be repackaged to be 'free of all religious influences'. In some cases, actual government guidelines have required this. Yet evidence suggests that it is often the 'faith' in faith-based programmes that makes them effective.[45] The White House has now begun a major effort to implement reforms, remove barriers and ensure that no group is excluded from becoming a partner with government simply because of the group's religious character. The goal of the new policies is to create a level playing field for all groups, religious or secular.

The Initiative has attracted much media attention as a high profile, top agenda item of the Bush Administration. However, less well known is that several evangelicals serving inside and outside of government have helped shape the basic policies behind the Initiative. The case of the Faith-Based Initiative provides an excellent example of Christians seeking to shape public policy according to biblical norms of justice.

Stanley Carlson-Thies, a social policy expert with a background

---

43. Bush 2001a: 6.

44. Bush 2001c. Monsma notes that government policies have often been inconsistent, sometimes lenient, sometimes overly restrictive.

45. Johnson, Tomkins & Webb 2002.

in welfare policy, served as the White House Office's Associate Director for Law and Policy. Don Eberly, another evangelical who has written extensively about civil society, served as Deputy Director and helped launch the Initiative. The legal mind behind the public policy at the heart of the Initiative is Carl Esbeck, a Christian lawyer who led the Department of Justice's Taskforce on Faith-Based and Community Initiatives. Together with John DiIulio – the first Director of the Office and a leading Catholic social scientist and expert on public administration – these and other leaders have worked to shape public policy at the highest level of American government.

The innovations they have sought to advance in public policy represent important new developments in American politics. But within the world of Christian reflection on government, the ideas behind the Initiative are not entirely new or unprecedented. Both Protestant and Catholic traditions of political thinking have pioneered well developed understandings of how different social and political institutions can work together in partnership to promote the public good as the Faith-Based and Community Initiative intends to do. Historically, both traditions have long held that caring for the poor is not the exclusive responsibility of the government, nor is it the exclusive responsibility of the church or other religious institutions. It is a shared responsibility. 'The main challenge, then', writes Luis Lugo, 'lies in properly structuring the relationship between government and those institutions of civil society involved in ministering to the poor.'[46]

As of 2003, the Initiative has slowly begun to revolutionize how government and faith-based organizations collaborate to serve people in need. While the work of many 'Good Samaritans' in society has often been hindered by misguided government policies in the past, the President's Initiative now requires the government to adopt a new set of rules, overturning many unnecessarily restrictive (and arguably unconstitutional) policies. The set of new rules is known as Charitable Choice.

---

46. Lugo 1998: 17. For a closer look at the Protestant and Catholic roots behind the Initiative, see also Marshall 2002: 59–61; Hoover 2000: 4–7, 26.

Under Charitable Choice, the government must now give faith-based organizations the same access to public funds to provide social services that other organizations have long enjoyed. They can no longer be discriminated against because they are perceived as being 'religious' or 'too religious' to work with government. The law protects their right to use public funds to provide social services (although government contracts and grants cannot be used to pay for worship services, evangelism or religious instruction). Nor can faith-based programmes be pressured to set aside the faith that often makes them successful. To keep these programmes true to their foundations, they are also free under the law to hire staff who will be committed to the particular religious basis of an organiza-tion's programmes. The new standard requires the government to maintain a respectful partnership, so both faith-based organizations and government agencies can reach their shared goal of helping people.

Charitable Choice also protects the religious liberty of people receiving services from the government. Under Charitable Choice no one can be denied services because of their religious affiliation. Also, people in need choose for themselves whether or not they will receive services from a faith-based provider. Charitable Choice requires the government to provide a referral to an alternative pro-gramme if a person objects to receiving assistance in a faith-based programme.

The changes in government policy and practice now underway reflect the fruit of serious Christian engagement in policymaking and in the political process. The idea for Charitable Choice came about in the mid-1990s when Carl Esbeck researched the unconsti-tutional barriers that religious groups faced in collaborating with government social welfare programmes. Instead of simply docu-menting the problems, he went a step further. He drafted a set of legal rules that could be adopted into legislation to address unfair discrimination against faith-based organizations. Senator John Ashcroft of Esbeck's home state of Missouri included Charitable Choice in a welfare reform bill he sponsored in Congress. Evangel-icals and other religious and community groups built a coalition and met with legislators on many occasions to explain the need for these new rules. In August 1996, under the previous President, Bill

Clinton, Congress adopted Charitable Choice's 'faith-friendly' guidelines into law as part of a series of major reforms to the nation's social service programmes. Today, the President's Initiative seeks to build on this legislative accomplishment that many evangelicals helped achieve.

A similar initiative is also under way in the United Kingdom. In several speeches British Prime Minister Tony Blair has encouraged the growth of strategic partnerships between national and local governments and religious social service groups. 'And where the two do go together,' he has stated, 'the government fully recognizing its obligations, looking to the voluntary sector as partner and not substitute – the impact is far greater than government acting on its own.'[47] William Hague, the former leader of the opposition Conservative Party, has also endorsed closer collaboration.

As in the United States, evangelicals in Britain have been at the forefront of this new movement. One evangelical ministry, the Oasis Trust, led by Steve Chalke, organized a petition drive that delivered 75,000 signatures to the Prime Minister to encourage the government to give faith-based organizations equal access to public funding to serve the poor through empowerment programmes. In 2000, the UK Parliament enacted the Local Government Act, which like Charitable Choice, provides a strong encouragement to government authorities to include previously excluded community and faith-based organizations as necessary partners in the delivery of local social welfare programmes. Since passage of the Act, the Oasis Trust has launched a major campaign to educate and help equip organizations interested in this new opportunity. The organization has also educated and lobbied government officials and departments to ensure that legislation fully respects the rights of faith-based organizations to retain their distinctive character and hiring practices.

The struggle for change has not been easy. For example, opponents in both countries have mounted campaigns to deny faith-based organizations the right to consider religious commitment as an important qualification in hiring staff. Some European

---

47. Butler 2001.

Community directives and US regulations forbid the practice as 'religious discrimination'. However, this restriction creates a difficult burden on faith-based organizations that desire to hire only staff who are fully committed to the religious basis of their programmes. In the US political opponents have sought to undermine the Initiative by portraying faith-based groups as biased or bigoted. However, in reality, faith-based groups are only insisting on the basic freedoms that other organizations enjoy to hire people who share their vision and mission.

To address this concern, and to counter the arguments of critics who seek to maintain such restrictions, evangelicals have had to develop and fight for public policies that will honour this right and safeguard the independence of faith-based organizations. They have had to refute other criticisms: 'Isn't the government just dumping its responsibility to care for the poor on to the churches?' Or 'Surely this is an unconstitutional violation of the separation of church and state! The government shouldn't use my tax dollars to promote religion.'

To answer these charges in newspapers, on television and in the corridors of power, advocates have had to advance an argument about what justice requires in the relationship between government and faith-based organizations. They have had to articulate in the public square their basic political principles. This requires a coherent political framework and an ability to express one's basic position in a shared public language that all citizens can understand to build broad support. Evangelicals have had to explain why this set of policies is more just than the way things were done before.

To do this, leading evangelicals in the movement have drawn on the principles of structural and confessional pluralism discussed earlier. The idea of structural pluralism illuminates how the actions of the Initiative help restore a proper relationship between government, faith-based organizations and citizens in need. When family members are struggling with drug addiction or seeking work because they are unemployed, they need different types of help from different institutions in society. Families, schools, churches, drug treatment programmes, governments and businesses can all play important and unique roles in helping out. As President Bush has stated: 'Governments can spend money, but they can't put hope in our hearts or a sense of purpose in our lives.'[48]

By building partnerships and providing resources to Christian drug treatment programmes, for example, to provide the moral challenge, one-on-one encouragement, and care that government cannot, the new rules recognize the legitimate and essential role community organizations play in collaboration with government efforts. This is not to shirk government's duty to advance justice, but to uphold it. 'The best mentoring program will never be a substitute for Medicaid for poor children', Bush has stated, articulating this principle. 'The best effort to renovate housing will never be a substitute for fair housing laws. But we strongly believe [faith-based and community groups] can do more. We must find creative ways to expand their size and increase their number.'[49]

The ideas of structural and confessional pluralism also help answer other criticisms. The Initiative does not violate the separation of church and state or privilege a particular religion. To the contrary, Charitable Choice, based on the principle of confessional pluralism, requires that government programmes provide equal access to funding for all, whether a programme is run by 'Methodists, Muslims or Mormons, or good people of no faith at all' as the President has stated. The government recognizes the public service of many different faith communities in society without 'taking sides'. These new rules overturn prior unfair policies and regulations that were rooted in a non-neutral, secular world-view, ensuring that now there is no bias either for or against faith-based (or secular) programmes. Instead of unconstitutionally establishing religion, Charitable Choice prevents the unjust establishment of a secular bias against religious groups that the Initiative's critics seek to maintain.

Charitable Choice also restrains the use of government power to its own area of competence. The government now simply evaluates whether a particular programme achieves legitimate public

---

48. From a speech by then Texas Governor George W. Bush on the campaign trail in Indianapolis, Indiana; Bush 1999.

49. From the President's speech to the US Conference of Mayors, Bush 2001b.

social service goals and outcomes effectively. The state can no longer misuse its authority by first seeking to inquire how religious a programme is, or whether it is 'pervasively sectarian', that is, unable to separate its religious and public missions. A just state that respects religious freedom and diversity does not perpetuate religious prejudice.

Similarly a just state that recognizes institutional and religious diversity in society will not require faith-based groups to change their hiring policies when they accept the government's invitation to help address society's most pressing social crises. The state violates the political norm of justice if it denies to all the different kinds of religious organizations in society the right to hire a staff who will model and live by the faith-basis of these programmes. If a Jewish programme is not free to hire like-minded staff to lead the organization, or if over time it becomes run by a staff of Baptists or atheists, it will lose its distinctive Jewish character and no longer be able to carry out its mission. The principle of confessional pluralism recognizes that different faith communities must be free to live by their religious principles not only in private, but also in public and governmental matters. Different faith communities have different needs and approaches to hiring staff for their programmes. The government should not impose a one-size fits all approach that requires all organizations to regard religious commitment as irrelevant to the staffing and operation of their programmes.

The government can avoid imposing such an unwelcome and unjustified form of orthodoxy on organizations by recognizing their independent right to formulate their own hiring policies. The principle of structural pluralism holds that God created faith-based organizations to have their own special nature, separate from the identity of their government partner. Therefore, they should not be viewed as an 'arm' of the government. They are subject in part to a different set of norms than those that hold for government agencies. If government laws fail to honour the unique character and independence of faith-based organizations, then these 'power cells' of civil society are likely to lose the very energy and effectiveness government hopes to find in them as partners for people in need.

The case of the Faith-Based Initiative highlights the important role principles like structural and confessional pluralism can play in a Christian framework for politics. But some justice questions that governments must address require the use of other tools or modes of analysis from the Christian's political toolbox. Often political debates do centre on matters of dollars and cents (or pounds and pence.) How much should a government spend? A proper education system or health care programme, for example, requires adequate public funding, even if, in some cases, this might require increased taxation or a slowdown of economic growth. To contribute to these debates, Christians and their fellow citizens should feel free to bring their convictions and world-views into the public debate over the facts and figures.

When considering these issues, it is important to remember that the public good is seldom as simple as just maximizing economic efficiency, as some reductionist approaches would suggest. Funding debates about spending more or less always presuppose answers to deeper questions that involve important principles. When the government funds schooling, who should provide that schooling? When debates over the proper amount of welfare benefits rage, other questions are often taken for granted. What *kind* of assistance should be given to help a person move from welfare to work and better support themselves and their family? The Christian in politics has a licence to investigate all these matters in God's good creation as part of a divine calling to pursue justice.

The challenge ahead

So what are some basic steps evangelicals can take to shape the future of politics and engage the public square as a service to Christ's kingdom? First, we must consider afresh that the God we serve desires justice in this world – and discover the role we have to play. Many problems the world faces today simply cannot be addressed apart from the responsible use of political power. God, the source of all power and authority, has given citizens and public officials together the task of seeking and advancing justice for all. Obedience to God includes learning how we can discern and obey

God's call to do justice as citizens and leaders in the exercise of political responsibility. If we are in covenant with God, we must ask what this call requires of us personally and corporately.

Second, in seeking justice, we can be inspired by the biblical story and the stories of those engaged in this work and those who have preceded us in the faith. Genesis and the Lord's Prayer remind us that as creatures of God in a good but fallen creation, we are called to shape history and reshape our world to accord with the will of our loving Creator. Evangelicals can learn from the examples of leaders such as William Wilberforce whose labour of love in politics led to the abolition of slavery in Britain, and Abraham Kuyper, the Dutch theologian who served as Prime Minister of the Netherlands, whose political party advanced a Christian political platform based on the idea of justice for all.[50] We can also learn from those who are serving on the frontlines today in our time, such as those involved in the Faith-Based Initiative movement.

Third, evangelicals must work together to develop a coherent framework to guide their political activism. This ongoing work may take years or even decades. To begin, Christians called to governmental service can meet together and hammer out a manifesto of how biblical principles of justice should inform their work as public servants and servants of the kingdom of God.[51] They should work together with others in the church with special insight such as economists, sociologists, pastors, theologians, educators, business owners, environmentalists and interested citizens who long to see a viable Christian political option represented in the public square. To move from one's framework and basic principles to concrete policy proposals, evangelicals with special expertise must identify issues of concern and undertake detailed study and social analysis of the problems involved. How do a Christian world-view and a vision for justice address such issues as poverty, abortion, ethnic and racial reconciliation, human rights, bioethics,

---

50. To learn more about the lives of these Christian political leaders, see Langley 1984; Heslam 1998 and Belmonte 2002.

51. Ron Sider offers this and other useful recommendations in Sider 2000.

nuclear proliferation and international affairs? How can evangelical leaders begin to shape or reshape debate over these and many other issues for which biblically wise leadership is urgently needed? What role can principles such as structural and confessional pluralism play to resolve conflicts and promote greater justice?

Fourth, evangelicals must build strong organizations and coalitions to advocate for justice in the public square. Politics is a long-term communal task, not the work of individual 'Lone Ranger' Christians. Therefore, organizations such as the National Association of Evangelicals in the US and the Evangelical Alliance in the United Kingdom have vital roles to play in educating citizens about current issues and articulating a Christian voice for justice to government leaders. Other organizations such as Christian public policy think-tanks work to develop detailed policy proposals and new ideas to put before legislators to advance justice. To build support to enact legislative reforms into law, evangelical political organizations need to build coalitions with others, often including like-minded people from different faiths who share similar political goals. Because all true justice is God's justice, evangelicals should be bold to engage with others (including believers from other faith traditions and nonbelievers) in vigorous political debate over what a just course of action is for the government to take on a given issue. Again, this presumes we know why our faith leads us to support a given stance. We must also be able to communicate clearly why the position we support represents an attempt to advance true *public justice* for all and not an attempt to advance the narrow special interests of 'just us'.

Finally, advocating for justice in the public square is hard work. Evangelicals in politics need to develop a spirituality strong and deep enough to energize and sustain their labours for Christ's kingdom. Sometimes very good ideas that promote justice don't win the day (or at least not immediately). Opponents may be more effective at mobilizing support for their arguments. In England, William Wilberforce worked tirelessly for many decades to put an end to slavery, before it was officially abolished by an Act of Parliament in 1833, just days after he died. In working to advance justice, it is easy to get discouraged, lose heart, and forget that ultimately the God of justice is working out his purposes. He asks us only to trust, obey, and be faithful to our calling. As evangelicals overcome the mistakes of the past and confront the challenges of today and tomorrow with a new vision, we must remember that we are co-labourers with God. The final establishment of justice and the restoration of this world as God's kingdom will come one day as a gift from the king. We see the signposts today. Until then, we take to heart the true word of the Lord to sustain our efforts: 'He has showed you, O man, what is good. And what does the LORD require of you? To act justly and to love mercy and to walk humbly with your God.' And 'Let us not become weary in doing good, for at the proper time we will reap a harvest if we do not give up.'[52]

Bibliography

Aquinas, Thomas (Summa), *The Summa Theologica* (trans. Fathers of the English Dominican Province, 1948), vol. 1, New York: Benziger.

Belmonte, Kevin (2002), *Hero for Humanity: A Biography of William Wilberforce*, Colorado Springs, CO: NavPress.

Blamires, Harry (1963), *The Christian Mind*, London: SPCK.

Brown, Ruth Murray (2002), *For a 'Christian America': A History of the Religious Right*, New York: Prometheus Books.

Bush, George W. (1999), 'The Duty of Hope', campaign speech, Indianapolis, IN, 22 July.

——, (2001a), 'Rallying the Armies of Compassion', Administration document, Washington, DC: The White House, January.

——, (2001b), 'Remarks by the President to the United States Conference of Mayors', Detroit, MI, 25 June.

——, (2001c), 'Unlevel Playing Field: Barriers to Participation by Faith-Based and Community Organizations in Federal Social Service Programs', Administration document, Washington, DC: The White House, August.

Butler, Patrick (2001), 'Blair invites religious groups to deliver public services', *The Guardian*, 29 March.

Calvin, J. (Inst), *Institutes of the Christian Religion* (trans. F. L. Battles, 1960),

---

52. Mic. 6:8 and Gal. 6:9, NIV.

Library of Christian Classics, vols. XX and XXI, Philadelphia: Westminster Press.

Carlson-Thies, Stanley and James W. Skillen (1996), *Welfare in America: Christian Perspectives on a Policy in Crisis*, Grand Rapids: Eerdmans.

Dooyeweerd, Herman (1979), *Roots of Western Culture: Pagan, Secular, and Christian Options*, Toronto: Wedge Publishing Foundation.

Freston, Paul (2001), *Evangelicals and Politics in Asia, Africa and Latin America*, Cambridge: Cambridge University Press.

George, Robert P. (2001), *The Clash of Orthodoxies: Law, Religion, and Morality in Crisis*, Wilmington, DE: ISI Books.

Hamilton, Alexander, James Madison and John Jay (1961), *The Federalist Papers*, ed. Clinton Rossiter, New York: Penguin Books.

Heslam, Peter S. (1998), *Creating a Christian Worldview: Abraham Kuyper's Lectures on Calvinism*, Grand Rapids: Eerdmans.

Hitchens, Peter (1999), 'The False Religion of Politics', speech given at Morpeth Arms, Westminster, October, Conservative Christian Fellowship, ccfwebsite.com.

Hoover, Dennis (2000), 'Charitable Choice and the New Religious Center', *Religion in the News*, A Publication of The Leonard E. Greenberg Center for the Study of Religion in Public Life, Trinity College, Hartford, CN, 3.1: 4–7, 26.

Jackson, Timothy P. (2003), *The Priority of Love: Christian Charity and Social Justice*, Princeton: Princeton University Press.

Johnson, Byron R. with Ralph Brett Tompkins and Derek Webb (2002), *Objective Hope – Assessing the Effectiveness of Faith-Based Organizations: A Review of the Literature*, Philadelphia: Center for Research on Religion and Urban Civil Society.

Langley, McKendree R. (1984), *The Practice of Political Spirituality: Episodes from the Public Career of Abraham Kuyper, 1879–1918*, Jordan Station, Ontario: Paideia Press.

Lugo, Luis E. (1998), *Equal Partners: The Welfare Responsibility of Governments and Churches*, Washington, DC: Center for Public Justice.

Marshall, Paul (2002), *God and the Constitution: Christianity and American Politics*, Lanham, MD: Rowman & Littlefield.

Monsma, Stephen V. (1984), *Pursuing Justice in a Sinful World*, Grand Rapids: Eerdmans.

—— (1996), *When Sacred and Secular Mix: Religious Non-Profit Organizations and Public Money*, Lanham, MD: Rowman & Littlefield.

Neuhaus, Richard John (1986), *The Naked Public Square*, Grand Rapids: Eerdmans.

Noll, Mark (1994), *The Scandal of the Evangelical Mind*, Grand Rapids: Eerdmans.

O'Donovan, Oliver (1996), *The Desire of the Nations: Rediscovering the Roots of Political Theology*, Cambridge: Cambridge University Press.

O'Donovan, Oliver and Joan Lockwood O'Donovan (eds.) (1999), *From Irenaeus to Grotius: A Sourcebook in Christian Political Thought*, Grand Rapids: Eerdmans.

Runner, H. Evan (1974), *Scriptural Religion and Political Task*, Toronto: Wedge Publishing Foundation.

Sherman, Amy (1999), *Sharing God's Heart for the Poor: Meditations for Worship, Prayer, and Service*, Indianapolis: Hudson Institute; Charlottesville: Trinity Presbyterian Church.

Sider, Ron (2000), 'Toward an Evangelical Political Philosophy', in David P. Gushee (ed.), *Christians and Politics Beyond the Culture Wars: An Agenda for Engagement*, Grand Rapids: Baker.

Skillen, James W. (1981), 'Politics, Pluralism and the Ordinances of God', in Henry Vander Goot (ed.), *Life is Religion: Essays in Honor of H. Evan Runner*, St Catharines: Ontario.

——, (1990), *The Scattered Voice: Christians at Odds in the Public Square*, Grand Rapids: Zondervan.

——, (2000a), *A Covenant to Keep: Meditations on the Biblical Theme of Justice*, Grand Rapids: CRC Publications; Washington, DC: Center for Public Justice.

——, (2000b), 'American Statecraft: A New Art for the 21st Century', the Sixth Annual Kuyper Lecture, Washington, DC: Center for Public Justice.

Skillen, James W. with Jerry S. Herbert and Joshua Good (2001), *At A Political Crossroads: Christian Civic Education and the Future of the American Polity*, Washington, DC: Center for Public Justice.

Spykman, Gordon J. (1992), *Reformational Theology: A New Paradigm for Doing Dogmatics*, Grand Rapids: Eerdmans.

Thomas, Cal and Ed Dobson (1999), *Blinded by Might: Can the Religious Right Save America?* Grand Rapids: Zondervan.

Willis, Ellen (2001), 'Freedom from Religion', *The Nation*, 19 February.

Wolters, Al (1985), *Creation Regained: Biblical Basics for a Reformational Worldview*, Grand Rapids: Eerdmans.

Wright, N. T. (1999), *New Heavens, New Earth: The Biblical Picture of Christian Hope*, Cambridge: Grove Books.

Zylstra, Bernard (1970), 'The Crisis of our Times and the Evangelical Churches', *Out of Concern for the Church*, Toronto: Wedge Publishing Foundation.